PERGAMON RUSSIAN CHESS SERIES

ENDGAME STRATEGY

ENDGAME STRATEGY

By

M. I. SHERESHEVSKY

Translated by

K. P. NEAT

PERGAMON PRESS

OXFORD · NEW YORK · TORONTO · SYDNEY · PARIS · FRANKFURT

U.K.	Pergamon Press Ltd., Headington Hill Hall, Oxford OX3 0BW, England
U.S.A.	Pergamon Press Inc., Maxwell House, Fairview Park, Elmsford, New York 10523, U.S.A.
CANADA	Pergamon Press Canada Ltd., Suite 104, 150 Consumers Road, Willowdale, Ontario M2J 1P9, Canada
AUSTRALIA	Pergamon Press (Aust.) Pty. Ltd., P.O. Box 544, Potts Point, N.S.W. 2011, Australia
FRANCE	Pergamon Press SARL, 24 rue des Ecoles, 75240 Paris, Cedex 05, France
FEDERAL REPUBLIC OF GERMANY	Pergamon Press GmbH, Hammerweg 6, D-6242 Kronberg-Taunus, Federal Republic of Germany

English translation copyright © 1985 K. P. Neat

First edition 1985

Library of Congress Cataloging in Publication Data

Shereshevsky, M. I.
Endgame strategy.
(Pergamon Russian chess series)
Includes indexes.
1. Chess — End games. I. Title. II. Series.
GV1450.7.S54   1985   794.1'24   84–19042

British Library Cataloguing in Publication Data

Shereshevsky, M. I.
Endgame strategy. — (Pergamon Russian chess series)
1. Chess — End games
I. Title
794.1'24   GV1450.7
ISBN 0–08–029746–3 Hardcover
ISBN 0–08–029745–5 Flexicover

This is a translation of the Russian edition, published in 1981 by Polimya, Minsk.

CONTENTS

FOREWORD TO THE ENGLISH EDITION

M. Shereshevsky's book *Endgame Strategy* was published in the USSR in 1981 in an edition of 50,000 and was immediately sold out.

The author, one of the strongest players in Byelorussia, has recently been working as a trainer. In his lessons with young players Shereshevsky has made use of the endgame teaching methods of one of the country's leading trainers, M. Dvoryetsky, and has worked out a definite system.

This book contains an interesting selection of endings. Along with classic examples there are endings both of leading modern grandmasters, as well as of less well known players. The author aims in the first instance to explain the course of the struggle, penetrate into the psychology of the players' actions, and to focus the readers' attention on the turning points and characteristic mistakes. In contrast to the majority of works on the endgame, the book is divided into chapters not according to material, but according to the playing methods which are most characteristic of the given group of endings. The names of certain chapters have an unusual ring: "Do not hurry", "The problem of exchanging", "The principle of two weaknesses", and so on. For this English edition the author has added a number of endings played in recent times, as well as endings from games by the strongest English players.

The main value of the book, in my opinion, lies in the fact that it contains specific advice and recommendations on how to improve endgame technique, for which the practical player will sometimes search in vain when studying multi-volume reference books on the endgame.

A. Yusupov
International Grandmaster

INTRODUCTION

From the practical point of view, the endgame is the least well studied stage of chess. Chess literature contains very few works on the endgame, and in the main these are reference works, in which theoretical and not practical positions are analyzed.

The present book is an attempt to study and systemize certain basic practical principles of the playing of chess endings.

The necessity for a systematic approach to the study of chess endings occurred to me mainly as a result of my teaching experience. It is no secret that, in the preparation of young players, many trainers and teachers devote most attention to the study of numerous opening systems and the forms of middlegame resulting from them. The endgame is always allotted very little time.

Some trainers give their pupils the most elementary conceptions of the endgame, assuming that with the general development of a player his mastery of endgame play will also rise. Others demonstrate long and complex analyses from reference books, although the probability of such positions being repeated in a practical game is slight. It is evident that both approaches are a long way from the truth: the mastery of a player is directly dependent not so much upon his amount of theoretical knowledge, as upon his understanding of the general principles of conducting chess endings.

In 1976 I happened to be the second of international master Mark Dvoryetsky during the USSR Championship 1st League in Minsk. Dvoryetsky adjourned his game with grandmaster Taimanov in a superior position. In one of the lines of analysis a rook ending with f- and h-pawns was reached. Dvoryetsky referred to a book on rook endings, and began studying the appropriate chapter. I was surprised: after all, Dvoryetsky is a great expert on the endgame. To my question he replied that he knew the basic principles of playing such endings, but did not even attempt to remember lengthy concrete analyses. Later during the tournament we frequently discussed the question of how to study the endgame. Dvoryetsky considers it essential to know the classics, to analyze complicated practical rather than theoretical endings, and to find general rules and principles of play in complex endings. And in theoretical endings it is sufficient to know whether the ending is won or drawn, and to have a rough impression of the plan of play.

Of course, every trainer has his own style of working, and his own system for preparing players. But it is worth recalling that Mark Dvoryetsky, an Honoured Trainer of the Russian Federal Republic, has prepared three Junior World Champions. And all three – Valery Chekhov, Artur Yusupov and Sergey Dolmatov – are very strong in the endgame.

Of course, the role of exact knowledge in the endgame should not be underestimated. It is no accident that *Fizkultura i Sport* has begun publishing a second edition of the multi-tome study of the endgame edited by grandmaster Yuri

Averbakh*. And even so, in the introduction to this series it is emphasized that a sure indication of a strong player is good playing technique in complex endings.

The present book studies such basic principles of play in complex endings as centralization of the king, schematic thinking, prophylaxis, and the principles of "do not hurry" and of two weaknesses. The majority of these were formulated with amazing precision and conciseness in an article by a talented Soviet master who was killed during the Second World War, Sergey Byelavyenets, an extract from which is given after this introduction. Also examined are typical endgame positions with the advantage of two bishops, an isolated d-pawn, and a 3—2 Q-side pawn majority. Some examples are given to study the problem of exchanging, and ways of battling for the initiative in the endgame. In conclusion we give a number of complex endings, in which the various principles expounded in the previous chapters are put into practice.

The knowledge of many rules, and the choice of a specific plan based on them, is mainly of a psychological nature. Therefore in certain examples, especially where Byelorussian players are involved, I have laid particular emphasis on the competitive situation in which the game was played.

Of course, the rules and recommendations given in the book cannot be regarded as unshakeable and universal endgame laws. Chess is too complex and diverse for that. Latent or manifest in each position are its rules, principles and regularities, many of which a player will often sense intuitively.

Without pretending to offer universal recommendations, the author has aimed mainly to help players to be better oriented in endings, and to be more correct and accurate in taking the necessary decisions in practical play.

---

*   An English translation, *Comprehensive Chess Endings*, is currently being published in five volumes by
    Pergamon Press.

CHAPTER 1

BASIC PRINCIPLES OF ENDGAME PLAY

S. BYELAVYENETS

During the fierce battles of the middlegame, passions are aroused. Sacrifices and striking combinations are in the air, and each of the players watches intensely for tactical blows, clever traps, and subtle unexpected moves. Then suddenly, mass exchanges take place, the heated combinational skirmishes come to an end, and a prosaic endgame ensues. Sometimes the transition into the endgame occurs at the will of one of the players, who assumes that here it will be easier to exploit his advantage.

In the endgame, technique becomes of primary importance. First of all a player must retune his thinking and his mood. One can virtually forget about 'brilliancy' and tactics. I would advise every player, if time on his clock permits, to spend several minutes on 'calming the passions aroused in him'. Subsequently this loss of time will without fail be justified, since the player will be examining the position correctly, from the 'endgame' point of view. What does this mean?

This question must be dwelt on in some detail, since multi-tome endgame books, with their countless examples and positions, do not devote sufficient attention to the course of a player's thinking in the endgame.

In the middlegame his thoughts are mainly occupied by the calculation of variations, which are subordinate to some aim. The main things that a player is occupied with in the middlegame are the checking of all kinds of tactical blows, and the calculation of combinations and variations. In the endgame things are different. Only in rare, so-called combinational endings, must the attention be focused on calculation, on tactics. In the overwhelming majority of endings it is essential to think in terms of plans. Variations play a secondary role. The main role belongs to schematic thinking, and the possibility of setting up this or that position is checked by calculating variations. We plan the deployment of our own pieces that we require, taking account, of course, of what the opponent may do. Then we check by a calculation of variations whether it is possible to achieve this position. For example: in the following position from the game Capablanca–Ragozin, Moscow, 1936, White formulated his tasks very concisely.

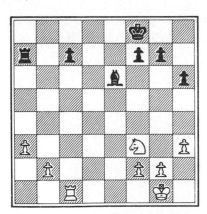

Capablanca writes about his thoughts during the game:

"White's plan is to prevent the advance of the c-pawn (after which the b-pawn could become weak) and to control the entire board up to the fifth rank.

1

This is achieved by moving the king to e3, and by placing the rook at c3, the knight at d4, and the pawns at b4 and f4. After he has attained such a position, White will be able to advance his Q-side pawns."

As we see, variations did not interest Capablanca, and he was not even interested in the time and speed with which the planned position would be attained. The main thing was that the required type of position had been selected, and the subsequent play followed according to plan.

1	Nd4	Rb7
2	b4	Bd7
3	f4	Ke7
4	Kf2	Ra7
5	Rc3	Kd6
6	Rd3	Ke7
7	Ke3	Ra4
8	Rc3	Kd6

The set-up planned by White is complete. He is now faced with a new problem — that of advancing his Q-side pawns. To do this he must first take his king to the aid of the pawns which are to be advanced.

9	Rd3	Ke7
10	Rc3	Kd6

A few words about repeating moves. A basic rule of the endgame is: do not hurry! If there is a possibility of advancing a pawn two squares or one, advance it first one square, look carefully around, and only then advance it a further square. Of course, you should not hurry in quiet positions, whereas in combinational endings things are different. To many the rule of "do not hurry" may seem paradoxical, but in fact it is seen in practically all the endings of games by great masters of the endgame. Look carefully at the endings of Capablanca and Flohr, and you will see with what slowness, sometimes bordering on tedium, they realize an advantage.

The repetition of moves in the endgame plays an important role. Disregarding the fact that it gains time for thinking, it can be mentioned that, by repeating moves, the active side acquires certain psychological gains. The defender, whose position is inferior, often cannot stand it, and creates a further weakening which eases his opponent's task. In addition, repeating moves enables the position to be clarified to the maximum extent. We know that many upholders of 'pure' chess will severely criticize us for this advice. But we cannot refrain from advising players: you should sometimes repeat moves in the endgame! In the struggle every chance has to be exploited, and there is nothing ugly or unethical in repeating moves.

11	Ne2	g6
12	Rd3+	Ke6
13	Kd4	Ra6
14	Re3+	Kd6
15	Nc3	f5
16	b5	

The pawns begin their advance and the white pieces are able to support them. It should be noted that Capablanca began advancing his pawns only when his pieces had occupied their strongest possible positions. Of course, now Black cannot capture on a3 due to 17 Ne4+.

16	...	Ra8
17	Kc4	Be6+
18	Kb4	c5+
19	bxc6	Bg8
20	Nb5+	Kxc6
21	Rd3	

White can now manage without the advance of his a-pawn. Black's K-side pawns are weakened, and one of them falls.

21	...	g5		
22	Rd6+	Kb7		
23	fxg5	hxg5		
24	Rg5	Rf8	26	...	Rc8
25	Rxg5	f4	27	Rg7+	Kb6
26	Nd4		28	Rg6+	Kb7

associated with ... f3.

A very important move. Capablanca deprives his opponent of any chance

26	...	Rc8
27	Rg7+	Kb6
28	Rg6+	Kb7
29	Nb5	Rf8
30	Nd6+	Kb8
31	h4	Resigns.

CHAPTER 2

CENTRALIZATION OF THE KING

In the transition of a game into the endgame it is the role of the king that changes most of all. In the opening and the middlegame the king endeavours to find a safe shelter and to observe the battle from afar, without as a rule taking any direct part in it, but in the endgame, when the probability of a mating attack is greatly reduced, the king is transformed into an active fighting unit. Often an experienced player, anticipating the transition into an ending, will in advance bring his king closer to the centre, so as then to obtain a playing advantage.

Centralization of the king is one of the main principles of endgame play, but, paradoxically, many players sometimes disregard it. Centralization of the king in the endgame is hardly ever incorrect. It can only be inopportune. Very often, when one side has several apparently equally good plans, the correct one will be that in which the main factor is the centralization of the king. We can therefore advise the reader: if the game has gone into an endgame and you are considering what plan to adopt, never forget about the king!

Capablanca—Reshevsky

Nottingham, 1936

(See next diagram)

White stands better. Black, apart from his isolated pawn, has a whole complex of weak dark squares on the Q-side, especially c5. The winning procedure seems fairly straightforward: it should be sufficient to transfer the king to d4 and the knight to c3, when Black will practically be in *zugzwang*. But in White's

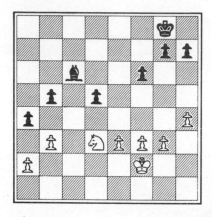

position too there are vulnerable points: his pawn formation is not flawless. Were his rook's pawn at h2, all would be clear. As grandmaster Bondarevsky aptly put it, the white pawn at h4 is that hook which, by holding on to, Black creates counter-play. This is a classic ending and it has been annotated by many authors, but the most correct and accurate analysis is that given by Bondarevsky in *Shakhmatny Bulletin*, 1973 No. 1.

1 . . .	g5!
2 hxg5	

White is forced to fix the K-side pawn structure, otherwise Black, by exchanging on h4, will give White a weak pawn. 2 h5 came into consideration.

2 . . .	fxg5
3 Nb4	

After 3 f4 gxf4 4 exf4 d4! Black would in time lose his d-pawn, but would activate his bishop and have good drawing chances in view of the limited material remaining.

3 . . .	axb3
4 axb3	Bb7

5 g4

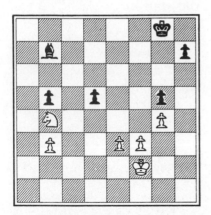

The position has clarified. Black's only counter-chance is . . . h5. There are two fundamentally different ways of preparing this advance. The first, which occurred in the game, is to prepare the advance of the rook's pawn using the king. The second is to centralize the king to defend the weaknesses and to support . . . h5 with the bishop.

5 . . .	Kg7
6 Ke2	Kg6
7 Kd3	h5
8 gxh5+	Kxh5
9 Kd4	Kh4
10 Nxd5	Kg3

Black's idea becomes clear — he has counter-play on the K-side.

| 11 f4 | g4 |

Black loses after 11 . . . Bxd5 12 Kxd5 g4 13 f5 Kh3 14 f6 g3 15 f7 g2 16 f8=Q g1=Q 17 Qh8+ Kg2 18 Qg8+.

| 12 f5 | Bc8 |

Not 12 . . . Bc6 13 Nc7.

| 13 Ke5 | Bd7 |
| 14 e4 | |

Here 14 Nc7 no longer works: 14 . . . Bxf5! 15 Kxf5 Kf3.

| 14 . . . | Be8 |
| 15 Kd4? | |

A mistake, which was noticed only by Bondarevsky. The grandmaster shows that White could have won by 15 f6! Kf3 16 Nf4 g3 17 Kf5 Bd7+ (otherwise *e4—e5—e6*) 18 Kg5 Be6 19 Nxe6!! g2 20 f7 g1=Q+ 21 Kf6.

15 . . .	Kf3
16 e5	g3
17 Ne3	

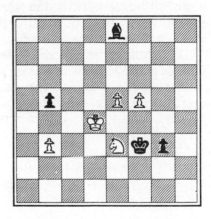

| 17 . . . | Kf4? |

The decisive mistake in a drawn position. Alekhine showed that 17 . . . Bd7 would have lost to 18 e6 Bc8 19 e7 Bd7 20 f6 Be8 21 Nf5, but Bondarevsky found a draw by 17 . . . Bf7!! 18 e6 Bg8 19 e7 (or *19 b4 Kf4!*) 19 . . . Bf7 20 f6 Kf4!, when White is unable to improve his position. By the brilliant manoeuvre 17 . . . Bf7!! Black gains a tempo for playing his king to f4.

But now the rest of the game is clear without any explanation.

18 e6	g2
19 Nxg2+	Kxf5
20 Kd5	Kg4
21 Ne3+	Kf4

22 Kd4

Black resigned, since there is no defence against **23 e7** followed by the transfer of the knight to c7.

We will now analyze the second possible plan: **5 ... Kf7 6 Ke2 Kf6 7 Kd3 Ke5**. Now, as Bondarevsky pointed out, White has to reckon with the possibility of ... d4 followed by ... Kf4, therefore: **8 Nc2 Bc6 9 Nd4 Be8 10 Kc3 h5 11 gxh5 Bxh5 12 Kb4 g4 13 fxg4 Bxg4 14 Kxb5 Ke4 15 Kc5 Kxe3**, and Black gains a draw.

Of course, in a practical game it would be impossible to calculate all the above variations. Therefore it is the general assessment of the position which assumes primary importance. Had Reshevsky chosen the second path, he would have gained a draw. Centralization of the king does not always give the desired result, but in the majority of cases it is necessary.

Em. Lasker—Ed. Lasker

New York, 1924

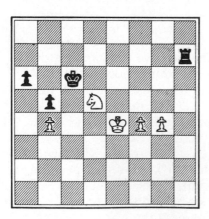

Black is the exchange up. Annotating this game in the tournament book, Alekhine showed that after **1 ... Rd7!** **2 Ne3** (*2 Nf6 Rd8! 3 g5 a5 4 bxa5 b4 5 g6 b3*) **2 ... a5 3 bxa5 b4 4 g5 Kc5 5 Nc2 b3 6 Na3 b2 7 g6 Kb4**

8 Nb1 Rd1 9 g7 Rg1 Black wins.
In the game Black played

| 1 ... | Rh8 |

with the threat of giving check and winning the knight.

2 Ne3

Forced, since **2 Nc3** merely strengthens the effect of ... a5.

2 ...	Re8+
3 Kd4	Rd8+
4 Ke4!	

One of the most difficult moves in this ending. It would seem that Emanuel Lasker evaluated the position intuitively. After **4 Kc3** Black does not have a forced win, but the probability of defeat for White would be considerable. Black, for instance, could play **4 ... Rd6**. If now the knight moves from e3, the black rook reaches d1, while if the white pawns advance the black king transfers behind the back of the rook to e7. The main drawback to White's position after **4 Kc3** is that his king is cut off from the K-side, and he therefore has no real counter-play.

Emanuel Lasker chooses a plan which, though risky, is the only correct one. He keeps his king in the centre, from where it can easily be switched to either wing. By threatening the advance of his pawns, White forces Black to play ...a5, and he hopes to be able to cope with the one black pawn. This plan demands coolness and an accurate appraisal of all the subtleties in the position. Had the black rook been on the seventh rank, White's play would not have succeeded.

4 ...	a5
5 bxa5	b4
6 a6!	

This is the tactical basis of White's play. He would have lost after 6 g5 b3 7 Nc4 Kc5 8 Nb2 Rd2 9 Nd3+ Kc4 10 Ne5+ Kc3.

6 ...	Kc5

6 ... b3 does not succeed: 7 Nc4 Kb5 8 Nb2 Kxa6 9 Ke3 Kb5 10 g5 Kb4 11 g6 Kc3 12 Na4+ with a draw.

7 a7	b3
8 Nd1	

The pawn at a7 makes this move possible.

8 ...	Ra8
9 g5	Rxa7
10 g6	Rd7
11 Nb2	Rd2
12 Kf3!	

White is rescued by the centralized position of his king. Black is forced to retrace his steps, since after 12 ... Rxb2? 13 g7 White wins.

12 ...	Rd8
13 Ke4	Kd6

Now White's king rushes across to the Q-side to the black pawn, sacrificing his own passed pawns.

14 Kd4!	Rc8
15 g7!	Ke6
16 g8=Q+	Rxg8
17 Kc4	Rg3

After 17 ... Rb8 Black again loses his pawn: 18 Kc3 Kf5 19 Nd3 Rb6. Now 20 Kb2 is bad due to 20 ... Ke4, but if White coolly waits with 20 Nb2 Kxf4 21 Na4 Rb8 22 Nb2, Black has no possibility of winning. As soon as the black king reaches e1 with the white king at c3 and knight at b2, there immediately follows Na4 Kd1;

Kb2, forcing the win of the pawn by Nc5.

18 Na4	Kf5
19 Kb4	Kxf4
20 Nb2	Ke4
21 Na4	Kd4
22 Nb2	Rf3
23 Na4	Re3
24 Nb2	Ke4

The final attempt to break through.

25 Na4	Kf3
26 Ka3!	

Now 26 ... Ke2 is met by 27 Kb2.

26 ...	Ke4
27 Kb4	Kd4
28 Nb2	Rh3
29 Na4	Kd3
30 Kxb3	Kd4+

Drawn. A very difficult ending, in which the white king saved his army from defeat.

Fyedorov—Chernikov

Krasnodar, 1974

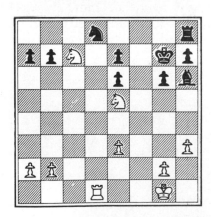

We give the commentary to this game by grandmaster Averbakh in *Shakhmaty v SSSR*, 1978 No. 9:

"White has a powerful initiative. His knights have broken into the enemy position and with the support of the rook have created the grounds for various tactical blows. Black's pieces are restricted, and only his bishop is displaying some semblance of activity, by attacking the e3 pawn. Fyedorov played

1 Kf2

following the good old rule that in the endgame the king should head for the centre. But this natural move gave Black a respite, and by

1 ... Nc6

he began exchanging off White's attacking pieces. It is true that after

2 Nxc6   bxc6
3 Rc1

Fyedorov won the c-pawn, but Black gained the opportunity to activate his rook, and in the end, not without the help of his opponent and . . . time trouble, he gained a draw.

Yet in the diagram position White had the possibility of an elegant three-move manoeuvre which would have tied the opponent hand and foot: 1 Ng4! Nc6 (*2 Rxd8* was threatened) 2 Rf1! Nd8 3 h4!, and Black's position is hopeless.

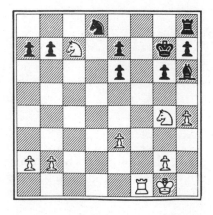

White plays 4 Rf2 and takes his king across to the Q-side, winning.

Why did Fyedorov, an undoubtedly talented master, fail to find this quite straightforward forcing manoeuvre?

It seems to me that he played his king to f2 without much thought. A pawn is attacked, it has to be defended, and the king is better placed in the centre."

The position demanded thinking in terms of schemes, and the centralization of the king should have been deferred for the moment.

Dvoryetsky—Smyslov

Odessa, 1974

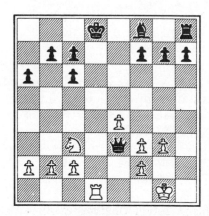

White's K-side pawn majority is more of a reality than Black's on the Q-side. Black has to decide which pawn formation to leave White with on the K-side: e4/e3/f3/g3, or (after *1 ... Qd4*) e4/f3/f2/g3.

1 ...   Kc8?

Black should have concentrated all his forces, including his king, on the K-side to parry the opponent's onslaught. Perfectly reasonable was either 1 ... Qd4 2 Rxd4+ Ke8, or 1 ... Bd6 2 fxe3 Ke7.

2 fxe3   g6?!

This allows White to seize the initiative completely on the K-side. 2. . .Be7 is preferable.

3 e5!	Bg7
4 f4	f6

Otherwise after 5 Ne4 Black is in a bind.

5 exf6	Bxf6
6 e4	h5
7 Kg2	Bxc3
8 bxc3	

After this exchange the difference in the positions of the two kings is especially noticeable.

8 . . .	b5
9 e5	a5
10 Kh3!	

Black has no way of opposing the break-through of the white king.

10 . . .	b4
11 Kh4!	Re8
12 Kg5	Re6
13 Kh6	

Black resigned, since against Kg7—f7 there is no defence.

Roizman—Mikhalevsky

Minsk, 1979

(See next diagram)

Black's passed pawn is blockaded, while White has all the preconditions for creating an outside passed pawn on the Q-side. In the event of the knights being exchanged the game should end in a draw, while after the exchange of queens much will depend on the mutual placing of the kings. Black therefore begins

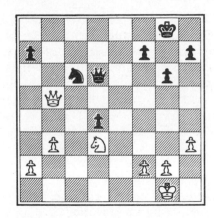

centralization.

1 . . .	Kg7
2 b4?!	

White's king is too far from the centre, and any transition into a knight ending will favour Black. He should have played 2 Kf1.

2 . . .	Nc7
3 a4?!	

Not 3 Qe5+ Qxe5 4 Nxe5 Kf6 5 Nf3 Ke6 6 Nxd4+ Kd5 7 Nb5 Kc4 8 Nd6+ (after *8 Nxa7 Kxb4* the knight is lost) 8 . . . Kxb4 with advantage to Black, but White should have activated his king and only then advanced his pawns.

3 . . .	Nd5
4 g3?	

White still thinks that he has the advantage, and he parries the threat of 4 . . . Nf4 with a transition into a drawn queen ending. But the black pieces are already pretty active. After this move it is difficult for White to avoid the exchange of queens, and in the knight ending, thanks to the activity of his king, Black gains the advantage.

4 . . .	Nc3
5 Qe8	

9

Risky is 5 Qa5 Qe6 6 Qxa7 Qe4 7 Qa6 Qf3, while after 5 Qc5 the difference in the positions of the kings becomes important — Black is the first to reach c4.

5 ...	Qe6!
6 Qxe6	fxe6
7 a5	Kf6
8 Kf1	

White cannot prevent the advance of the e-pawn by 8 f4 due to 8 ... Kf5 9 Nc5 e5, and after the exchange the black king penetrates to c4.

8 ...	e5
9 Nc5	

Here too 9 f3 does not help: 9 ... Ke6 10 Ke1 Kd5 11 Nb2 e4.

9 ...	e4
10 Ke1	Ke5
11 Nd7+	Kd5!

The main thing is to activate the king!

12 b5

12 Nf6+ should also be examined. Before looking at any variations, we must dwell on the principles of playing such endings. Black wins if his king can control the queening square of the d-pawn, i.e. stand on one of the critical squares c2 or c1 without being pursued by the white knight. The defender must attack the king in such a way that he can control one of the critical squares and check the king when it steps onto the other. We will consider an example.

(See next diagram)

Black is in check, and on 1 ... Kb2 there follows 2 Nd4! when the knight controls one of the critical squares c2, and can attack the king if it returns to

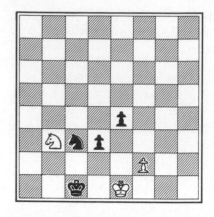

the other critical square c1. The position is drawn. But if White moves his knight to another square, e.g. d2, the black king acquires a choice of critical squares, and White loses: 2 Nd2 Kc2 3 Nc4 Nb1 4 Ne3+ Kc1 5 Nc4 Na3! (5 ... d2+ is also good enough).

Let us now continue our analysis of the game after the possible 12 Nf6+ Kc4 13 Nxh7 Kd3 14 Ng5 (or *14 Nf6 Kc2 15 Ng4 e3! 16 fxe3 d3 17 Nf2 d2+ 18 Kf1 Ne4*) 14 ... Kc2 15 Ne6 Nb5! 16 Ng5 Nd6! (it was essential to vacate c3 for the black king) 17 Ne6 d3 18 Nd4+ Kc3 19 Ne6 d2+ 20 Ke2 Nc4, and wins.

12 ...	Nxb5
13 Nf6+	Kc4!

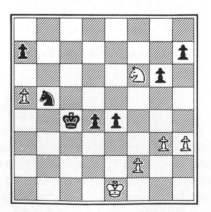

14 Kd2?

After this Black wins very easily.

White had two other possibilities:

(a) 14 Nxe4 (the weaker alternative) 14 . . . Kd3 15 Nd2 Kc2 16 f4 d3 17 g4 Nd4 18 h4 Kc1 19 Ne4 Nc2+ 20 Kf2 d2, with an easy win.

(b) 14 Nxh7! (attempting to create an outside passed pawn on the K-side) 14 . . . Kd3 15 Ng5 (*15 Nf6 Nc3 16 Ng4 Kc2 17 Ne5 d3 18 Nc4 Nb1 19 Ne3+ Kc1 20 Nc4 Na3!*) 15 . . . Nd6! (not *15 . . . e3 16 h4*). Here White again has two possibilities. We give some sample variations:

(b1) 16 Ne6 Kc3 17 Kd1 Nc4 (not *17 . . . d3 18 Nc5* with a draw) 18 Ng5 (after *18 Nc5* White loses in a pawn ending: *18 . . . Nb2+ 19 Ke1 Nd3+ 20 Nxd3 Kxd3 21 Kd1 e3 22 fxe3 Kxe3 23 g4 g5!* − not 23 . . . Kf3 24 g5 Kg3 25 Kd2 with a draw − *24 a6 d3 25 Ke1 d2+ 26 Kd1 Kd3 27 h4 gxh4*, and mates) 18 . . . Kd3! 19 Ne6 (if *19 h4 e3*) 19 . . . Nxa5! 20 Nc5+ Kc4 21 Nxe4 Nb3 22 h4 a5 23 Kc2 d3+ 24 Kb2 a4 25 g4 Kd4 26 Nd6 a3+ 27 Kxb3 d2 28 Nb5+ Kd3 29 Nc3 a2.

(b2) 16 Kd1 e3 17 fxe3 Kxe3 18 Ne6 Ne4 19 Nc7 (*19 Nf4* loses to *19 . . . Nf2+* and *20 . . . Nd3+*) 19 . . . Nxg3 20 Nd5+ Ke4 21 Ne7 (*21 Nf6+ Kd3 22 a6 Ne4 23 Nd7 Ke3 24 Ne5 d3 25 Nc4+ Kd4 26 Nb6 axb6 27 a7 Ke3 28 a8=Q Nf2+*) 21 . . . g5 22 Kd2 Nf1+ 23 Ke1 Ne3 24 a6 Nc4 25 Kd1 d3 26 Ke1 Kd4 27 Kd1 d2 28 Ke2 (if *28 Kc2 Ke4*) 28 . . . Kc3 29 Nd5+ Kc2 30 Nb4+ Kb2 31 Kd1 Kc3 32 Nd5+ Kd4 33 Nb4 Ke3 34 Nd5+ Kf2 35 Nc3 Kf3 36 Kc2 Ke3 37 Nd5+ Ke2 38 Nc3+ (were f4 available to the white knight, the game could end in a draw) 38 . . . Ke1. When the black pawn is at d2 and the white king at d1, the critical squares are d3 and e3, while with the white king at c2 the critical squares became e2 and e1.

The game actually concluded:

14 . . .	Nd6
15 Nxh7	e3+
16 fxe3	Ne4+
17 Kd1	d3
White resigns.	

CHAPTER 3

THE ROLE OF PAWNS IN THE ENDGAME

In the endgame the main task is not usually the immediate mating of the opponent's king, but the queening of a pawn. Therefore, in comparison with the middlegame, in the endgame the value of the pawns increases. This must be taken into account when solving exchanging problems. Right in the opening stage of the game examined below White carried out a complex and deep combination, as a result of which play went into an ending, by-passing the middlegame. For the sacrificed piece White gained three pawns.

Schlechter—Duras

San Sebastian, 1911

1 e4	e5
2 Nf3	Nc6
3 Nc3	Nf6
4 Bb5	Bb4
5 0—0	0—0
6 d3	d6
7 Bg5	Ne7
8 Nh4	c6
9 Bc4	Ne8

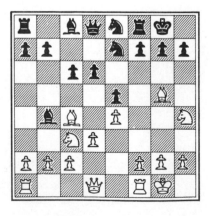

10 f4!?

A piece sacrifice, the consequences of which had to be judged accurately.

10 ...	Bxc3
11 bxc3	d5
12 Bb3	f6
13 fxe5	fxg5
14 Rxf8+	Kxf8
15 Qf3+	Kg8
16 Rf1	Nc7
17 Qf7+	Kh8
18 exd5	cxd5
19 Qf8+	Qxf8
20 Rxf8+	Ng8
21 Nf3	

As a result of his combination White for the moment has only one pawn for the piece, but the dominating position of his rook enables him to acquire two further pawns.

21 ...   Be6?

Probably the decisive mistake. Black incorrectly approaches the exchanging problem. The advance of White's passed pawns will be best supported by his long-range bishop, and the black cavalry will clearly be unable to cope with it and the three enemy infantrymen. After the correct 21 ... Bd7 22 Rxa8 Nxa8 23 Bxd5 Bc6! (leaving the opponent with a knight, not a bishop) 24 Bxc6 bxc6 25 Nxg5 Ne7 a hard struggle would have been in prospect. It should be added that on 21 ...g4 White can continue 22 Nd4! Bd7 23 Rxa8 Nxa8 24 Bxd5, obtaining three pawns for a piece in a favourable version.

22 Rxa8   Nxa8

23	Nxg5	Nc7
24	Nxe6	Nxe6
25	Bxd5	Nd8
26	d4	

Black is unable to prevent the advance of the central pawns.

26	...	Ne7
27	Bb3	Nec6
28	Kf2	

The white king hurries to the aid of the pawns.

28	...	Na5
29	e6!	Nac6

Not 29 ... Nxb3 30 e7.

30	d5	Ne7
31	d6	

The pawns sweep away everything in their path.

31	...	Ndc6
32	dxe7	Nxe7

The rest is clear.

33	Kf3	Kg8
34	Ke4	Kf8
35	Ke5	Ke8
36	Bd5	b6
37	Be4	h6
38	Kd6	Kd8
39	Bd3	h5
40	h4!	b5
41	Bxb5	Nf5+
42	Ke5	Nxh4
43	Bd3!	

44 Be4 is threatened, and on 43 ... Nxg2 there follows 44 Kd6. **Black resigned.**

Lukov–Syemkov

Bulgarian Championship, 1977

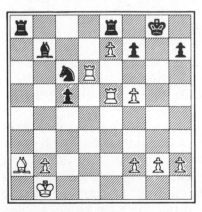

White has sacrificed a knight, obtaining three pawns in return, one of which has reached the seventh rank. But with his last move ... Nb8—c6 Black has simultaneously threatened the white rook and passed pawn. In the event of 1 Rxc5 Rxe7 2 Bd5 Nb4! 3 Bxb7 Re1+ 4 Rc1 Ra1+ the white king is mated. Nevertheless White has a way to maintain his initiative.

1 Rxc6!

Now Black has an extra rook for only three pawns! But in the endgame there is a difference between the absolute and relative values of pawns. Follow the advance of the white infantry, which the opponent's superior forces is unable to prevent.

1	...	Bxc6
2	f6	h6

The threat was 3 Rg5+ followed by Bxf7.

3	Re3	c4!

A clever defence. By sacrificing a fourth pawn, Black opens the c-file and gains counter-play.

4	Bxc4	Rec8
5	b3!	

Reinforcing the bishop and opening an escape for the king. Not 5 Rg3+ Kh8 6 Bxf7?? Be4+.

5	...	Ra5

To be able to answer 6 Rg3+ with 6 ... Rg5.

6	g4!	Be8
7	f4	

The pawns advance in strict battle formation.

7	...	Rca8
8	Rd3	

The d8 square is put under attack.

8	...	Kh7

Rook checks do not achieve anything.

9	Rd6

Not allowing the black king to come out: 9 ... Kg6?? 10 Bd3+.

9	...	Rc8
10	h4	Ra7
11	Kb2	

White can improve the position of his king, since the advance of his pawns cannot be prevented.

11	...	Rd7

This hastens the inevitable.

12	Rxd7	Bxd7
13	Bxf7	Rb8
14	g5	hxg5
15	fxg5	Be8
16	g6+	Resigns.

Miller—Weltmander

Izhevsk, 1949

Black has some compensation for the exchange in the form of his superior pawn formation, his well-placed pieces and his extra pawn. But it is White to move, and he carries out what appears to be a winning combination.

1	Nxd5!	Kxd5
2	Rf1	

There appears to be no defence against 3 g4, but Black finds a counter-combination.

2	...	a5!
3	g4	Nxc3!!
4	Rxc3	b4
5	Rcf3	Bxc2!
6	Rxf6	b3

(See next diagram)

A curious situation. The black bishop and two pawns prove no weaker than the white rooks.

7	Ra6	Kxd4
8	Rxa5	b2
9	Rb5	c3
10	Rb8	Bd3
11	Re1	Kc5

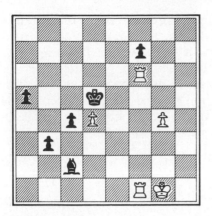

Black prepares to block the b-file with his bishop.

	12	Kf2	Bb5
	13	Re5+	Kd6!
	14	Rexb5	c2
	15	Rxb2	c1=Q

Drawn

Botvinnik—Keres

19th USSR Championship
Moscow, 1951

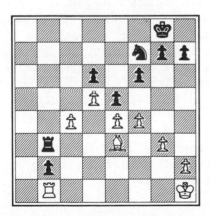

Black has a decisive positional advantage. His passed b-pawn, supported from behind by his rook, ties down White's entire forces. The white bishop is attacked, and if it moves the game will be concluded by Black bringing his knight over to the Q-side via f7—d8—b7—c5 or a5. Botvinnik finds the best practical chance,

which involves sacrificing his bishop.

1 c5!

All White's hopes are pinned on this pawn.

1 ...   Rxe3

As shown by Keres, 1 ... dxc5   2 Bxc5 Nd8? gets Black nowhere due to 3 fxe5 fxe5   4 Bd6!, but 2 ... g5! came into consideration.

2 Rxb2   g6?

In time trouble, Keres makes a mistake which leads to a draw. He should have answered with a counter-sacrifice of a piece to eliminate the enemy passed pawn in the variation 2 ... h5! 3 Rb8+ Kh7   4 Rf8 dxc5! 5 Rxf7 exf4   6 gxf4 Rxe4,   and Black must win the rook ending. White is not saved by 3 c6 Rc3   4 Rb7 Nh6   5 Rd7 Ng4   6 Rxd6 Rc1+   7 Kg2 Rc2+ (pointed out by Botvinnik).

| | 3 | c6 | Rc3 |
| | 4 | Rb7!! | Kg7 |

Botvinnik showed that Black could also hardly have hoped to win after other moves, for example: 4 ... Kf8 5 Rb8+ (*5 c7 Ke8*) 5 ... Kg7 (if *5 ... Ke7*, then *6 Rb7+ Ke8   7 Rb8+ Nd8   8 Rc8!* with the threat of *9 c7*) 6 Rb7. Black has gained a tempo, but it is difficult to make use of it, since on 6 ... f5 there follows 7 fxe5 dxe5   8 exf5 gxf5   9 Rd7, threatening c6—c7 and d5—d6.

5 c7

(See next diagram)

The players have exchanged roles. Black's passed pawn has been eliminated

at the cost of the white bishop. White's passed pawn has reached the seventh rank and is worth no less than the black knight. Not one black piece has freedom of movement. The rook cannot move off the c-file, the knight is restricted by the threat of c8=Q+, and king moves are met by Rb8+ or c8=Q. A positional draw! The game continued:

5 ...	Rc2
6 Kg1	h5
7 h4	Rc4
8 Kg2	Rc2+
9 Kf1	Rc4

Drawn

Timman—Gligoric

Bad Lauterberg, 1977

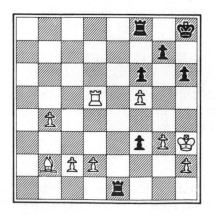

On the previous move the queens were exchanged. A brief glance at the position shows it to favour Black. Formally White has sufficient compensation for the exchange — two pawns, but it is difficult for him to deal with the enemy pawn at f3. White's only hope lies in his Q-side pawn armada.

1 Bd4	Rfe8
2 Kg4	Rf1
3 Kf4	

3 ... Re4+ was threatened.

3 ...	Re2
4 Be3	Rxh2
5 b5	f2
6 Kf3	Rc1
7 Bxf2	Rf1
8 c4	Rfxf2+
9 Ke4	Re2+

The ending after 9 ... Rxd2? 10 Rxd2 Rxd2 11 b6 favours White.

| 10 Kd4 | Rxd2+ |
| 11 Kc5 | Rb2 |

Here too the exchange of rooks favours White. Annotating this game in Volume 23 of *Chess Informator*, grandmaster Marjanovic gives the variation 11 ... Rxd5+? 12 Kxd5 Kg8 13 c5! Kf7 14 Kd6 Ke8 15 Kc7. The white king 'shoulder-charges' his black colleague away from the passed pawns, after which Black is unable to prevent them from queening.

| 12 Kc6 | Rhc2 |
| 13 c5 | |

As a result of an almost forced series of moves Black has an extra rook for just one pawn, but White's passed pawns on the Q-side, supported by his king, are a formidable force.

13 ...	Rc3
14 Kb6	h5
15 c6	Rbc2
16 Kc7	Kh7
17 Rd6	Rxg3
18 b6	

Black is now a whole rook up, which he would be glad to give up for the opponent's passed pawns, but the pawns, having reached the sixth rank, are worth more.

18 ...	Rb3
19 b7	Rcb2

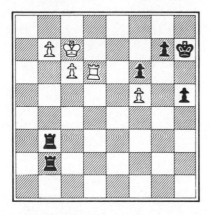

By skilful play Glogiric has stopped the enemy pawns at the last line, and has created a passed pawn of his own. It appears that White is faced with having to suffer in the queen ending after 20 Rd8 h4 21 b8=Q Rxb8 22 Rxb8 Rxb8 23 Kxb8 h3 24 c7 h2 25 c8=Q h1=Q, but Timman finds a brilliant defensive idea.

20 Rd4!!

It transpires that the situation on the board is a positional draw. If Black plays 20 ... Kh6, White replies 21 Rd8, and Black cannot go into the queen ending, since after queening his pawn White wins by a check at h8. In the event of the exchange of the f- and g-pawns after 20 ... g6 21 fxg6+ Kxg6 22 Rd8 h4

23 b8=Q Rxb8 24 Rxb8 Rxb8 25 Kxb8 h3 26 c7 h2 27 c8=Q h1=Q White must give perpetual check by 28 Qg4+. The game continued:

20 ...	Rb5
21 Ra4	Rb1
22 Rd4	R1b3
23 Ra4	Rb2
24 Rd4	R5b3
25 Ra4	Rb1

Drawn

Model–Kubbel

Leningrad, 1929

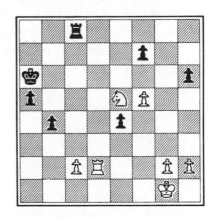

White is a knight up for only a pawn. Apart from his central pawn, which can easily be blockaded, Black has no far-advanced passed pawns. But the position is of a concrete nature, and White's apparent well-being is deceptive.

1 ...	e3
2 Rd6+	

Leonid Kubbel, now an acknowledged classic of chess composition, gives the following variations after 2 Re2: "... Black wins by the study-like 2 ... b3 3 Nd3 Rc3 4 Kf1 (or *4 g4*) 4 ... Rxd3 (Black gives up the exchange and obtains two connected passed pawns against a rook) 5 cxd3 a4 6 Rb2 Kb5

17

etc., or 3 c4 Rd8 4 Re1 (*4 g4 Rd1+ 5 Kg2 Rd2*, and after the exchange of rooks the b-pawn queens) 4 . . . b2 5 Nxf7 (attacking the rook; if *5 Nf3 e2*) 5 . . . Rd2 etc.".

| 2 . . . | Kb5 |
| 3 Nf3 | |

There is no other way of defending the c-pawn.

| 3 . . . | Rxc2! |

Nevertheless!

| 4 Nd4+ | Kc5 |
| 5 Nxc2 | |

5 Rc6+ Kxd4 6 Rxc2 b3 is completely hopeless.

5 . . .	Kxd6
6 Kf1	b3
7 Na3	Kc5
8 g4	Kb4
9 Nb1	a4

White resigns.

CHAPTER 4

THE PROBLEM OF EXCHANGING

As material is reduced the problem of exchanging becomes of primary importance. In the opening or middlegame the consequences of an incorrect piece exchange can sometimes subsequently be repaired, but in the endgame such a mistake can be fatal. Of course, in the majority of cases an experienced player will easily determine which exchange favours him. But situations often arise where an exchange which seems plausible on general grounds turns out to be routine and not in accordance with the demands of the position, whereas a decision which is at first sight paradoxical proves to be the only correct one. We will also consider cases where there is only one reply to the question "to take or not to take?", but there are several different captures leading to play of a different nature. In addition, this chapter contains examples where one of the sides is faced with loss of material. We will see how difficult it can be to choose the least out of several evils.

Simplification is often the best way of realizing a material or positional advantage. The outcome of a game may depend mainly on the ability of a player to solve correctly the problem of exchanging, whether to make a timely simplification of the position or, on the contrary, maintain the tension.

Klein—Capablanca

New York, 1913

(See next diagram)

As yet this is far from being an endgame position. Black has a big advantage: the better bishop and an 'eternal'

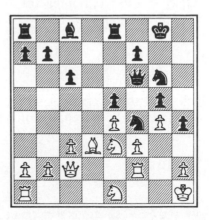

knight at f4 — the pride of his position. In the game there nevertheless followed:

1 ...   Nxd3!

Capablanca gives up his splendid knight for White's bad bishop, demonstrating a subtle assessment of the position. It would seem that in the joke prevalent among chess players "the worst bishop is better than the best knight" there is a grain of truth. The black knight at f4 occupies an ideal position, of course, but how can any real advantage be extracted from this? White's bishop seems to be bad, but it holds together his K-side pawn formation, and has fair prospects in the event of possible play on the Q-side. Black aims to take play into an ending where his bishop may prove stronger than the white knight, taking account of the K-side pawn formation.

2 Nxd3   Be6
3 Rd1   Red8
4 b3   Nf4
5 Ng2?!

A strange move. 5 Nf5 or 5 Nxf4 more natural.

5	...	Nxd3		
6	Rxd3	Rxd3		
7	Qxd3	Rd8		

Possibly White was hoping for 7 ... Bxg4? 8 Nxh4 gxh4 9 Rg2.

8	Qe2	h3!
9	Ne3	a5

Black sets about creating weaknesses on the Q-side. The advantage of bishop over knight is obvious.

10	Rf1	a4
11	c4	

Now the d4 square is weakened, but 11 bxa4 is even worse due to 11 ... Qf4! followed by ... Ra8.

11	...	Rd4
12	Nc2	Rd7
13	Ne3	Qd8
14	Rd1	Rxd1+
15	Nxd1	

After 15 Qxd1 Black's 15 ... Qd4 is again very strong.

15	...	Qd4
16	Nf2	b5
17	cxb5	axb3!
18	axb3	Bxb3
19	Nxh3	Bd1

Black's passed b-pawn and the weakness of White's K-side decide the outcome of the game.

20	Qf1	cxb5
21	Kg2	b4
22	Qb5	b3
23	Qe8+	Kg7
24	Qe7	b2
25	Nxg5	Bb3

White's threats are easily parried, while the black pawn is about to queen.

26	Nxf7	Bxf7
27	Qg5+	Kf8
28	Qh6+	Ke7
29	Qg5+	Ke8

The checks are at an end, and **White resigned.**

It is curious that in his book *My Chess Career* Capablanca does not even comment on 1 ... Nxd3! For him such a plan was the natural continuation.

Flohr–Spielmann

Bled, 1931

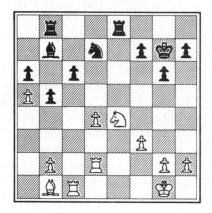

On the Q-side Black has a weak c-pawn and a badly placed bishop at b7. He makes a desperate attempt to escape from the vice.

> 1 ...   f5!

Preparing the freeing break ... c5.

> 2 Nd6!!

A solution which is convincing in its simplicity. The white knight is forced to move, but where to? 2 Nc5 can immediately be discarded, since after 2 ... Nxc5 3 dxc5 White loses the greater part of his advantage. On 2 Nc3 or 2 Nf2 there follows 2 ... c5!, when the worst for Black is over. That

20

only leaves moves to g3, g5 and d6.
In the first two cases it is unfavourable
for Black to play . . . c5, e.g. 2 Ng5
c5? 3 dxc5 Nxc5 4 Rxc5 Re1+ 5
Kf2 Rxb1 6 Rc7+ with decisive
threats. But at g3 the knight is badly
placed, and 2 Ng5 can be met by
2 . . . h6, driving the knight to the edge
of the board and obtaining counter-play
after . . . Rbc8. Flohr does not try to
cling to the advantage he has already
achieved, but converts it into a different
form.

2 ...	Re6
3 Nxb7	Rxb7
4 d5!	cxd5
5 Rxd5	

Black's weak c-pawn and his bad bishop have disappeared from the board,
but his position has not improved. After
the series of exchanges White's advantage
is not as obvious as it was before, but it
is of a stable nature. All the black pawns
are on white squares, the a6 pawn being
especially weak. The bishop is clearly
superior to the knight, which has no
strong points, and White's rooks are
significantly more active than the opponent's. By the following manoeuvre
Flohr improves the deployment of his
forces, exchanges one pair of rooks, and
then sets about implementing his strategic plan of giving Black a second weakness on the K-side.

5 ...	Nf6
6 Rdc5	Rbe7
7 Kf1	Ne8
8 Ba2	Re2
9 R5c2	Rxc2
10 Rxc2	

With the exchange of one pair of
rooks the white king can advance without fear.

| 10 ... | Nc7 |

11 Rc6

The black pieces are tied to the defence of the a6 pawn. To win White
needs to create one further weakness in
the opponent's position.

11 ...	Kf8
12 h4	Kg7
13 Kf2	Kh6
14 Bb3	

The immediate 14 g4 is also possible,
but since Black is deprived of the slightest counter-play, White operates according to the principle "do not hurry!".

14 ...	Kh5
15 Kg3	Rd7
16 Kh3	Kh6
17 Kg3	Re7
18 Kf4	Kh5
19 g3	

Black is in an unusual form of *zugzwang*. His knight has no moves due to
the loss of his a6 pawn, and his rook
must not allow the white king to e5.
Therefore his king must retreat from h5,
allowing g3—g4.

| 19 ... | Kh6 |
| 20 Bg8! | |

A continuation of the previous tactics.
The bishop will return to a2 and will
stand better than at b3, being defended
by the b2 pawn against a horizontal
attack by the black rook.

20 ...	Kg7
21 Ba2	Kh6
22 g4!	fxg4
23 fxg4	Kg7
24 g5	

The noose tightens. There is practically nothing that Black can move.

21

24 ...	Kf8
25 Kf3	Ke8

Black's game is lost. White has many ways to win, e.g. 26 Rf6 followed by the exchange of rooks at f7 at an appropriate moment. Flohr chooses a different, more consistent plan: he completely breaks up the black pawns on the K-side, giving his opponent a second weakness. In passing White sets a clever, camouflaged trap, into which Black falls.

26 h5!?	gxh5
27 Rh6	b4
28 Rxh5	Re5?!
29 Kf4!	Rxa5
30 g6!!	

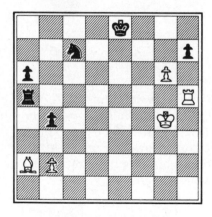

Black resigns.

Szabo—Fischer

Buenos Aires, 1970

(See next diagram)

Black has slightly the more active position, but a draw is the most likely outcome. But the Hungarian grandmaster plays

1 Nd4?

committing a serious, but by no means

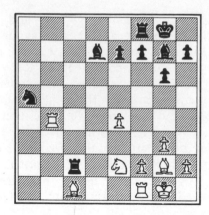

obvious mistake. After the correct 1 Nf4 it is unlikely that Black would have been able to realize his insignificant positional advantage.

1 ...	Bxd4!

A deeply-conceived exchange. In the King's Indian Defence, which was played in this game, the black-squared bishops are especially valuable. Fischer exchanges his fianchettoed bishop, foreseeing a forcing manoeuvre, as a result of which Black remains with two rooks and a knight against White's two rooks and a bishop.

2 Rxd4	Bb5
3 Re1	

3 Rfd1 Nb3 4 Rb4 Be2 is bad for White.

3 ...	Nb3
4 Rb4	Nxc1
5 Rxb5	

All the pawns are on one wing, which slightly favours the side with the knight. But how is this advantage to be transformed into something real? After 5 ... Nd3 6 Rf1 Black does not have any serious advantage. The American grandmaster finds a fine knight manoeuvre.

5 ...	Ne2+!

6 Kf1?!

This natural move is the decisive mistake. White would have retained some drawing chances after 6 Kh1, leaving f1 free for his rook.

6 ...	Nc3!

The knight has taken up an ideal position. The manoeuvre ... Rd8—d2 cannot be prevented.

7	Rc5	Rd8
8	Bh3	Rdd2
9	Rc8+	Kg7
10	Re3	Nd1!

Ten moves ago it was impossible to imagine such a turn of events. The loss of two pawns is inevitable for White. The finish was:

11	Rf3	Rxf2+
12	Rxf2	Rxf2+
13	Kg1	Re2
14	Bg4	Rxe4

White resigns.

Mikhalyevsky—Akopov

Rostov, 1977

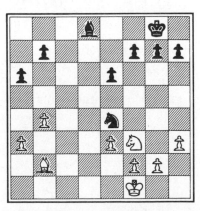

The position looks roughly equal, and after the exact 1 ... Nd6 2 Nd2 f6

followed by the centralization of his king, Black would have had every right to count on a draw. But instead he played

1 ...	Bf6?

Black should have aimed for the exchange of knights, and not bishops, since in a knight ending a spatial advantage is often a decisive factor.

2 Bxf6	Nxf6?!

Now the white king breaks through in the centre, ahead of Black's. It would have been better to allow the spoiling of his pawn formation, but restrain the white king, by capturing on f6 with the pawn. After 2 ... gxf6 3 Ke2 Kf8 the pawn sacrifice 4 Kd3 Nxf2+ 5 Kd4 does not achieve anything due to 5 ... Nd1, and White would have had to waste time on driving the black knight from e4.

3 Ke2	Kf8

3 ... Ne4 is dangerous due to 4 Kd3! Nxf2+ 5 Kd4, and here 5 ... Nd1 is well met by 6 e4, if there is nothing better.

4	Kd3	Ke7
5	Kd4	Nd7
6	Nd2!	

White avoids the unclear complications which could have arisen after 6 e4 Kd6 7 e5+ Kc6 8 Ng5 Kb5, and prevents Black from activating his king, since 6 ... Kd6 can be met by 7 Nc4+ Kc6 8 e4, cramping Black still further.

6 ...	Nb6
7 e4	

The pawn ending after 7 Ne4 Na4 8 Nc5 Nxc5 9 Kxc5 Kd7 is most probably drawn.

23

7 ...	Na4	20 ...	fxg4
		21 fxg4	Nd1
		22 g5?!	

After 7 ... Kd6 8 e5+ Kc6 9 Ne4 Kb5, apart from 10 Nd6+ with unclear complications, White has the simple 10 Nc3+, retaining all the advantages of his position.

This move should not have been made, since Black acquires counter-play by ... Kf7—g6. 22 a4! was good, when a possible variation would be 22 ... Nb2 23 a5 b5 24 Kc5 g5 25 hxg5 hxg5 26 Ng6+! Kf7 27 Kb6 Nd3 28 Kxa6 Nxb4 29 Kxb5 Nd5 30 a6 Nc7+ 31 Kb6 Nxa6 32 Kxa6 Kxg6 33 Kb6, winning.

8 e5	f5

Instead of the backward f7 pawn, Black acquires a weakness at e6.

9 Nc4	Kd7
10 Nd6	b6
11 f3	Nb2
12 h4!	

White aims to weaken the opponent's K-side, which Black is unable to prevent.

12 ...	Na4
13 Nf7	Ke7
14 Ng5	h6
15 Nh3	Kd7
16 Nf4	Ke7
17 Kc4?!	

By subtle play White has gained the better position. He should now have shut the black knight out of the game by 17 Nd3, when Kc4 followed by b4—b5 is decisive, e.g. 17 Nd3! Kd7 18 Kc4 Kc6 19 Nf4! Kd7 20 Nh5.

17 ...	Nb2+
18 Kc3	Nd1+
19 Kd4	Nb2
20 g4?!	

It would have been simpler to give the opponent the move by 20 Kc3 Nd1+ 21 Kd3 Nb2+ 22 Kd4, when 22 ... Na4 is bad due to 23 Nd3, while 22 ... Nd1 is very strongly met by 23 a4!, e.g. 23 ... Nb2 24 a5 b5 25 Nd3, with a won pawn ending.

22 ...	hxg5
23 hxg5	Nb2
24 g6	

White cramps Black's position to the maximum, but uses up his reserve tempo. However, after 24 Kc3 Nd1+ 25 Kd3 Nb2+ 26 Kd4 Na4! (26 ... Nd1 is bad due to 27 a4) 27 Nd3 Kf7! 28 Kc4 Kg6 29 Kb3 b5 30 Nc5 Kxg5 31 Nxa6 Black has serious counter-play.

24 ...	Na4
25 Nd3	Kd8
26 Kc4	Kd7??

A fatal blunder. After 26 ... b5+ 27 Kd4 Kd7 28 Nc5+ Nxc5 29 Kxc5 Kc7 White does not have the tempo move g5—g6, and the game ends in a draw.

27 b5	axb5+
28 Kxb5	Nc3+
29 Kxb6	Nd5+
30 Kb7	Ne7
31 a4	Nxg6
32 a5	Resigns.

Najdorf—Averbakh

Candidates Tournament
Zurich, 1953

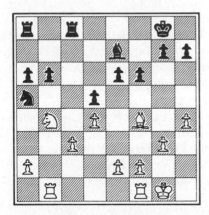

White's Q-side pawns are weak, and he has the inferior bishop and a 'hole' at c4. The c3 pawn is attacked, and the Argentinian grandmaster plays

1 Bd2?

An incorrect decision. The knight should have been retained at all costs, since after its exchange there is nothing with which to defend the white squares on the Q-side. After 1 Nd3! Nc4 2 Rfc1 followed by the approach of the king to the centre, White would have had hopes of saving the game.

| 1 ... | Nc4 |
| 2 Be1 | Bxb4! |

The decisive exchange. White's backward pawn on the c-file is removed, but the file itself comes under the command of the black rooks.

3 cxb4

3 Rxb4 is also unpromising.

3 ...	Na3!
4 Rb3	Nb5
5 e3	Rc2
6 a4	Nd6

| 7 a5?! | b5 |

All White's pawns are on dark squares, which emphasizes the unfortunate position of his bishop at e1.

8 Rc3	Rc8
9 Rxc8+	Nxc8
10 f3	Ne7
11 Bf2	Kf7!

After 11 ... Rb2? 12 Rc1 White would have seized the c-file. Black has no reason to hurry.

12 Rb1	Nf5
13 Kf1	Nd6
14 Rb3	Nc4
15 Kg2	f5

Zugzwang! 16 f4 or 16 e4 fails to 16 ... Nd2, king moves are impossible for the same reason, and 16 Rd3 is decisively met by 16 ... Rb2.

16 Rb1	Nxe3+
17 Kg1	f4!
18 gxf4	Nf5
19 Kf1	g6!
20 Rb3	Ke7!
21 Rb1	Kd7!

White resigns, since after ... Rc4 Black wins a pawn in the most favourable situation. By simple moves and with inexorable consistency Averbakh realized his advantage, without allowing his opponent the slightest chance.

Panno—Bronstein

Candidates Tournament
Amsterdam, 1956

(See next diagram)

Black is a pawn up with a good position, although there are opposite-

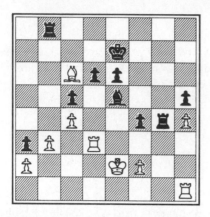

coloured bishops on the board. It is his move and, exploiting the poor position of the enemy bishop, he sets his central pawns in motion.

1 ...	d5!
2 cxd5	Kd6
3 Kf3	Bd4
4 Ba4	

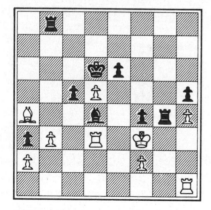

Black is faced with an exchanging problem. Bronstein makes a natural move

| 4 ... | exd5? |

and... throws away the win. Here is the commentary on this move by the Soviet master Goldberg in the tournament book:

"At the board it is unlikely that anyone would have resisted the temptation to connect his pawns, since it appears that after 4 ... Kxd5 White can set up a white-square blockade at e4. Bronstein could hardly have imagined that, a pawn up and with the white bishop badly placed, he would be unable to win the game. Only after a painstaking analysis did it transpire that by this move Black threw away the win. After 4 ... Kxd5 White is seemingly unable to organize a defence, e.g. 5 Rd2 e5 6 Re2 Rg7 (the rook cannot be moved off the b-file, since then the white bishop will come into play by *Bb5*) 7 Rd1 Re7 8 Re4 Rb6 9 Rd2(d3) Rg6 10 Bb5 Rg4, winning a second pawn. But now White unexpectedly acquires counter-play."

| 5 Rd2! | Bf6 |
| 6 Re2! | Rg7 |

On 6 ... Bxh4 there follows 7 Be8!, while if 6 ... Rxh4 7 Rxh4 Bxh4 8 Be8.

| 7 Be8 | Re7 |

Rhe1 was a possible threat.

| 8 Rxe7 | Kxe7 |
| 9 Bxh5 | |

White has regained his pawn. He can meet 9 ... Rh8 with 10 Kg4.

9 ...	c4
10 bxc4	dxc4
11 Rc1	c3
12 Bg6	Be5
13 h5	Kf6
14 Rc2	

A draw is now inevitable. The finish was:

14 ...	Kg5
15 Re2	Rb5
16 Rc2	Rc5
17 Rc1	Rd5
18 Re1	Bd6

19	Rg1+	Kh6
20	Re1	Bc5
21	Re2	Kg5
22	Rc2	Bb4
23	Re2	Bd6
24	Rc2	

Drawn

This ending shows how an insignificant mistake when exchanging can reduce to nought the fruits of a player's previously excellent play.

Svyeshnikov–Kasparov

47th USSR Championship
Minsk, 1979

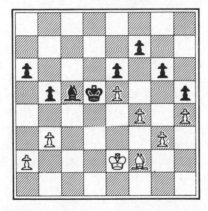

Four of White's pawns are on squares of the same colour as his bishop, and the black king occupies a dominating position in the centre. Nevertheless it is not clear whether or not this advantage is sufficient for Black to win, since he has no pawn breaks on the K-side. With his last move Black offered the exchange of bishops, and White, after an insufficiently deep analysis of the position, agreed to the exchange.

1 Bxc5?

1 Be1 is of course correct.

1	...	Kxc5

| 2 | Kd3 | |

Events now develop by force. Hopeless for White is 2 a3 Kd4 3 Kd2 a5.

2	...	Kb4
3	Kc2	Ka3
4	Kb1	a5
5	Ka1	a4
6	bxa4	Kxa4
7	Kb1	

7 Kb2 b4 would not have changed anything. When he went into the pawn ending Svyeshnikov may possibly have thought that he would reach this position with him to move, when White is saved by Kc2! Ka3; Kc3. This ending shows how seriously the problem of exchanging must be approached when going into a pawn ending.

7	...	Ka3
8	Ka1	b4
9	Kb1	b3

White resigns.

Son–Khorovyets

Tashkent, 1978

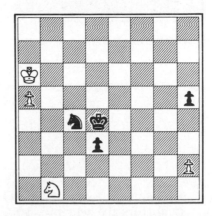

Black's passed pawn is much more dangerous than the opponent's, and in addition her king and knight occupy ideal positions.

1 ...   h4!

This move was sealed by Black, setting her opponent a difficult choice.

2 Kb5

White gives up a piece, but 2 h3 Kc5 3 Nc3 Kb4 was equally cheerless.

2	...	Na3+!
3	Kb6	Nxb1
4	a6	d2
5	a7	d1=Q
6	a8=Q	Qb3+
7	Kc7	

As a result of a practically forced series of moves, Black has a material advantage and an easily won position. Now 7 ... Qf7+ 8 Kb6 Qf6+ 9 Kc7 Nc3 would have won quickly.

7	...	Qc4+
8	Kd6	Qc5+
9	Ke6	Qe5+
10	Kf7	

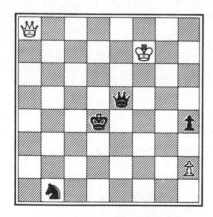

10 ...   Qd5+??

The problem of exchanging! There was a straightforward win by 10 ... Qf4+ followed by ... Nc3. With the queens on the board the extra knight quickly decides matters, whereas after their exchange the position reached is almost a pawn ending, where a win is possible only by exceptionally subtle play.

11	Qxd5+	Kxd5
12	Kf6	Nd2

13 Kf5!

The routine 13 Kg5? would have lost after 13 ... Nf3+ 14 Kg4 Ke4, or 14 Kf4 Nxh2 15 Kg5 Nf3+ 16 Kf4 Ng5. Bad for White is 13 h3 Ke4 14 Kg5 Nf3+. We again see how dangerous the transition into a pawn ending can be (here the play develops in analogy with pawn endings).

13 ...   Nf3

There is nothing better.

14 h3!

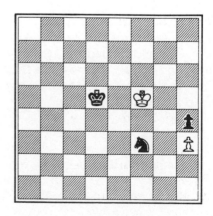

Here is the result of the incorrect queen exchange. White threatens to drive away the knight by 15 Kf4 and then attack Black's only pawn.

It is true that Black has a study-like way to win. We suggest that the reader himself should try to find the win from the diagram position, and only then play through the game continuation.

14 . . .	Kd4
15 Kf4	Ne1!
16 Kg4	Ng2
17 Kf3	Ne3!
18 Kf4	

Black has found the only moves to defend her pawn, but how can the white king be forced out of opposition?

| 18 . . . | Kd3 |
| 19 Kf3 | Nf5 |

Repeating moves to gain time on the clock.

| 20 Kf4 | Ne3 |
| 21 Kf3 | Kd2! |

Black drives the white king, which is forced to maintain the opposition, a little further from the h4 pawn.

| 22 Kf2 | Nd5! |

The decisive manoeuvre.

23 Kf3	Ne7!
24 Kg4	Ng6
25 Kg5	Ke3
26 Kxg6	Kf4!

It was still possible to go wrong: 26 . . . Kf3?? 27 Kf5 Kg3 28 Ke4, with a draw. But now **White resigned.**

Aronin—Smyslov

19th USSR Championship
Moscow, 1951

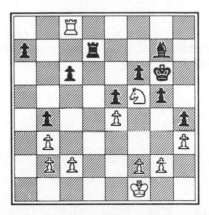

White has a decisive advantage. In comparison with the white pieces, Black's occupy pitiful positions. The fine knight at f5 is greatly superior to the black bishop obstructed by its own pawns, while the white rook holds sway in the enemy rear. In addition to all this it is now White to move, and he can calmly pick up the c6 pawn, retaining all the advantages of his position. To Aronin's misfortune, he had to seal the next move.

1 Rg8?!

This move in itself is strong enough, but the question mark is attached because it is made with the faulty idea of transposing into what appears to be an easily won pawn ending.

| 1 . . . | Kh7 |
| 2 Rxg7+? | |

A mistake which shows how easily a certain win can slip away, due to an incorrect evaluation of an ensuing pawn ending. In Aronin's defence, it has to be said that it was very difficult to foresee Smyslov's brilliant defensive idea. Besides, a player who is faced with defeat mobilizes all his strength and clutches at the slightest chance, however improbable, like a drowning man at a straw. The player who is winning, on the other hand, is reluctant to seek saving chances for the opponent, especially if they are of a very difficult nature. Even great players have been known to relax in such a situation, and chess history knows of numerous similar examples. White would have won most easily by 2 Re8!, answering 2 ... Kg6 with 3 Re7.

	2 ...	Rxg7
	3 Nxg7	Kxg7
	4 g4	

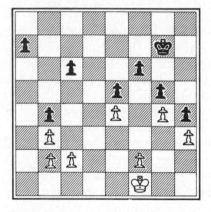

It appears that Aronin's idea should guarantee him an easy win. With his last move White has deprived Black of counter-play on the K-side involving ... f5 and ... g4. He has in mind the following variation: 4 ... Kf7 5 Ke2 Ke6 6 Kd3 Kd6 7 Kc4 a5 8 f3 Kd7 9 Kc5 Kc7 10 c3 bxc3 11 bxc3 Kb7 12 Kd6 Kb6 13 c4 Kb7 14 c5, and White wins. But Smyslov has prepared a series of surprises.

	4 ...	hxg3!

In addition to all his other advantages, White gains the prospect of creating an outside passed pawn.

	5 fxg3	g4!!

The outside passed pawn also gains the opportunity to become protected.

	6 h4	c5
	7 Ke2	Kh7!
	8 Kd3	Kh6

Smyslov's brilliant plan begins to reveal itself. On the natural 9 Kc4 White even loses after 9 ... f5! 10 exf5 e4!, when the black pawn queens. No better is 10 Kd3 f4 11 gxf4 exf4 12 Ke2 Kh5 13 e5 Kg6, when the black king eliminates White's passed pawns. The game continued

	9 c3	a5
	10 cxb4	axb4

and the players agreed a draw.

On the other hand, the transition into a pawn ending, where all the nuances have been correctly worked out to the end, can be the quickest way to win.

Marovic—Stein

Yerevan, 1971

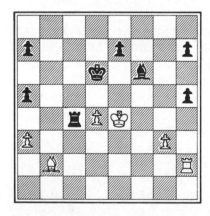

Black is two pawns up, but since both are doubled one gains the impression that the winning path will be long and hard. But the Soviet grandmaster finds a forced win, which involves going into a pawn ending.

1 ...	h4!
2 gxh4	Bxd4!
3 Rd2	e5
4 Bxd4	

What is Black to do now? In the event of 4 ... exd4 White, of course, does not fall into the trap 5 Rxd4+? Kc5!, but plays 5 Rf2!, after which Black's winning chances in the rook ending are highly problematic. If Black plays 4 ... Rxd4+, the pawn ending after 5 Rxd4+ exd4 6 Kxd4 must end in a draw, e.g. 6 ... h5 7 a4 a6 8 Kc4! Ke5 9 Kc5 Kf4 10 Kb6 Kg4 11 Kxa5 Kxh4 12 Kxa6 Kg5 13 Kb7, with a draw. But Stein had envisaged in advance

$$4 \ldots \quad \text{Ke6!!}$$

by which Black gains a decisive tempo.

5 h5	Rxd4+
6 Rxd4	exd4
7 a4	Kf6
8 Kxd4	Kg5
9 Ke5	

In the variation 9 Kc5 Kxh5 10 Kb5 Kg4 11 Kxa5 h5 12 Ka6 h4 13 Kxa7 h3 14 a5 h2 15 a6 h1=Q for a draw White is short of just one tempo. The game continued:

9 ...	Kxh5
10 Kf5	a6

White resigns.

It is difficult to solve the problem of exchanging when a transition into a rook ending is in prospect. In rook endings there are increased drawing tendencies, and we will see how even the best grandmasters in the world can go wrong when transposing into a rook ending.

Gufeld—Dolmatov

Daugavpils, 1978

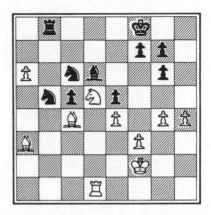

With his two strong bishops, outside passed pawn, superior pawn formation and well placed pieces, White has an undisputed advantage.

1 Bxb5

Gufeld decides to take play into a rook ending which appears highly promising for White. As became clear on the conclusion of the game, 1 Bc1 would have been stronger, retaining the advantage in a complicated ending.

1 ...	Rxb5
2 Nc3	Rb3
3 Rxd6	Rxc3
4 Rxc6	Rxa3
5 Rc8+	Ke7
6 Rc7+	Ke6
7 a7	

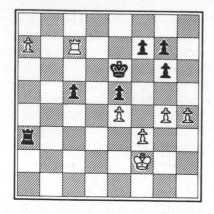

As a result of forcing play, White has reached the position for which he was aiming in carrying out the exchanging operation. Black's position is difficult. White threatens 6 g5, after which his king approaches the c-pawn, and Black ends up in *zugzwang*.

| 7 ... | Ra2+! |
| 8 Ke1! | |

White sees through his opponent's camouflaged positional trap. On the natural 8 Ke3? there would have followed 8 ... c4!, and if 9 g5 f5, with the threat of mate by ... f4.

| 8 ... | g5! |
| 9 hxg5 | |

After 9 h5 White is not threatening to place his opponent in *zugzwang*, since the black king acquires the additional square f6.

9 ...	g6
10 Kd1	c4
11 Kc1	Kd6!

In a rook ending the possibility of active counter-play often proves more important than a material deficit.

12 Rxf7	Kc5
13 Kb1	Ra4
14 Rd7!	

The strongest continuation. After 14 Rg7 Kd4 15 Rxg6 Rxa7 16 Rf6 Kd3 Black has good counter-play.

| 14 ... | Kb4 |
| 15 Kb2 | Ra5! |

15 ... c3+ 16 Kc2 Kc4 17 Rc7+ Kd4 was bad due to 18 Kb3.

16 Re7

After 16 Rg7 Black gains counter-play by 16 ... Kc5!, e.g. 17 Kc3 (*17 Rxg6 Rxa7 18 Rf6 Kd4 19 g6 Kd3*) 17 ... Ra3+ 18 Kd2 Ra2+ 19 Ke1 Ra1+ 20 Kf2 Ra2+ 21 Kg3 c3 22 Rxg6 Rxa7 23 Rh6 (*23 Rg8 Rc7!*) 23 ... Ra1! 24 Rh8 Ra6! 25 Rc8+ Rc6 26 Rxc6+ Kxc6 27 g6 c2 28 g7 c1=Q 29 g8=Q Qf4+ 30 Kh3 Qh6+! (but not *30 ... Qxf3+ 31 Kh4 Qxe4?? 32 Qa8+*), and Black gives perpetual check.

16 ...	c3+!
17 Kc2	Ra2+
18 Kb1	

On the natural 18 Kd3 Black should not lose after 18 ... Rd2+ 19 Ke3 Rd8 20 Rb7+ Kc4 21 Rc7+ Kb3 22 f4 exf4+ 23 Kxf4 c2 24 e5 Ra8 25 e6 Rxa7 26 Rxc2 Kxc2 27 Ke5 Kd3 28 Kf6 Ke4 29 e7 Ra8 30 Kxg6 Kf4, and the black king succeeds in latching on to the 'tail' of the white pawns.

18 ...	Ra6
19 Rxe5	Rxa7
20 Re6	Kc4
21 Rxg6	

(See next diagram)

White has now won a third pawn, yet the game ends in a draw. Tartakover was probably right when he said: "If it

comes to that, a rook ending can be won only thanks to the quality of the pawns, but not the quantity".

21 ...	Kd3
22 Rd6+	Ke3
23 Kc2	

On 23 e5 there would have followed 23 ... Kxf3 24 e6 Re7!

23 ...	Kxf3
24 Re6	Rc7
25 g6	

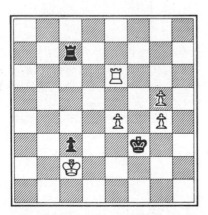

One gains the impression that White will nevertheless win. If 25 ... Kxg4, then 26 Rf6 Kg5 27 Rf7, winning. But Dolmatov, who has conducted a difficult defence splendidly, crowns it fittingly with a brilliant king move.

| 25 ... | Kf4!! |

It transpires that White does not achieve anything by 26 Rf6+ Kxe4 27 Rf7 Rc6, when the position is a draw. The finish was:

26 Re8	Kg5
27 g7	Rxg7
28 Kxc3	Kf6
29 Kd4	Rxg4
30 Kd5	Kf7

Drawn.

In the transition to a rook ending the stronger side must weigh up everything 'for' and 'against' just as carefully as in the transition to a pawn ending.

We will now analyze a famous ending between Capablanca and Alekhine, which played, in Alekhine's words, a very important role in his subsequent battle for the World Championship in his match with Capablanca.

Capablanca—Alekhine

New York, 1924

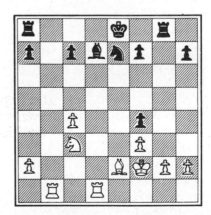

Black's position is difficult, practically lost. He has five pawn 'invalids', inferior minor pieces, and unco-ordinated rooks. Alekhine's opponent was the then World Champion, the great master of endgame technique, Capablanca, and so no one was in any doubt that Black would lose. Only Alekhine himself was not yet ready

33

to lay down his arms, and he was able to demonstrate that, even on the sun, spots can occur.

| 1 ... | Bc6 |
| 2 Rd4 | |

White tries to gain a material advantage as soon as possible, but allows Black to co-ordinate his forces. 2 Nb5! was preferable.

2 ...	Ng6
3 Bd3	Nh4
4 Bf1	Ng6
5 Ne2	Ke7!
6 Re1	Rgb8!
7 Nxf4+	Kf8

Black has lost a pawn, but has significantly improved his position.

8 Nxg6+

Capablanca connects his opponent's pawns, but gains the prospect of creating an outside passed pawn on the K-side.

| 8 ... | hxg6 |

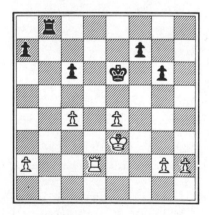

9 Bd3?

The solving of an exchanging problem can sometimes be such a difficult matter that mistakes can be made even by World Champions. Here is Alekhine's

comment:

"White overestimates his chances in the resulting rook ending. He should have aimed not for the exchange of bishops, but for the exchange of at least one pair of rooks, since this would have practically eliminated his opponent's only counter-chance — the advance of his a-pawn. He should have played, for example, 9 Rd2 a5 10 Bd3 a4 11 Rb1 Rxb1 12 Bxb1 Rb8 13 Bd3 a3 14 Be2, with the threat of Rd3, tying the black rook to the a-file, after which it would not have been difficult for White to realize his advantage on the K-side."

9 ...	Rb2+
10 Re2	Rab8
11 Be4	

Otherwise White cannot defend his a2 pawn.

11 ...	Rxe2+
12 Kxe2	Bxe4
13 fxe4	Ke7
14 Rd2	Ke6
15 Ke3	c6!

16 h4?

With his last move Alekhine had prepared veiled counter-play, hoping for this very reply by White.

16 c5 would not have achieved any-

thing due to 16 ... Rb5 17 Rd6+ Ke5 18 Rxc6 Ra5, but correct, as shown by Alekhine, was 16 h3! with the idea of playing Kd4—c3 and c4—c5, when Black would have been faced with difficult problems.

16 ...	Rh8!
17 g3	Rh5!

Capablanca obviously overlooked this deep manoeuvre by his opponent. On the fifth rank the black rook occupies an ideal position, and due to the possible counter-attack by Black on the Q-side, White is unable to exploit his extra pawn and to create a passed pawn.

18 Rh2	Ra5
19 Kf4	

19 g4? is very strongly met by 19 ... Ke5.

19 ...	f6!

Black forestalls 20 g4, on which there would follow 20 ... g5+!

20 Rc2	Re5

21 c5 was threatened.

21 c5	

"After this move, which restricts the mobility of the black rook, the white rook is also tied to the c5 pawn, and Black has to reckon only with the threat of Kg4—h3 and then g3—g4." (Alekhine).

21 ...	Rh5
22 Rc3	a5

Defending against 23 Ra3.

23 Rc2	Re5
24 Rc3	Rh5

25 Kf3	Ke7
26 Kg4	Kf7!

Precise defence. Now on 27 Kh3 Alekhine had prepared 27 ... g5! and if 28 Kg4 Kg6 followed by ... gxh4 and ... Re5—h5.

27 Rc4	Kg7!
28 Rd4!	

Capablanca gives back his extra pawn and tries to exploit the remoteness of the black king from the centre.

28 ...	Rxc5
29 Rd7+	Kf8

Not 29 ... Kh6 30 Rf7.

30 Kf4	Kg8
31 Ra7	Kf8
32 a4	Kg8
33 g4?!	

"After 33 Ke3! Rc3+ 34 Kd4 Rxg3 35 Rxa5 Kf7 36 Ra8 Black would still have had to defend accurately, in view of White's dangerous a-pawn. But thanks to the small amount of material remaining, he would probably have been able to draw. At any rate, this would have been the logical continuation of the manoeuvre begun by White on the 28th move." (Alekhine).

33 ...	g5+!
34 hxg5	Rxg5
35 Ra6	Rc5
36 Ke3	Kf7
37 Kd4	Rg5
38 Rxc6	Rxg4
39 Rc5	Rg5!

In this position the players agreed a draw, since the pawn ending after 40 Rxg5 fxg5 41 Ke5 Kg6! 42 Kd6 Kf7! 43 Kd7 Kf6 ends in a draw by repetition of moves.

This game can be considered an historic one, since it played an important role in the subsequent battle between Alekhine and Capablanca for the World Championship. This is what Alekhine writes about it in his book *On the Road to the World Championship*:

"Despite this, I did take home with me from this tournament one valuable moral victory, and that was the lesson I learned from my first game with Capablanca, which had the effect of a revelation on me. Having outplayed me in the opening, having reached a won position in the middlegame and having carried over a large part of his advantage into a rook ending, the Cuban then allowed me to neutralize his superiority in that ending and finally had to make do with a draw."

Later Alekhine goes on: "I had finally detected a slight weakness in my future opponent: increasing uncertainty when confronted with stubborn resistance! Of course I had already noticed Capablanca committing occasional slight inaccuracies, but I should not have thought that he would be unable to rid himself of this failing even when he tried his utmost. That was an exceedingly important lesson for the future!"

So that the reader should not gain the erroneous impression that the stronger side should altogether avoid going into a rook ending, we will analyze two examples in which the transition to a rook ending is a good way of realizing an advantage.

Rubinstein—Alekhine

Carlsbad, 1911

(See next diagram)

White has the advantage thanks to his control of the only open file, but to pierce Black's defences, whose only real

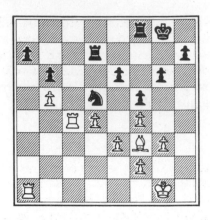

weakness is the a7 pawn, is far from easy.

1	Rc6	Kf7
2	Bxd5	

Grandmaster Razuvayev makes the following witty comment to this move:

"It is well known that 'rook endings are never won', but it can be assumed that Rubinstein received indulgence from Kaissa in this respect."

2	...	exd5
3	Rac1	Rfd8
4	Kf1	Ke7
5	Ke2	Rd6
6	R6c3	R6d7
7	Kd3	Ra8
8	Rc6	Rd6
9	Ke2	Rxc6
10	Rxc6	Kd7

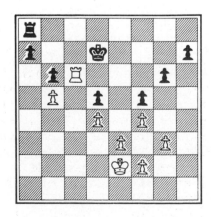

With the disappearance of one pair of rooks, White's advantage has not been reduced. But now both sides have to reckon with the possibility of a pawn ending, and the play becomes more tense and concrete.

11 f3!

Rubinstein begins preparing pawn advances in the centre (*e3—e4*) and on the K-side (*g3—g4*). At the same time the possibility of a pawn ending is eliminated: after 11 ... Rc8 12 Rxc8 Kxc8 13 e4 fxe4 (*13 ... Kb7? 14 exf5 gxf5 15 g4*) 14 fxe4 dxe4 15 g4 Kd7 (*15 ... h5 16 f5!*) 16 Ke3 Ke6 17 Kxe4 White wins. 11 ... a5 also does not work, since, as shown by Razuvayev, after 12 Rxb6 a4 13 Ra6! Rxa6 14 bxa6 Kc6 15 Kd3 Kb6 16 Kc3 Kxa6 17 Kb4 White obtains a won pawn ending.

11 ...	Re8
12 Kd3	Re7
13 g4	Re6
14 Rc1!	

Here White cannot go into the pawn ending. After 14 Rxe6 Kxe6 15 g5 (*15 e4? dxe4 16 fxe4 fxg4*) 15 ... Kd6 16 e4 Ke6 17 exd5+ Kxd5 18 Kc3 Ke6 19 Kc4 Kd6 20 d5 Kd7 21 Kd4 Kd6 the game is drawn.

14 ...	Re7
15 Rh1	

White's plan to improve his position is to play his king to g5 via h4. But when the opponent is deprived of counter-play and is forced to wait passively, it is useful for the stronger side to avoid taking positive action for a certain time, i.e. to play according to the principle of "do not hurry". Such tactics often bring good results.

15 ...	Ke6
16 Rc1	Kd7
17 Re1	Rf7
18 Ra1	Kd6
19 Rc1	Kd7
20 Rc6	Rf8

The illusion that Black's position is impregnable has been created. Rubinstein now embarks on his active plan.

21 Ke2!	Rf7
22 Kf2	Rf8
23 Kg3	Re8
24 Rc3	Re7
25 Kh4	h6

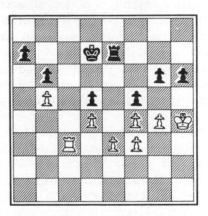

White has provoked an important weakening of his opponent's K-side, and Rubinstein now finds an excellent manoeuvre after which Black's defences collapse.

26 Kg3!	h5

As was shown by Kmoch, waiting tactics would not have saved Black. e.g. 26 ... Re8 27 Kf2 Re7 28 Ke2 Re8 29 Kd3 Re7 30 Rc6 Re6 31 gxf5! gxf5 32 Rxe6 Kxe6 33 e4, with a win in the pawn ending.

27 Kh4!

The white king reacts very keenly to the slightest advance of the black pawns.

27 . . .	Rh7
28 Kg5	fxg4!

Alekhine does not miss the chance to set his opponent a trap. After 29 Kxg6? g3 30 Kxh7 g2 31 Rc1 h4 it is Black who wins.

29 fxg4	hxg4
30 Kxg4	

White's positional advantage has become decisive.

30 . . .	Rh1

"Passive defence is no longer possible. If 30 . . . Re7, then 31 Kg5 Re6 32 Kh6! followed by Kg7—f7 and if necessary Rc7+ followed by Kxe6." (Spielmann).

31 Kg5	Rb1

After 31 . . . Rg1+ 32 Kf6 the white king transfers to e5.

32 Ra3	Rxb5
33 Rxa7+	Kd6
34 Kxg6	Rb3
35 f5	Rxe3
36 f6	

The black king is cut off along the rank and is unable to prevent the advance of the white f-pawn.

36 . . .	Rg3+
37 Kh7	Rf3
38 f7	Rf4
39 Kg7	Rg4+
40 Kf6!	

But not 40 Kf8? Rxd4, and the game ends in a draw.

40 . . .	Rf4+
41 Kg5	Rf1
42 Kg6	Rg1+

43 Ra8 was threatened.

43 Kf6	Rf1+
44 Kg7	Rg1+
45 Kf8	

By a subtle manoeuvre Rubinstein has forced the enemy rook off the fourth rank.

45 . . .	Rd1
46 Ke8	Re1+
47 Kd8	Rf1
48 Rd7+	Kc6
49 Ke8	Rf4
50 Re7	Kb5
51 Rc7!	

Much stronger than 51 f8=Q Rxf8+ 52 Kxf8 Kc4. Black resigned in view of the possible variation 51 . . . Re4+ 52 Kd7 Rf4 53 Ke7 Re4+ 54 Kd6 Rf4 55 Kxd5.

Karpov—Hort

Tilburg, 1979

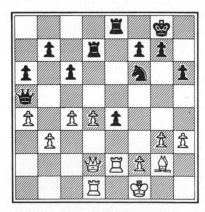

The position is roughly equal. With his last move the World Champion offered the exchange of queens, and Hort accepts the offer.

1 . . .	Qxd2?!

In the endgame White will have an initiative. Preferable was 1 ... Qf5, with equal chances.

2 Rexd2	e3
3 Re2	exf2
4 Rxe8+	Nxe8
5 Kxf2	a5!

It was for this position that Black was aiming when he went into the ending. Objectively speaking, the position is drawn, but only White can play for a win. If the pawn structure is appraised, White has a majority on the Q-side, and Black on the K-side. But there is no sense in White creating a passed pawn, since Black can easily blockade it. White's only active possibility on the part of the board where he is stronger is the advance b3—b4.

6 Ke3	Kf8
7 Rb1	Ke7
8 g4!	

A useful move.

8 ...	Kd8
9 b4	Re7+
10 Kd3	axb4
11 Rxb4	Kc7
12 Rb1	Nf6
13 a5	Nd7
14 Ra1	Nb8
15 h4	Na6

(See next diagram)

Black's defences are successfully holding. He has no weaknesses, and Karpov resorts to manoeuvring tactics, with the aim of provoking a weakening in the opponent's position and cracking his defences.

16 Rb1	Nb8
17 Bf3	Nd7
18 Ra1	Re8

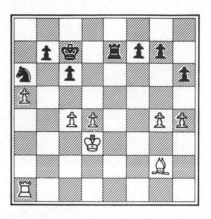

19 Rf1

19 a6? was bad due to 19 ... Ra8.

19 ...	Re7
20 Bg2	Nb8
21 Rf4	Nd7
22 Rf1	Nb8
23 Be4	Na6
24 Rb1	Nb8
25 Bf5	Nd7
26 Ra1	

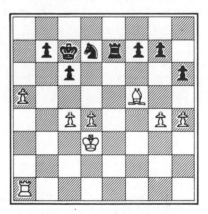

A brief glance at the position is sufficient to see that in the chess sense White has achieved little. But psychologically something has been done. Black senses that his position is impregnable, and weakens his vigilance. With his next move Hort tries to drive away the annoying white bishop, and commits a serious, possibly decisive, mistake.

26 ...   g6?

26 ... Nb8 was correct.

27 Bxd7!

In comparison with the position before the previous move, a slight change
has taken place: the g7 pawn has advanced one square. A slight change, but
one with enormous consequences. The
rook ending, which in the event of the
exchange on the previous move was
completely drawn, is now transformed
into one which is virtually won for
White. Karpov appreciates very subtly
the slightest change of position in the
endgame.

A pretty breakthrough, typical of the
endgame.

27 ...	Rxd7
28 Rf1!	Kb8
29 Rf6	Ka7
30 h5	Ka6?!

After this move Black loses by force.
His position was difficult, but he should
have tried 30 ... gxh5 31 gxh5 Ka6.

31 g5!

31 ...	hxg5
32 h6	Kxa5
33 h7	Rd8
34 Rxf7	b5
35 cxb5	Kxb5
36 Rb7+!	Ka6
37 Rg7	Rh8
38 Ke4	Kb5
39 Kf3	Kc4
40 Rd7	Kd3
41 Kg4	Rxh7
42 Rxh7	Kxd4
43 Rd7+!	Resigns.

CHAPTER 5

"DO NOT HURRY"

The ability to make use of this principle demands of a player great experience in the playing of chess endings. How many endings have not been won, merely because the stronger side tried to win as quickly as possible, and neglected to make simple strengthening moves before embarking on positive action. Following the principle of "do not hurry", it is possible to battle for a win in positions with a slight but persistent advantage. Only in this way can a player achieve weakenings in the enemy position, mask his plans, and lull the opponent's vigilance. But on no account should this principle be abused. One must be ready at the necessary moment to switch to sharp and positive action, otherwise the opponent may eliminate the weaknesses in his position, which are often of a temporary nature. The ability to sense and not miss this critical point is not something that comes easily. We will see in examples that in such situations even strong players often go wrong.

The logic behind the "do not hurry" principle is mainly psychological. It can be especially recommended to act according to this principle when the opponent is deprived of active counterplay.

Mikenas—Spassky

Moscow, 1955

(*See next diagram*)

Black's pieces are so cramped that he has practically nothing to move. In such a situation "do not hurry" tactics are normally best for the stronger side. White should quietly strengthen his

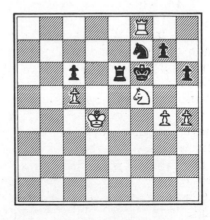

position, and should switch to forcing action only if there is an immediate way to win. Here the transfer of the king to b6 looks very strong, e.g. 1 Kc4 Re4+ 2 Kb3 Re5 (*3 Rxf7+ was threatened*) 3 Nd6 Re7 4 Ka4 Ke6 5 Rxf7 Rxf7 6 Nxf7 Kxf7 7 Ka5 Ke6 8 Kb6 Kd5 9 h5, and wins. But White hurries into taking specific action, and allows the win to slip from his grasp.

1 Nd6?!	Re7
2 Nxf7	Rxf7
3 Rc8	

This looks threatening, but not for nothing are rook endings regarded as the most drawish. Black finds a defensive manoeuvre which saves the game.

3 ...	Rd7+
4 Kc4	

Otherwise the black rook transfers to e6.

4 ...	Ke5
5 Rxc6	Rd4+
6 Kb5	Rxg4
7 h5	Rg5
8 Rg6	Rxh5

41

9 c6	Kf4+
10 Kb6	Rh1
11 c7	Rb1+
12 Ka6	Rc1
13 Kb7	Rxc7+
14 Kxc7	h5

and Black gained a draw.

Reti—Romanovsky

Moscow, 1925

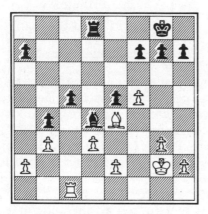

In this position the opposite-coloured bishops give White the advantage. The pawns at c5 and e5 create an impassable barrier to the black bishop, and White has a clear-cut plan to develop his initiative: transfer his rook to c4 and king to f3, and follow up with e2—e3 and Bd5. The black rook will be tied to the defence of the c-pawn, and White will be able to switch his rook to the K-side followed by the pawn break-through h2—h4, g3—g4 and g4—g5. Black is unable to hinder this plan.

1 Rc4	Kf8
2 Kf3	Rc8
3 e3	Bc3

(See next diagram)

This position is worth dwelling on in some detail. White's plan is well known

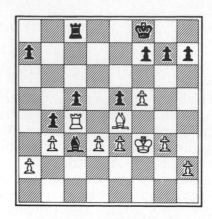

to us: Bd5, Rh4, Ke4, Rh5, h2—h4, g2—g4—g5 etc. Many players would have played this immediately, and would possibly have won. But endgame technique is not only thinking in schemes, and it dictates another move.

4 a4!

Do not hurry! White exploits the chance to improve the position of his a-pawn. Is the diversion worth while? Undoubtedly. If later such a "trifle" is all that is lacking to achieve a win, it will be a just punishment for disregarding the principle "do not hurry". If at a4 the pawn stands slightly better than at a2, it should be moved there, and then the implementation of the plan continued.

4 . . .	Ke7
5 Bd5	Rc7
6 Rh4	h6
7 Ke4	Kf6
8 Rh5	Rd7!
9 g4	

White clearly overlooked Black's latent counter-play. He could have prepared his offensive by Bc4, h2—h3 and g2—g4, without allowing the opponent any counter-chances. But no one is insured against such oversights. In the resulting complications the decisive role is played by the position of the white pawn at a4.

9 . . .	g6!?
10 Rxh6	Kg5
11 Rh7	Kxg4

Threatening mate.

12 Be6!

The only move to win.

12 . . .	fxe6
13 fxg6	Rd8
14 Rxa7	Kg5

"The bishop is exactly one tempo too late: 14 . . . Be1 15 a5 Bh4 16 a6 Bf6 17 g7 Rg8 18 Rb7 Bxg7 19 a7, and now in view of the threat of Rb8 Black is forced to play 19 . . . Ra8, when White takes the bishop and wins easily" (Reti).

15 g7	Kh6
16 a5	Kh7
17 a6	Rd6
18 h4	Be1
19 h5	Bh4
20 h6	Resigns.

Flohr—Bondarevsky

Moscow, 1939

(See next diagram)

The advantage is with White. His knight is obviously stronger than the black bishop, and his central pawns are more mobile. The mobility of Black's Q-side pawn mass is highly restricted, and his passed h-pawn is not very dangerous. White's plan is:

1. Provoke . . . a6 and thus safeguard himself against counter-play on the Q-side, while securing a post for his knight at c5.

2. Transfer the knight to c5, avoiding

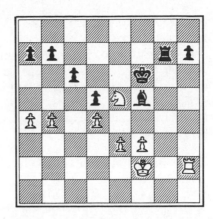

its exchange for the bishop, to do which he must play e3—e4.

3. After improving the position of his king, invade with his rook into the opponent's position, attacking the weak pawns at h7 and b7, then achieve the exchange of rooks and go into a won minor piece ending.

It is interesting to follow with what accuracy and artistry Flohr carries out his plan.

1 a5

With the threat of 2 a6.

| 1 . . . | Rc7 |
| 2 Rh6+! | |

It is such moves that reveal a mastery of endgame technique. To advance a5—a6 White needs his rook at c1. Therefore he could have played Rh1 immediately, but after the check any reply by Black will very slightly worsen his position. Perhaps this "very slightly" will not change anything, but nevertheless Flohr considers it necessary to give the check in this position.

| 2 . . . | Bg6 |

Now the g-file is blocked to the black rook.

| 3 Rh1 | Bf5? |

Probably the decisive mistake. Black should have played 3 . . . b6 4 Rc1 Be8, retaining the possibility of counter-play. After 3 . . . Bf5 White forces . . . a6, and Black's pawn formation becomes rigid.

| 4 Rc1 | a6 |

Forced, in view of the threat of 5 a6.

| 5 Rh1 | |

The rook has carried out its work on the Q-side, and returns to keep Black's passed pawn under control. The rook will then transfer to h4, where it will assist the advance e3—e4.

| 5 . . . | Rg7 |
| 6 Rh2! | |

Do not hurry! Black is deprived of the slightest counter-play, whereas White has a clear winning plan. This last rook move again forces Black to worsen the placing of one of his pieces. In such cases the absence of concrete threats exerts psychological pressure on the opponent. It can be assumed that by 6 Rh2! White gained a considerable amount of valuable time on the clock.

6 . . .	Rc7
7 Rh6+!	Bg6
8 Rh4	Bf5

8 . . . Kg5 would have been answered by a check from g4.

9 e4	dxe4
10 fxe4	Bg6
11 Rf4+	Ke6
12 Ke3	

White centralizes his king, since the transfer of his knight to c5 is assured.

| 12 . . . | Rg7 |

13 Nd3	Kd6
14 Nc5	Re7
15 Rf8	Kc7

16 Rb8 was threatened.

| 16 e5 | Re8 |

Black offers the exchange of rooks, because White's pressure is increasing with every move. The minor piece ending is lost for Black. After the loss of his h-pawn this becomes completely clear.

17 Rxe8	Bxe8
18 Kf4	b6
19 Na4!	bxa5
20 bxa5	Bf7
21 Nc5	Bc4
22 Kg5	Be2
23 Kh6	Kd8
24 Kxh7	Ke7
25 Kg6	Bf1

The plan White now chooses is possibly not the shortest, but on the other hand it is the safest: he transfers his king to c5 via b4.

26 Kf5	Bh3+
27 Ke4	Bg2+
28 Ke3	Bf1
29 Kd2	Kf7
30 Kc3	Kg6
31 Kb4	Kf5
32 Nb7	Resigns.

Boleslavsky—Goldenov

20th USSR Championship
Moscow, 1952

(See next diagram)

Black's isolated pawns may become a target for attack. However, only his a-pawn is a real weakness: his c- and e-pawns are excellently defended by his

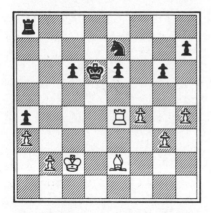

king, and also supported by his knight. Therefore White plans the advance of his pawn to h5, with the aim of giving Black a second weakness. But this move also has its drawbacks, since after the opening of the file White's g-pawn may become weak. Therefore, although he plans this advance, White deliberately delays it, and embarks on lengthy manoeuvring, with the aim of worsening the opponent's position and creating a favourable moment for h4—h5.

1 Bc4	Nd5
2 Re5	Rb8
3 Bd3	Rg8

Preventing h4—h5.

4 Kc1!

A very strong move. The king vacates a square from which the bishop can simultaneously attack the a-pawn and assist the h4—h5 advance. 4 Bc2 Nb6 5 Ra5 is now threatened, so that Black is forced to play ... c5, after which his position in the centre becomes less secure.

4 ...	c5
5 Bc4	Ra8
6 Re4	

Aiming at the a4 pawn. Since the advance of c-pawn has weakened Black's

control of b5, the a-pawn may be attacked by the bishop from this square, and Black has to take this into account.

6 ...	Ra7
7 Re2	Rb7
8 Kc2!	

At first sight this king move is a continuation of White's tactics of manoeuvring to improve his position. In fact it is a camouflage for a deeply-conceived plan.

8 ...	Rc7
9 Bb5	Ra7
10 Rd2	Ke7
11 Re2	Kd6

Black's vigilance has been weakened by the seemingly harmless and unthreatening nature of White's play. Now Boleslavsky begins carrying out his long-planned activity, a point which Black fails to perceive.

12 Re4!	Nb6
13 Bf1!	Nd5?

"After this imperceptible mistake Black loses his a-pawn. He should have made any move with his rook along the seventh rank, although even then his defence would not have been easy. For example: 13 ... Rb7 14 Bh3 Re7 15 Kd3, and Black is in an unusual *zugzwang*. If 15 ... Kd5 or 15 ... Re8, then White makes a favourable breakthrough by 16 f5". (Boleslavsky).

14 Bh3	Nc7
15 Bg4	Ra8

(See next diagram)

16 Kc1!!

Had the king been on this square earlier, Black would possibly have fore-

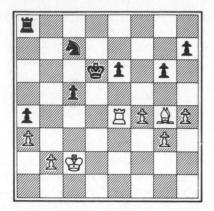

seen the manoeuvre threatening him. But by his eighth move Kc1—c2 White securely masked his plans from his opponent. It is interesting that earlier this king manoeuvre provoked the important weakening ... c5, while now Black cannot avert Bd1 and the loss of his a-pawn. Boleslavsky's play in this ending creates a strong impression.

16 ...	Ra7
17 Bd1	Nb5
18 Bxa4	Nd4
19 Bd1	Nf5
20 Bg4	Rb7
21 Bxf5	

Taking play into a rook ending.

21 ...	exf5

Otherwise the e6 pawn is weak.

22 Re3	Kd5
23 Kc2	c4
24 Re5+	Kd6

24 ... Kd4 25 a4 would also not have saved Black. Boleslavsky gives the following variations:

(a) 25 ... Rb3 26 a5 Rxg3 27 a6 Rg1 28 Ra5.

(b) 25 ... Ra7 26 a5 Ra8 27 b4 cxb3+ 28 Kxb3.

(c) 25 ... Rb4 26 a5 Ra4 27 h5, and:

(c1) 27 ... gxh5 28 Rxf5 h4 29 gxh4 Ke4 30 Rc5 Kxf4 31 Kc3 Kg3 32 Rxc4 Rxa5 33 b4.

(c2) 27 ... Ra2 28 h6 c3 29 Rb5 Kc4 30 Rb7 cxb2 31 Rxh7 Rxa5 32 Kxb2 Rb5+ 33 Kc2 Ra5 34 Rc7+ Kd4 35 Rg7 Ra2+ 36 Kb3 Rh2 37 Rxg6.

25 a4	Rb3
26 a5	Rxg3
27 a6	Kc7
28 Rb5	Rg1
29 Rb7+	Kc6
30 Rxh7	Ra1
31 Rg7	Resigns.

Botvinnik—Kottnauer

Moscow, 1947

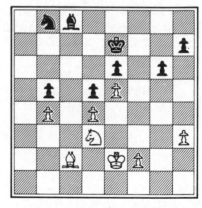

Black has a bad bishop, and his b-pawn is weak. Is this sufficient for White to win? After all, his b-pawn also requires defending. White must break up the opponent's K-side pawns, whereas for Black the transfer of his knight to c4 suggests itself.

1 Kd2

To free the knight from the defence of the b-pawn

1 ...	Nc6?!

Better was 1 ... Nd7 followed by ... Nb6—c4, but Black intends to transfer his knight to f5.

2	Kc3	Nd8
3	h4	Nf7
4	Nf4	

White prepares h4—h5.

4	...	Bd7
5	Kd2	Be8
6	Bd3	Nh6
7	h5!	

Earlier this would not have worked due to ...g5 followed by ...h6, but now h6 is occupied by the knight.

7	...	Nf5
8	hxg6	

After 8 Bxf5 gxf5 White would not have been able to win.

8	...	hxg6
9	Kc3	Kf7
10	Be2	Bd7
11	Nd3	Ke7
12	Nc5	Be8
13	Na6	Kd8
14	Bg4	Bd7
15	Nc5	Ke7
16	Kd3	

"Now White places his king on the f1—a6 diagonal, in order to lull Black's vigilance and divert his attention from the defence of the b5 pawn" (Botvinnik). The camouflaging of the plan resembles the previous example.

16	...	Bc8
17	Bh3	Ke8

The decisive mistake. Black overlooks White's threats. He should have prepared ...g5 by 17 ...Nh4. The immediate 17 ...g5 would not have worked due to 18 f4!

18 Kc3!

Black resigned, since after 18 ... Bd7 19 Bf1 he loses one of his pawns.

Vaganian—Shereshevsky

Minsk, 1972

White is the exchange up, but if he exchanges the white-squared bishops this leads to a theoretically drawn position.

White cannot approach the g6 pawn, and hence the position is a draw.

Confident of a draw, Black makes the first inaccurate move:

1 ...	Bg4+?!

He should not have voluntarily allowed the white king into the centre. To be considered was 1 . . . Be5, attacking the g3 pawn and the f4 square.

2 Kf4	Bc3
3 Bd5	Bd2+
4 Ke4	Bc3
5 Ra7+	Kf8
6 Rc7	Bf5+
7 Kf4	Bd4

With the idea that on 8 Kg5 there is a perpetual check by 8 . . . Be3+ and 9 . . . Bd4+.

8 Bf3	Bg7
9 Rb7	Bh6+?

There was no necessity to allow the white king forward. Had Black guessed at his opponent's plan, he would possibly have gained a draw. But Black's entire misfortune was precisely the fact that he did not imagine that he could lose this position. Note that White would not have achieved anything by 9 Bxh5 Bh6+ 10 Ke5 Bg7+, but since the pseudo-threat of capturing on h5 was maintained, Black wanted to get rid of it as soon as possible.

10 Ke5	Bg7+
11 Kd6	Bd4
12 Bd5	Bf2
13 Rb3	Bd4
14 Rb8+	Kg7
15 Rb7+	Kh8

On 15 . . . Kh6 White has the unpleasant 16 Bg8 g5 17 Rb5, while 15 . . . Kf8 did not appeal to Black due to 16 Rf7+ Ke8 17 Be6, when his king is in a dangerous position.

16 Rb4!

White's plan includes gaining control of f7 for his king. But on 16 Ke7 Black can reply 16 . . . Kg7! 17 Ke8+ Kf6, retaining drawing chances. There-fore White continues making harmless moves, masking his intentions.

16 . . .	Bc3
17 Rb3	Bd4
18 Bf7	Kg7
19 Rb7	

With the threat of a discovered check.

19 . . .	Kh8

But not 19 . . . Kh6 20 Bg8.

20 Kd5	Bc3
21 Rb3	Ba1
22 Kd6	Kg7
23 Rb7	

Again threatening a discovered check.

23 . . .	Kh8

Of course, not 23 . . . Kh6. I recall that at this point I jokingly regretted that it wasn't possible to claim a draw in view of the three-fold repetition of one and the same trap.

24 Bc4	Bd4

Let us compare this position with the one after Black's 15th move. We see that they are identical, except that the white bishop is at c4 instead of d5, which is of no significance.

25 Ke7!

The opponent has been influenced psychologically, and White can commence positive action.

25 . . .	Bc3?

The decisive mistake. Essential was 25 . . . Kg7 28 Ke8+ Kf6 followed by . . . g5. But Black reckoned that passive play would suffice for a draw, and did not want to bring his king out of its comfortable corner, since he did not attach any significance to the difference in the position of the white king at e7 and f7. Evidently if White had played his king to e7 on the 16th move, Black would have replied 16 ... Kg7!, but at the present time it was psychologically much more difficult for him to play this.

26 Kf7!

With the white king at f7 the ending after the exchange of white-squared bishops is lost, and Black had not taken this into account.

26 ...	Bd4
27 Rb5	Kh7
28 Rb3	

The pursuit of the black bishops begins. White has to hurry, since there are not so many moves to go before Black will be able to claim a draw on the 50-move rule.

28 ...	Be4

Parrying the threat of 29 Bd3.

29 Be6

With the threat of 30 Rb4.

29 ...	Bc2
30 Ra3	Be5
31 Bc4	Bd4

So that if 32 Bd3? Bb2!, with a draw.

32 Rf3	Be5
33 Re3	Bd4
34 Re2!	Ba4!

The only move. Bad is 34 ... Bf5 35 Be6 Bb1 36 Re1 Bc2 37 Rc1, winning.

35 Re7!	Bg7

On 35 ... Bc2 Black did not like 36 Bd3!?

36 Bd5	Bc2
37 Be4!	Bb3+
38 Ke8	Ba4+
39 Kd8	Bb3
40 Rb7	Be6

With a trap: 41 Rb6?! Bf7 42 Ke7 Bd4!, and after 43 ... Kg7 the game ends in a draw.

41 Ke7!

Black resigns. Against 42 Rb6 there is no defence.

Donchenko—Shereshevsky

Kaliningrad, 1973

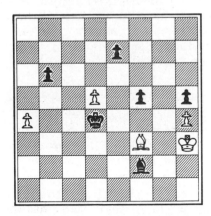

In this position the game was adjourned. Analysis showed that, in spite of his extra pawn, Black was unable to win, but that to achieve a draw White would have to defend accurately.

1 ...	Be1
2 d6	

Forced, since 2 Bxh5 is bad due to 2 ... Kxd5, while 2 Bg2 is met by

2 ... Ke3 followed by the advance of the f-pawn.

| 2 ... | exd6 |
| 3 Bxh5 | Bd2 |

Black achieves nothing by the direct 3 ... Ke3 4 Bf7 f4 5 h5 f3 6 h6 f2 7 Kg2.

4 Bf7	d5
5 h5	Ke4
6 Bg6	Bh6

After 6 ... d4 White can hold the position by 7 Kg2 d3 8 Kf2 Be3+ 9 Ke1 Ke5 (9 ... Kf4 10 h6) 10 Bf7 Kf6 (10 ... f4 11 h6) 11 Bc4 d2+ 12 Kd1 Kg5 13 Bd3 f4 14 Be2 Kh4 15 h6 Kg3 16 h7 Bd4 17 Kxd2 f3 18 Bxf3 Kxf3 19 Kd3, with a draw. Therefore Black does not force events, but begins manoeuvring with his bishop, so as to begin positive action in the most favourable situation (in accordance with the principle of "do not hurry").

7 Kg2	d4
8 Kf2	Bg5
9 Ke2	Be3
10 Ke1	Ke5
11 Ke2	Ke4
12 Ke1	Bg5
13 Ke2	Bh6
14 Kf2	

A move which indicates that White is confident of a draw.

| 14 ... | d3 |

Since the white king is in a dangerous position, Black begins playing actively.

| 15 Ke1 | Ke5 |
| 16 Kf2(?) | |

The king moves away from the d3 pawn.

| 16 ... | Kf6 |

It is important for Black not to frighten off his opponent.

| 17 Be8 | |

17 Ke1 is stronger. White fails to guess his opponent's intentions.

| 17 ... | Ke5 |
| 18 Bg6 | Kf4 |

The critical point of the ending has been reached. Had White played 19 Ke1 he could still have drawn, since after 19 ... Kg4 20 Kd1 d2 21 Be8 Be3 he has 22 Bd7! Kg5 23 h6! But White did not appreciate the fact that Black had embarked on active play.

| 19 Be8? | Bg5 |
| 20 Bf7? | |

The losing move. White was obviously expecting 20 ... Kg4 21 Be6, when he has everything in order. The best drawing chance was probably 20 Bd7. If instead 20 Bg6, then 20 ... Bh4+! 21 Kf1 Kg5 22 Be8 d2 23 Ke2 Be1, and by the advance of the f-pawn Black wins the h5 pawn, diverting the bishop from its defence. Note that it was already too late for 20 Ke1 due to 20 ... Ke3.

| 20 ... | Bh4+! |

This White had not foreseen. The rest is obvious.

21 Kf1	Ke3
22 h6	Kd2
23 Bb3	Kc1
24 h7	Bf6
25 Kf2	d2
26 Ke2	f4

White resigns.

In conclusion we will analyze two examples in which it was imperative for the stronger side not to delay taking positive action.

Kupreichik—Didishko

Minsk, 1980

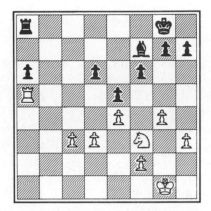

The white pawns constitute a compact mass, restricting the black bishop. The white rook is also much more active, and Black's outside passed pawn is securely blockaded.

1 ...   Kf8?!

Black has to take measures against Ne1 c2—b4. He can ensure the defence of his a-pawn using his bishop, while his king heads for the centre to cover the vulnerable points there. Black's plan is correct, but he implements it not altogether exactly. The king can reach e6 in two moves via f7, while the bishop has to go to c8 via e6. Therefore by 1 ... Be6 Black could have saved one move, e.g. 2 Ne1 Kf7 3 Nc2 Bc8 4 Nb4 Bb7.

Interesting, but probably inadequate, was the attempt to solve all the problems by tactical means: 1 ... Rc8?! 2 Rxa6 (if 2 c4, then 2 ... Re6 followed by the transfer of the bishop to c8) 2 ... d5 3 Ra3 dxe4 4 dxe4 Bg6 5 Nd2

Rd8 6 Ra2 Rd3 7 Rc2 Rxh3 8 f3, and for a long time the black rook is shut out of the game.

2 Ne1   Be8

Now the black bishop does not head for the defence of the a-pawn via the best route. To be considered was 2 ... Be6!? 3 Nc2 Bc8, so that if 4 Nb4 Bb7 or 4 Ne3 Be6, with drawing chances. It should be mentioned that at this point Didishko was in serious time trouble.

3 Nc2   Bc6
4 Ne3!

The point: 5 Nf5 is threatened.

4 ...   g6
5 Nc4

Loss of material for Black is inevitable.

5 ...   Rd8!

The best chance. After 5 ... Ke7 or 5 ... Bb5 White wins a pawn in a more favourable situation by 6 Nb6.

6 Rxa6   Bb5
7 Rxd6   Rxd6
8 Nxd6   Bxd3
9 f3   Ba6
10 c4

10 ... Ke7 was threatened.

10 ...   Ke7
11 c5   Kd7

If 11 ... g5 12 Nf5+, and the manoeuvre Ne3—d5 must win for White.

12 h4   Kc6
13 Ne8   g5!

51

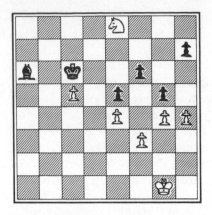

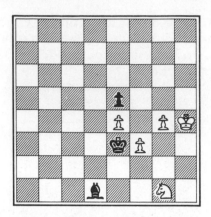

14 Nxf6?

White has gained a won position. But Kupreichik hastens to increase his material advantage, and makes the win much more difficult. Following the rule "do not hurry!", he should have played 14 h5!, winning.

14 ...	gxh4
15 Nxh7	Kxc5
16 Kg2	Be2
17 Ng5	Kd6!
18 Nh3!	

18 Kh3 Ke7 19 Kxh4 Kf6 leads to an amazing position, which, in spite of White's two extra pawns, is drawn.

18 ...	Kc5!

The black king reacts instantly to the movement of the white knight, and prepares to go onto the attack.

19 Ng1	Bd1
20 Kh3	Kd4
21 Kxh4	Ke3

(See next diagram)

22 Kg3?

But this is procrastination. It was imperative for White to hurry! Correct was 22 g5!, e.g. 22 ... Kf2 23 g6

Kxg1 24 g7 Bb3 25 Kg5! (but not *25 Kg3 Kf1 26 f4 Ke2 27 fxe5 Ke3*, with a draw) 25 ... Kf2 26 f4 Ke3 (no better is *26 ... exf4 27 Kxf4*, followed by *e4—e5*) 27 fxe5 Kxe4 28 Kf6, and wins. For a draw Black is short of one move, ... Bg8. Were his bishop on that square, 28 ... Kd5 would lead to a draw.

22 ...	Bb3!
23 g5	Bf7
24 Kg4	Bg6

The bishop blocks the g-pawn and prevents the advance of the white king. We have a positional draw.

25 Kg3	Bf7
26 Kg4	Bg6
27 Nh3	Be8
28 Kg3	

If 28 Kf5, then not 28 ... Bd7+? 29 Kxe5 Bxh3 30 g6 and wins, but 28 ... Kxf3! 29 Kxe5 Bg6 with a draw.

28 ...	Bh5
29 Kh4	Bf7

Black sticks to the proven defensive method, and avoids being diverted into calculating the variations after 29 ... Bxf3.

30 Kg4	Be8
31 Kg3	Bh5
32 Nf2	

White forces the opponent to capture on f3.

32 ...	Bxf3
33 g6	Be2
34 g7	Bc4
35 Kg4	Kxf2
36 Kf5	Ke3
37 Kxe5	Bg8

Drawn.

Lasker—Capablanca

World Championship Match
Havana, 1921

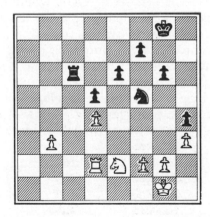

Black's pawn formation constitutes a compact mass, whereas White has two weaknesses — at b3 and d4. But the distance between these weaknesses is minimal, so that it is not easy for the stronger side to exploit them. All White's pieces are passively placed, and his king is a long way from the main battle sector — the b3 and d4 pawns. If in the diagram position the kings were at d3 and d6 respectively, the game would end in a draw. Therefore Black must all the time maintain the initiative, attacking White's weaknesses and trying not to allow the white king to come to their

defence.

1 ...	Rb6!

The aim of this move is to worsen the position of the opposing rook.

2 Rd3

Forced. 2 Rb2 or 2 Nc1 is met by 2 ... Rb4, winning a pawn.

2 ...	Ra6!

Creating a new threat of 3 ... Ra1+, for a long time shutting the white king out of play. Had Black not made the previous rook move to b6, White would have had the strong reply 3 Rb2, with counter-play.

3 g4	hxg3
4 fxg3	

Totally bad was 4 Nxg3 Ra1+ 5 Kg2 Nd6, when White has as many as four weak pawns.

4 ...	Ra2
5 Nc3	Rc2!

With the threat of 5 ... Nxd4.

6 Nd1	Ne7!

The black knight transfers to c6 to attack the opponent's weaknesses. With every move White's position deteriorates.

7 Ne3

7 b4 is bad due to ... Rc1—b1.

7 ...	Rc1+!

The white king can now be allowed into freedom, since the main role will be played by concrete variations. On the natural 7 ... Rb2 there could have

53

followed either 8 Nd1, with a continuation similar to the game, or 8 Rc3!? Rd2 9 Nc2 Nf5 10 b4 Nxd4 11 Nxd4 Rxd4 12 Rb3, with drawing chances. There is no point in Black allowing the opponent additional possibilities.

8	Kf2	Nc6
9	Nd1	Rb1!
10	Ke2?	

An oversight. White was bound to lose his b-pawn, but he should have aimed for the exchange of rooks, since in the knight ending Black would have encountered certain technical difficulties, in view of the limited number of pawns. Correct was 10 Ke1!, defending the knight (*10 Ke3? Nb4*), and if 10 ... Na5 11 Kd2 Rxb3 12 Rxb3, with drawing chances.

| 10 | ... | Rxb3! |
| 11 | Ke3 | Rb4 |

Black has won a pawn. Now the rhythm of the play changes sharply, and the principle of "do not hurry" comes into force. See how calm Capablanca's actions become.

| 12 | Nc3 | Ne7 |
| 13 | Ne2 | |

On 13 g4 there follows 13 ... g5.

13	...	Nf5+
14	Kf2	g5
15	g4	

Passive defence would not have changed anything.

15	...	Nd6
16	Ng1	Ne4+
17	Kf1	Rb1+
18	Kg2	Rb2+
19	Kf1	Rf2+!?
20	Ke1	Ra2
21	Kf1	

Forced. On 21 Nf3 Black wins by 21 ... Nf2, or 21 Ne2 Ra1+, 22 ... Rxd1+, 23 ... Nf2+ and 24 ... Nxh3.

| 21 | ... | Kg7 |

Black's plan includes playing his king to d6 followed by ... f6 and ... e5. It is interesting to note that during the twenty moves of this endgame Capablanca has not made a single move with his king — an exceptionally unusual occurrence in his games.

22	Re3	Kg6
23	Rd3	f6
24	Re3	Kf7
25	Rd3	Ke7
26	Re3	Kd6
27	Rd3	Rf2+
28	Ke1	Rg2
29	Kf1	Ra2
30	Re3	e5
31	Rd3	exd4
32	Rxd4	

Bad is 32 Ne2 Rd2 33 Rxd4 Ng3+!

32	...	Kc5
33	Rd1	d4
34	Rc1+	Kd5

White resigns, since on 35 Rd1 there follows 35 ... Ng3+ 36 Ke1 Rg2.

CHAPTER 6

SCHEMATIC THINKING

Chess history knows of a number of examples where, in a highly complex position, within literally a few minutes a player has taken a decision, the correctness of which has subsequently been confirmed by lengthy analyses, although to carry them out in actual play would be totally unrealistic. Capablanca's intuition was legendary, while Smyslov, Petrosian, Karpov and many other players are renowned for their exceptionally rapid and exact analysis of all the details of a position.

In the endgame, schematic thinking gives an experienced player the advantage over an opponent who may be superior to him in rapidity and depth of calculation, but who relies mainly on this calculation.

Schematic thinking should not be confused with the forming of a main strategic plan, although they have much in common. Both schematic thinking and a general plan follow from a concrete evaluation of the position. For example, in the Capablanca–Ragozin game (cf. p. 1) White's basic idea was to realize his extra pawn on the Q-side. The creation of a propitious moment for the implementation of this plan was preceded by a great deal of preparatory work on improving the positioning of the forces and on suppressing possible counter-play by the opponent. In doing so Capablanca used logical set-ups of his pieces, based on an evaluation of the position, and designed to solve specific and not very complicated problems. During the course of play one scheme was replaced by another, and at some point Capablanca gave up altogether the advance of his extra pawn on the Q-side, since Ragozin had acquired weaknesses on the K-side, and play against these weaknesses promised more certain success. All this is very characteristic of modern chess. Of course, it is possible to have positions which allow the outlining of an overall strategic plan, which the opponent is unable to oppose. More often plans have to be changed in accordance with changes in the situation on the board, caused by the actions of the opponent.

But thinking in schemes, in small components of a plan, is necessary all the time, except in highly tactical positions, where general considerations fade into the background and give way to specific calculation. In the Znosko–Borovsky v. Alekhine ending (p. 59) Black outlined a highly complex plan which was brilliantly justified. However, it seems to us that it is much easier to describe such a plan after the completion of a game than to form it during play. After all, had White on his second move played his pawn to f4, that would have been the end of Alekhine's plan and he would have had to form a completely different one. It is more probable that during the game Alekhine was thinking in small schemes: exchange one pair of rooks, retain the other, transfer the king to e6, create a weakness for White on the K-side, and so on. By thus improving his position, and not encountering any resistance by the opponent at the point when Znosko–Borovsky was completely deprived of counter-play, Alekhine was able to draw up his plan in all its details and implement it in full.

We give the following game in full, since soon after the opening it went into an endgame.

Janowski—Capablanca

New York, 1916

1	d4	Nf6
2	Nf3	d5
3	c4	c6
4	Nc3	Bf5
5	Qb3	Qb6
6	Qxb6	axb6
7	cxd5	Nxd5
8	Nxd5	cxd5
9	e3	Nc6
10	Bd2	

10 ...		Bd7!

No prejudices. Capablanca thinks schematically. Black's plan includes transferring his knight to c4 after the preparatory ... b5. To support the advance of the b-pawn the bishop retreats to d7, whereas at the seemingly active position f5 it was out of play.

11 Be2

In contrast to his opponent, Janowski develops his pieces without any definite plan. He should have considered playing his bishop to b5, preventing the advance of the black pawn and preparing the development of his king at e2 instead of castling.

11 ...	e6
12 0—0	Bd6
13 Rfc1	Ke7!
14 Bc3	Rhc8
15 a3?	

A quite unprovoked weakening of the position.

15 ...	Na5
16 Nd2	f5!

Suppressing possible counter-play with e3—e4.

17 g3	b5
18 f3	Nc4

"Black's first plan is completed. White now will have to take the knight, and Black's only weakness, the doubled b-pawn, will become a source of great strength at c4. Now for two or three moves Black will devote his time to improving the general strategic position of his pieces before evolving a new plan, this time a plan of attack against White's position" (Capablanca).

19 Bxc4	bxc4
20 e4	Kf7
21 e5?	

A positional mistake, after which it is unlikely that White's game can be saved. With the centre closed, Black's spatial advantage enables him without difficulty to prepare operations on the wings. Correct was 21 exd5 exd5 22 f4! followed by Nf3—e5.

21 ...	Be7
22 f4	b5

It is difficult for Black to achieve success by playing only on one wing, where White is able to hold the offensive. Therefore, after preparing a break-through on one of the wings and tying down the opponent's forces, a blow must be struck on the other, operating according to the principle of two weaknesses. Black first makes an attempt to break through on the Q-side.

| 23 Kf2 | Ra4 |
| 24 Ke3 | Rca8 |

Threatening ... b4.

25 Rab1	h6
26 Nf3	g5
27 Ne1	Rg8
28 Kf3	gxf4
29 gxf4	Raa8

Black readily switches his rooks from wing to wing. White's lack of space, or, as Nimzowitsch put it, his inferior 'lines of communication', prevents him from keeping pace with his opponent.

30 Ng2	Rg4
31 Rg1	Rag8
32 Be1	

White has prepared for the defence of his K-side. After the transfer of his bishop to f2 followed by Ne3 he will gradually neutralize Black's pressure on that part of the board. But just at this point, when the co-ordination of the white rooks is destroyed, the breakthrough comes on the opposite wing!

| 32 ... | b4! |

The inclusion in the game of the white-squared bishop quickly decides matters.

33 axb4

In the event of the exchange of bishops, the advance of the black h-pawn is decisive.

| 33 ... | Ba4 |

34 Ra1

Or 34 Rc1 Rxf4+!

34 ...	Bc2
35 Bg3	Be4+
36 Kf2	h5

Loss of material is inevitable.

37 Ra7	Bxg2
38 Rxg2	h4
39 Bxh4	Rxg2+
40 Kf3	Rxh2
41 Bxe7	Rh3+
42 Kf2	Rb3
43 Bg5+	Kg6
44 Re7	Rxb2+
45 Kf3	Ra8
46 Rxe6+	Kh7

White resigns.

Bogoljubov—Lasker

Moscow, 1925

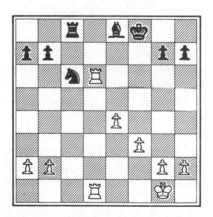

White has an undisputed advantage — a rook and two connected pawns against knight and bishop. It is very difficult for Black to find a reasonable plan of defence, but he hit upon a brilliant defensive formation and managed to save the game. Not without reason have FIDE awarded a Lasker medal for the best game of the year in which defence triumphs.

| 1 ... | Ne5 |
| 2 Rd8 | |

It is advantageous for White to exchange rooks.

| 2 ... | Rc2 |
| 3 R8d2 | Rc7 |

An interesting point. 3 ... Rc6 was objectively stronger. It would seem that Lasker was masking his plan, hoping for a greater effect if White should play routinely. He had obviously made a good study of Bogoljubov's at times over-temperamental character, and was assuming that White would try to advance his pawns in the centre without sufficient preparation. There is also another possibility which cannot be ruled out: Lasker had not yet formed the plan in all its details.

4 Kf2?

An inaccuracy. This centralization of the king is untimely. Bogoljubov plans f3—f4, without considering any counter-play by the opponent. He should first have broken up Black's position by 4 Rd5 Nf7 (4 ... Nc4 5 Rc1) 5 Kf2! (if immediately 5 Ra5 Rc2, while on 5 R1d2 Black gains counter-play by 5 ... Rc1+ 6 Kf2 Bc6! 7 Ra5 a6, when it is not easy for the white rook at a5 to return to play) 5 ... Ke7 6 R1d2 Rc1 7 Rh5 h6 8 Ra5 a6 9 Rad5 Bc6 10 Rd1 Rc2+ 11 R5d2 Rc5 12 Ke3. White has provoked the advance of the black pawn to h6, which is useful for him, and also the very important (as will be seen from the further course of the game) advance of the pawn to a6.

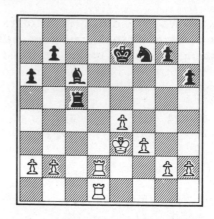

White's subsequent plan could be as follows: drive the black rook from c5, transfer his own rook to c5, and by the threat of exchanging wrest control of the fifth rank, and only then begin advancing the pawns over the entire front. Of course, it is easy to give such advice after the analysis of the position, but in a practical game it would be extremely difficult to perceive the difference between the positions of the pawns at a7 or a6.

4 ...	Ke7
5 h3	Rc6!
6 f4	Nf7
7 Rd5?	

An incomprehensible move. True, after 7 Ke3 Ra6 8 b3 Re6 Black probably should not lose, since White has advanced his pawns too early.

7 ...	Ra6!
8 a3	Bc6
9 R5d4	

Now Black's plan of defence takes shape. The bishop has put the central e4 pawn under fire, and it can advance only to a square attacked by the knight. The black knight is also ready at any point to switch to f5 (with the white pawns at f4 and e5) and can assist the undermining of White's centre at an appropriate moment by ...g5. While Black's minor pieces and king are holding the defence in the centre, his rook breaks out via the Q-side and begins a counter-attack.

9 ...	Rb6!
10 b4	a5!
11 bxa5	Ra6
12 R1d3	Rxa5
13 Kf3	Rc5

Each black piece is working to maximum effect.

14 h4

White would like to play g2—g4, but this is met by ... g5!

14 ...	h5!
15 g4	hxg4+
16 Kxg4	Nh6+!

Before beginning a counter-attack with his rook from the rear, the enemy king must be driven back.

17 Kg3	Rc1
18 a4	Rg1+
19 Kf3	Ra1

19 ... Nf5 also looks good.

20 Rd1	Ra3+
21 R1d3	Rxd3+!

Lasker avoids the repetition of moves, rightly assuming that after the exchange of rooks it is White who will have to fight for a draw. Unfavourable for Black was 21 ... Rxa4?! 22 Rxa4 Bxa4 23 f5! followed by 24 Kf4.

22 Rxd3	Nf5
23 h5	Ke6!

Black threatens 24 ... Nd6 25 Re3 Nxe4! with serious winning chances, but White has a possibility of gaining a draw.

24 Rc3!	Nd6
25 Rxc6!	bxc6
26 a5	

The position has changed sharply. Now Black is required to display a certain accuracy, to avoid ending up in an inferior position.

26 ...	c5!
27 a6	Nb5
28 Ke3	c4

The actions of the knight and the c-pawn are co-ordinated to the maximum extent. The white king's passage to the Q-side is blocked, and we have a positional draw.

29 Kd2	Kd6
30 Ke3	Ke6

Drawn.

Znosko—Borovsky v. Alekhine

Paris, 1933

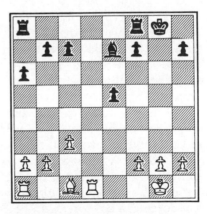

This ending is highly instructive. The position appears to be a 'dead' draw. It is hard to imagine that, without the opponent blundering, one of the sides can hope for success. But that is precisely what happened. Let us hand the word over to Alekhine himself:

"The play in this ending is by no means so simple as it appears — especially for White. Black's plan, which will prove completely successful, consists of the following parts: (1) exchange one pair of rooks; (2) transfer the king to e6 where, being defended by the e-pawn, it can prevent the invasion at d7 by the remaining white rook; (3) operating with the rook on the open g-file and advancing the h-pawn, force the opening of the h-file; (4) after this White's king, and possibly his bishop, will be tied to the defence of h1 and h2 against invasion by the rook; (5) Black meanwhile, by advancing his a- and b-pawns, will sooner or later also open one of the files on the Q-side; (6) since at this point his king will still be on the opposite wing, White will be unable to prevent the invasion of the first or second rank by the black rook. It must be admitted that, had White from the very beginning realized that there was a real danger of him losing this ending, by careful defence he might have been able to save the game. But what happened was that Black played according to a definite plan, whereas White played only with the conviction that the game was bound to end in a draw. The result was an instructive series of typical patterns and stratagems, much more useful to students of the game than the so-called 'brilliancies' of short one-sided games."

To Alekhine's words we can add that this deeply conceived active plan is based on the principle of two weaknesses. The first weakness of White's position will be the occupation by the black rook of the h-file, the invasion squares along which White succeeds in covering with his king. The second and decisive weakness becomes the open file on the Q-side, where the invasion cannot be prevented. It should also be mentioned that a part of any plan is the centralization of the king.

1 Bh6	Rfd8

2 Kf1?	

After the correct 2 f4! White's chances would have been in no way worse.

2 ...	f5
3 Rxd8+	Rxd8
4 g3	

Defending against a possible . . . f4.

4 ...	Kf7
5 Be3	h5
6 Ke2	Ke6
7 Rd1	Rg8!

Black confidently carries out his plan. Three stages are already complete. It is unfavourable for White to prevent the advance of the rook's pawn by h2—h4, due to . . . Rg4.

8 f3	h4
9 Bf2	hxg3
10 hxg3	Rh8
11 Bg1	Bd6
12 Kf1	

The first weakness has been created, and White's king and bishop are tied to defending against the threats of the black rook. Now the decisive stage of the game commences. Black embarks on his Q-side pawn offensive.

12 ...	Rg8
13 Bf2	b5!

Starting the attack. If White plays passively there will follow . . . c5, . . . c4, . . . a5, . . . b4 etc. But this would have been a lesser evil than that which occurs in the game.

14 b3?	a5
15 Kg2	a4
16 Rd2	

On 16 b4 Black would have transferred his rook to c6 via a8 and a6.

| 16 ... | axb3 |
| 17 axb3 | Ra8 |

The triumph of Black's strategy! His
plan has been carried out. White has
acquired a second weakness: the a-file
occupied by the black rook. But the
game is not yet over.

| 18 c4 | Ra3! |

Very strong.

19 c5	Be7
20 Rb2	b4
21 g4!?	

Realizing that his game is lost, White
seeks counter-chances.

21 ...	f4
22 Kf1	Ra1+
23 Ke2	Rc1
24 Ra2	

Otherwise after ... Rc3 the white
pieces would be stalemated.

24 ...	Rc3
25 Ra7	Kd7
26 Rb7	Rxb3
27 Rb8	Rb2+
28 Kf1	b3
29 Kg1	Kc6
30 Kf1	Kd5
31 Rb7	e4!

This energetic realization of his advantage is typical of Alekhine.

32 fxe4+	Kxe4
33 Rxc7	Kf3
34 Rxe7	Rxf2+
35 Ke1	b2
36 Rb7	Rc2
37 c6!	

Black might just play 37 ... Rc1+?,
when 38 Kd2 b1=Q 39 Rxb1 Rxb1
40 c7 follows.

37 ...	Kg3
38 c7	f3
39 Kd1	Rxc7
40 Rxb2	f2
White resigns.	

Gligoric—Smyslov

Candidates Tournament
Zurich, 1953

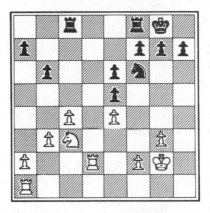

In his book on the tournament,
Bronstein makes the following comment
on this position: "There exists a wide-
spread and therefore dangerous delusion
that with an extra pawn the win is
achieved automatically. Meanwhile, in
the given position Black's main advantage lies not so much in his extra pawn,
which cannot be realized for some time,
as in his control over many squares in
the central region of the board: d4, d5,
c5, f4 and f5.

White has his counter-chances: a Q-
side pawn majority and the d-file. How
many such games have ended in a draw
after inaccurate play! But Smyslov con-
ducts such endings with an iron hand.
His plan divides into the following parts:

(1) Immediately exchange one rook,
but retain the other for a possible battle

61

against White's Q-side pawns and an attack on the c4 and e4 pawns.

(2) By the threat of creating an outside passed pawn, divert the white rook onto the h-file, when his own rook can occupy the d-file.

(3) By the advance of the g-pawn to g4, undermine the support of the e4 pawn — the white f-pawn.

(4) Tie down the white pieces by attacking the e4 pawn.

(5) Advance the king to win the opponent's weak pawns.

As we see, the winning plan is simple — for Smyslov, of course."

1	...	Rfd8
2	Rad1	Rxd2
3	Rxd2	Kf8
4	f3	Ke7
5	Kf2	h5!
6	Ke3	g5
7	Rh2	Rd8
8	Rh1	g4

Black successfully advances towards his goal.

9	fxg4	Nxg4+
10	Ke2	Nf6
11	Ke3	Rd4
12	Rf1	Ng4+
13	Ke2	Kf8

Smyslov embarks on the final stage of his plan — he directs his king along the route e7–f8–g7–g6–g5–g4.

14	Rf3	Kg7
15	Rd3	Kf6!
16	Rxd4	

A desperate attempt to obtain counter-chances.

16	...	exd4
17	Nb5	Ke5
18	Nxa7	Kxe4
19	Nc8	d3+!

But not 19 ... e5?? 20 Nd6 mate!

20	Kd2	Kd4
21	c5	bxc5
22	Nd6	Ne5

White resigns.

Polugayevsky—Vasyukov

34th USSR Championship
Tbilisi, 1967

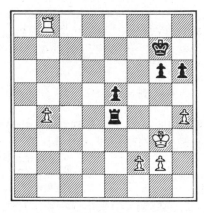

In this book there is hardly any analysis of pure rook endings. In our opinion, rook endings occupy a special place in the classification of chess endings. They are extremely complex and are subject to their own special rules and principles, which often have nothing in common with the principles of handling complicated endings. Frequently in rook endings, due to the abundance of possibilities, the actions of the two sides are difficult to describe, the resulting positions are of an irrational nature, and the choice of move has to be made mainly on the basis of concrete variations. But often we observe completely the opposite picture. Concrete variations have practically no significance, and the thinking is exclusively schematic.

It is to this second type that the Polugayevsky—Vasyukov ending belongs. The weaker side's method of defence in such endings has long been known.

Black's rook stands behind White's passed pawn, and while the latter is advancing to b6, Black waits. When the white king goes to the aid of the passed pawn, Black wins one of the K-side pawns and sets up a passed pawn on that part of the board. After this he is ready to give up his rook for White's passed pawn, and the ending normally reduces to king and rook against king and pawn. The result depends on the specific features of the resulting position, of course, but the game is more likely to be a draw than for the side with the extra pawn to win. It would appear that in the given position the play should proceed according to the scheme described.

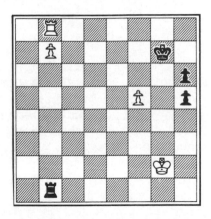

1 b5?

White's sealed move is a serious mistake, after which he should no longer have been able to win. Let us hand over the commentary to grandmaster Polugayevsky:

"Only when I began my analysis did I discover a nuance in this position, and a highly important one. The point is that, by advancing his pawn to b7, White ties down the opposing king and rook, and then, by an encircling manoeuvre with his king, utilizing once again the 'triangulation' method, he wins the e5 pawn. But even after this, victory can be achieved only if he creates a passed pawn on the f-file.

(See next diagram)

By playing f5—f6+, White prevents the black king from moving between the squares g7 and h7, and after ... Kf7 he wins by Rh8, while in the event of ... Kxf6 he has the opportunity for a deadly check: Rf8+ and b8=Q.

In the adjourned position the white f-pawn has no opposite number, but the black g6 pawn stands in its path. This pawn could have been cleared out of the way immediately, by the dagger-blow 1 h5! If Black captures on h5 or allows White to take on g6, White's idea of creating a second passed pawn is achieved in pure form, and a theoretically won ending is reached.

During the game I was intending to play h4—h5 on my next move, but in my analysis I became aware that such a hope was not feasible. After all, it was now Black's turn to move, and before posting his rook behind the white b-pawn, he could radically prevent all his opponent's aggressive intentions on the K-side, by first playing 1 ... h5!

If in this case the white king were to head for the b-pawn, play would proceed as described at the very beginning, and (I have to ask you to take my word for this) White would at best be one tempo away from a win. However much I racked my brains, I couldn't find a win for White.

If instead White wins the e5 pawn by 'triangulation' — which is possible — then he succeeds in creating a passed pawn only on the g- or h-file, which is not good enough to win."

1 ...   Rb4?

Obviously Black had failed to discover the essence of the position, and with his very first move after the adjournment he commits a decisive mistake. As already mentioned, 1 ... h5! was correct.

| 2 h5! | gxh5 |
| 3 b6?! | |

It is easy to understand Polugayevsky's joy on seeing the first move after the resumption. But emotions, even positive ones, are not always a good help in chess. Pleasurably anticipating the implementation of his plan, White plays too hastily and allows his opponent a latent possibility of counter-play, which Vasyukov fails to exploit. 3 Kf3! was correct.

| 3 ... | h4+? |

Let us again hand over to grandmaster Polugayevsky:

"Saving chances were offered by 3 . . . Rb3+!, when an amazing, study-like draw results after 4 f3 e4 5 b7 (or *5 Kf2 Rb2+ 6 Ke3 Rxg2 7 b7 Rb2 8 fxe4 h4*, and the black h-pawn is no weaker than either of its white opponents) 5 . . . h4+! (but not *5 . . . e3 6 f4 e2 7 Kf2*), and after 6 Kf2 Black is saved by the straightforward 6 . . . h3, and after 6 Kxh4 e3 7 Kg3 by the highly subtle 7 . . . Rb4!!, when White is in *zugzwang*.

He has no other move than 8 f4 (the exchange of the b7 pawn for the e3 pawn leads to a theoretically drawn ending), but then 8 . . . e2 9 Kf2 Rxf4+ 10 Kxe2 Rb4 once again gives White

nothing.

Therefore, in reply to 3 . . . Rb3+ White would have had to try 4 Kh4. But after 4 . . . e4! (*4 . . . Rb2*, however, is also possible) the tempting 5 Kxh5 leads only to a draw after the quiet 5 . . . Rb4!!, when White is doomed to carrying on the fight 'a king down', since he dare not step onto the 'mined' 4th rank. The thematic 6 f4 is just one tempo too slow: 6 . . . e3 7 f5 e2 8 Re8 Rxb6 9 Rxe2 Rb1. Also, 6 g4 does not change anything: the further advance g4—g5 is all the same impossible, in view of the reply . . . Rb5!''

| 4 Kf3 | Kh7 |

No better is 4 . . . Kg6 5 b7 Kh5 6 g4+! hxg3 7 fxg3, when Black is unable to defend against the break-through 8 g4+ and 9 g5!

| 5 b7 | Kg7 |
| 6 Ke3 | e4 |

Waiting tactics would also have been unsuccessful. If 6 . . . Kh7, then 7 Kd3 Kg7 8 Kc3 Rb1 9 Kc4 Rb2 10 Kd5 and the e-pawn is lost, since 10. . .Rb5+? loses immediately to 11 Kc6!, when White's king approaches the b7 pawn with gain of tempo, after which he wins by moving his rook along the eighth rank.

7 Kf4	Kh7
8 Ke5	Kg7
9 Kd5	Rb2

The e-pawn was doomed. If 9 . . . Kh7, then 10 Kc5 Rb2 11 Kc6 Rc2+ 12 Kd5 Rb2 13 Kxe4.

10 Kxe4	Rb4+
11 Kd3	Rb3+
12 Kc4	Rb1
13 f4	

This was the sort of position White

was aiming for at the start of the adjournment session. The game concluded:

13	...	Rc1+
14	Kd3	Rb1
15	f5	Rb6
16	f6+	Resigns.

We will now analyze another rook ending which in many respects resembles the previous one.

Smirnov—Shereshevsky

Minsk, 1979

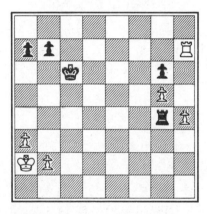

On the K-side an exchange of pawns is bound to take place, after which White will remain with an extra passed pawn on the g-file. The black rook will stand behind it, and, if the white king should head for the g6 pawn, Black will pick up the b-pawn and set up a passed pawn on the Q-side. The game will end in a draw. This would be the normal procedure in this ending.

1 ...	a5

It is useful for Black to remove his pawns from the seventh rank. Besides, the further the a-pawn is advanced, the more quickly it will be possible to create a passed pawn, if White should give up his b-pawn to take his king across to his passed pawn.

2	Kb3	b5
3	Kc2	a4
4	Rh6	Kc5
5	Rxg6	Rxh4
6	Rg8	Rg4

Both sides follow the pre-planned scenario.

7	g6	Kb6

But not 7 ... Kc4? 8 g7 Rg2+ 9 Kb1 Kb3 10 Rc8!, when on 10 ... Rg1+ there follows 11 Rc1 Rxg7 12 Rc3 mate!

8	g7!	

The advance of the king towards the pawn at g6 was totally unpromising.

8	...	Kb7
9	Kd3	

White's plan begins to take shape. After the arrival of the white king at f3 the black rook will be forced to allow it across the fourth rank. The white king then intends to break through at a5.

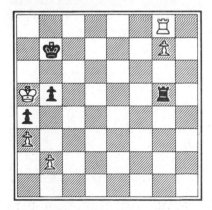

Here White sacrifices his g-pawn by Rf8, and after .., Rxg7 plays Rf5, picking up Black's Q-side pawns and winning. But Black finds a defence.

9 ...	Ka7
10 Ke3	Kb7
11 Kf3	Rg1
12 Kf4	Rg2
13 Ke5	Rg3
14 Kd5	Rg5+
15 Kd6	

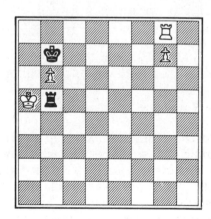

Up till now Black has stuck to waiting tactics, but now he is in *zugzwang*. His rook must not allow the white king to reach c5, while his king must guard c6. By the method of elimination it is easy to find the only move, but one which proves sufficient for a draw.

15 ...	b4!

Black sacrifices his Q-side pawns, but breaks up his opponent's pawn formation. An amazing ending is reached, in which White is three pawns up, but there

is no win!

16 axb4	Rg6+
17 Kc5	Rg5+
18 Kc4	Ka7
19 b5	Rg4+
20 Kc5	Kb7
21 b6	Rg5+
22 Kb4	Rg4+
23 Kb5	

Black is again in *zugzwang*. He is forced to give up his a-pawn, but this is of no significance.

23 ...	Rg5+
24 Kxa4	Rg4+
25 b4	Rg1
26 Ka5	Rg5+
27 b5	Rxb5+!

Drawn.

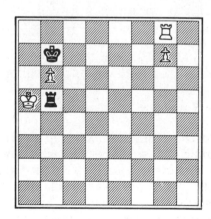

CHAPTER 7

THE PRINCIPLE OF TWO WEAKNESSES

In this elementary pawn ending White wins by sacrificing his a-pawn to take his king across to the K-side and eliminate the black pawns.

The first weakness in Black's position is the white passed a-pawn; the second is his K-side. If we slightly change the position by adding a white pawn at c4 and a black one at c5, White will be unable to win, since one weakness — the extra a-pawn — is insufficient, and Black's K-side is impregnable. As Nimzowitsch expressed it, in this second example White lacks a 'manoeuvring pivot' — the square d4 for his king. The principle of two weaknesses frequently determines the plan in an endgame, as we will see in numerous examples.

Shereshevsky—Belyavsky

Lvov, 1977

After a rather uninteresting opening and a complex but transient middlegame, in which White gained an advantage by tactical means, he was faced with a choice: to win the exchange with a sharp and unclear position, or to go into an ending with material level, but with

Black having two obvious weaknesses (pawns at b4 and e6). White chose to go into the ending, since Black had no compensation for the two pawn weaknesses on opposite wings.

1	d4	Nf6
2	Nf3	b6
3	e3	Bb7
4	Bd3	e6
5	0—0	Be7
6	Nbd2	d5
7	b3	0—0
8	Bb2	c5
9	Ne5	Nc6
10	a3	a6
11	f4	b5
12	dxc5	Bxc5
13	Qf3	Nxe5
14	Bxe5	a5

14 ... Ne4 was seriously to be considered.

15	Qg3	g6
16	f5	Nh5
17	fxg6!	fxg6

A sad necessity. Of course, 17 ... Nxg3 failed to 18 gxh7 mate, while on 17 ... hxg6 there would have followed 18 Rxf7!!, and now:
(a) 18 ... Rxf7 19 Qxg6+ Kf8 (*19 ... Ng7 20 Qh7+ Kf8 21 Bxg7+ Ke7 22 Bf6+*) 20 Qh6+ Ke7 21 Bg6.
(b) 18 ... Nxg3 19 Rg7+ Kh8 20 Rxg6+ Kh7, when White has at least a draw by perpetual check, but can also continue his attack with 21 Rxg3+ Rf5 22 Rf1, with very dangerous threats:
(b1) 22 ... Bc8 23 Rff3 (*23 Rh3+ Kg6 24 g4 Qg5 25 Rg3 is also possible*) 23 ... Bf8 (otherwise *Rh3+* wins) 24 Rg4 Bh6 25 Rh3 with a decisive

attack.

(b2) 22 ... Bxe3+ 23 Rxe3 Qb6 24 Rff3 Kg8 25 Bxf5 exf5 26 c3, with a big advantage.

18 Qh3?!

After 18 Rxf8+ Qxf8 19 Qh3 White would have won the b-pawn.

18 ...	Qb6
19 Qg4	Rf5

The threat of Bxg6 had to be parried, but Black should have included the intermediate check 19 ... Bxe3+ 20 Kh1 Rf5, with some counter-play for the exchange, although after 21 Bxf5 exf5 22 Rxf5 Bxd2 (22 ... Bc8 23 Qf3) 23 Rxh5 White has an obvious advantage. Now White has a choice.

20 Bd4!?

Forcing an ending in which Black has two pawn weaknesses on opposite wings, and his minor pieces are unable to defend them. In addition Black is deprived of counter-play.

20 ...	Bxd4
21 Qxd4	Qxd4
22 exd4	Rxf1+
23 Rxf1	b4
24 g4	Ng7

25 axb4	axb4
26 Nf3	

White's plan is to transfer his knight to e5 and his king to e3, and only then to lay siege to the weaknesses. Black is powerless to avert loss of material.

26 ...	Ne8
27 Ne5	Nd6
28 Kf2	

Allowing the exchange of bishops, but this is no longer of any importance.

28 ...	Ba6
29 Ke3	Bxd3
30 Nxd3	Rc8
31 Nxb4	Rc3+
32 Kf4	Kf8
33 Rf3	Rc7
34 Ke3+	Ke7
35 Kd2	Ne4+
36 Kc1	

White has won a pawn while maintaining a positional advantage.

36 ...	Nc3
37 Re3	Kd7?
38 Na6	Resigns.

In the above ending White exploited two black pawn weaknesses on opposite wings. But the concept of a 'weakness' is much wider than that of a lone (isolated) pawn which can be subjected to attack. A weakness may be the occupation of an open file by an enemy major piece, an enemy outside passed pawn, an immobile piece, a king which is cut off, and so on. In short, a weakness is primarily a positional defect.

Alekhine—Sämisch

Baden Baden, 1925

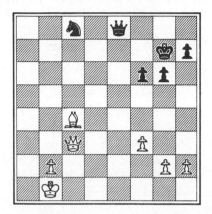

White has an extra passed b-pawn (Black's first weakness). However, the immediate advance of this pawn would expose the white king and give Black serious drawing chances. Therefore Alekhine sets about creating a second weakness in Black's position.

1 Qd4

"By this and his following move White selects the correct winning plan, which is the advance of his K-side pawns. The passed b-pawn must be advanced only later, when with the exchange of queens the danger of perpetual check will be eliminated" (Alekhine).

	1 ...	Qe7
2	Bd3!	Qc7
3	g4	Kf7
4	h4	Nb6
5	h5	gxh5
6	gxh5	

The second weakness — the pawn at h7 — has been created.

	6 ...	Qc6
7	Be4!	

Avoiding the exchange of queens

which was possible after 7 Qe4, and with the aim of fixing the weak pawn at h7. Of course, not 7 Bxh7 Qxf3 8 Qxb6? Qd1+ with a draw.

	7 ...	Qb5
8	h6	Qb3
9	Bc2!	Qb5
10	Qd3	Qxd3
11	Bxd3	

White has achieved the exchange of queens in the most favourable circumstances: the black king is tied to the defence of the h-pawn, and the knight is quite unable to cope with the passed b-pawn supported by king and bishop.

	11 ...	Nc8
12	Bxh7	Resigns.

Tartakover—Boleslavsky

Groningen, 1946

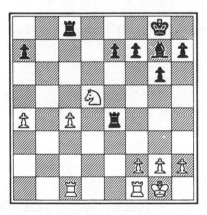

Black has an undisputed positional advantage, and he carries out a manoeuvre which wins a pawn by force.

	1 ...	Rcxc4
2	Nxe7+	Kf8
3	Nd5	Rxc1!
4	Rxc1	Bb2!
5	Rc8+	Kg7
6	Kf1	Rxa4

Thus White's first weakness is Black's passed pawn on the Q-side. Guided by the principle of two weaknesses, Black directs his efforts towards giving White a second weakness — on the K-side.

7 Ne3	Bd4
8 Nc2	Bb6
9 f3	Kf6

The creating of weaknesses in the opponent's position is normally preceded by improving the placing of the pieces: the black bishop has taken up an excellent post at b6. Now Black activates his king.

10 Ke2	Ke6
11 Kd3	Kd7
12 Rf8	Ke7
13 Rb8	h5

Black at last sets about creating a second weakness in White's position.

14 g3

This move could have been avoided, but after . . . h4 and . . . Bg1 White would have been left with a weak square at g3.

14 . . .	Bg1
15 h3	Bb6
16 g4	h4
17 Rh8	g5
18 Rg8	f6

Black has carried out his plan: White has been given weak pawns at f3 and h3. Now Black decides the game by advancing his king. Since he too has acquired a weak pawn at f6, care and accuracy are essential.

| 19 Rc8 | Kd6 |
| 20 Re8 | Kd5?! |

Too hasty. Black should first have

worsened the position of the white king by 20 . . . Rf4 21 Ke2, and only then played 21 . . . Kd5, when 22 Ne3+ can be met by 22 . . . Bxe3 22 Kxe3 a5, advancing the pawn to a4.

| 21 Ne3+ | Bxe3 |

"After 21 . . . Kc6 22 Nf5 Black is unable to win, due to the weakness of his f-pawn. For example: 22 . . . Kd7 23 Re7+ Kc8 24 Rf7 Bd8 25 Nd6+ Kb8 26 Rb7+ Ka8 27 Rf7 Ra6 28 Nb7 Bb6 29 Nd6 Bc7 30 Rf8+ Bb8 31 Ne4 Ra3+ 32 Ke2 Ra2+ 33 Kd3 Rh2 34 Rxf6 Bf4 35 Rf5 Rxh3 36 Nxg5, with a draw" (Boleslavsky).

| 22 Kxe3 | a5 |
| 23 Rd8+? | |

Missing a chance to save the game. Had White anticipated his opponent's plan, by 23 Ra8 he would have prevented the regrouping . . . Rf4 and . . . a4, followed by the advance of the black king on the Q-side.

| 23 . . . | Kc6! |

The game is decided. The remainder does not require any explanation.

24 Rc8+	Kb7
25 Re8	Rf4
26 Ke2	Kb6
27 Re3	Kb5
28 Kd2	a4
29 Kc3	Kc5
30 Kc2	Rb4
31 Re6	Rb6
32 Re4	Rb3!
33 Rxa4	Rxf3
34 Ra6	Kd4
35 Kd2	Ke5
36 Ke2	Rxh3
37 Kf2	Rd3
38 Ra5+	Rd5
39 Ra3	Rd4

40 Ra5+	Ke6
41 Ra6+	Kf7

White resigns.

Alekhine—Vidmar

Hastings, 1936

White has an extra pawn at b4. Alekhine himself assessed this position as follows: "White's winning plan is easy to explain, but rather difficult to carry out. White exploits the fact that the black pieces are occupied on the Q-side to create, by the gradual advance of his pawns and their exchange, vulnerable points in Black's position in the centre and on the K-side. Only after this preparatory work can the decisive offensive be begun". In other words, Alekhine indicates the need to give the opponent a second weakness.

1 g4!	Ke7
2 b5	e5

Depriving the white rook of d4.

3 f4	f6(?)

It was better to exchange on f4, since now Black's e-pawn is isolated.

4 fxe5	fxe5
5 Ra2	

Preventing . . . Kd6.

5 . . .	Rb6
6 Rb2	h6
7 Kf2	Ke6
8 Kf3	Nd5

Black offers to go into a rook ending, but White declines and continues breaking up the opponent's position on the K-side.

9 h4!	Ne7
10 Be4	Nd5
11 Rb3	Kd6

After a move by his rook Black would have had to reckon with the exchange of minor pieces and the advance of White's passed pawn.

12 g5!

Alekhine consistently carries out his plan.

12 . . .	hxg5
13 hxg5	

The preparatory work is complete. The black pawns at e5 and g7 are separated and weak.

13 . . .	Ke6
14 Bd3	Kd6
15 Ra3	Nc7
16 Ra7!	Rb8

16 . . . Nxb5 17 Rxg7 would not have left Black any chance of saving the game.

17 Ke4	g6

18 Kf5 was threatened.

18 Ra3!	Rb6
19 Bc4	Rb8

71

ES–F

19 ... Kc5 is well met by either 20 Ra7 or 20 Be2, and the knight cannot take on b5 due to Ra5.

20 Rd3+	Kc5
21 Rd7!	

The outcome of the game is decided.

21 ...	Ne8
22 Bf7	Nd6+
23 Kxe5	Rb6
24 e4	Nxb5

Black has succeeded in eliminating White's passed pawn on the Q-side, but on the K-side White has become total master of the position.

25 Rd5+	Kb4
26 Rd8	Na7
27 Rd6	Nc6+
28 Kf6	Kc5
29 Rd5+	Kb4
30 e5!	Kc4
31 Rd1+	Kc5
32 Rc1+	Kd4
33 e6	Ke3
34 Bxg6	Nd4
35 Bf7	Ne2
36 Re1	Kf2
37 Rxe2+	Resigns.

Kovalyev—Azos

Tashkent, 1978

(See next diagram)

White has an extra passed pawn at h4 — Black's first weakness. White's plan is to give Black a weakness on the Q-side (provoke ... c5 or ... d5), and then use the passed h-pawn to divert Black's forces, giving it up when necessary to be able to attack Black's weakened Q-side.

1 Ke3+	Kg4

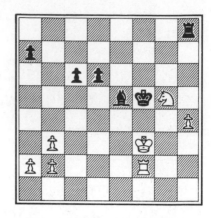

2 Rg2+!	Kf5

Equally cheerless for Black is 2 ... Kxh4 3 Nf3+! Kh3 (*3 ... Kh5 4 Rg5+ Kh6 5 Nxe5*) 4 Rg6 Re8 (or *4 ... Bg3 5 Ng5+ and 6 Ne4*) 5 Nxe5 Rxe5+ 6 Kd3 Rd5+ 7 Kc2, when the rook ending is easily won for White, since the black king is cut off, e.g. 7 ... Kh4 8 a4 Kh5 9 Rg7 a5 10 Rg2 c5 11 Rd2 Rxd2+ 12 Kxd2 c4 (otherwise *b2—b4*) 13 Ke3 Kg6 14 Kd4, and wins.

3 Nf3	Bf4+

On 3 ... Bf6 White has the unpleasant 4 Rd2 Re8+ 5 Kf2, with numerous threats.

4 Kd3	c5

The first part of White's plan is complete: Black's Q-side has been weakened.

5 Kc4	Ke4
6 Ng5+	Kf5

6 ... Ke3 can be met by 7 Rg4 Re8 8 Kd5 Re5+ 9 Kxd6 Rxg5 10 Rxf4.

7 Kd5	

The h-pawn can now be given up: the invasion of the white king is decisive.

7 ...	Rxh4
8 Nf7	Rh5
9 Nxd6+	Bxd6
10 Kxd6	

The outcome is decided, although in the rook ending White has to overcome certain technical difficulties.

10 ...	Ke4
11 Rg7	a6
12 Rc7	Rh2
13 Rb7	c4
14 Kc5	Kd3
15 a4	Rh5+
16 Kb6	Rh6+
17 Ka7	a5

18 a5 and 19 Rb6 was threatened.

18 Rb6	Rh8
19 Ka6	Ra8+
20 Kb5	Ra7
21 Rb8!	

Within a few moves **Black resigned**.

Alekhine—Euwe

London, 1922

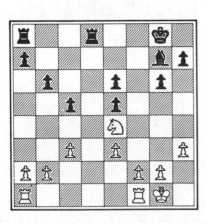

White has the advantage. The difference in strength between the white knight and the black bishop is obvious. But to realize his advantage he must:

(a) fix Black's K-side pawns, since otherwise the bishop may escape from its 'prison'; (b) wrest the d-file from the opponent (in doing so he must weigh up whether or not the minor piece ending is won or whether a pair of rooks must be retained); (c) give Black a second weakness on the Q-side, since he already has one, and a very serious one at that — the bishop at g7; (d) if possible, invade the opponent's position with decisive effect.

1 Rfd1

White begins the battle for the d-file, exploiting the fact that 1 ... c4 loses a pawn to 2 Nd6.

1 ...	Kf8
2 Kf1	

The two players centralize their kings. White is not tempted into winning a pawn by 2 Ng5 Ke7 3 Nxh7 Bh6 4 h4, after which his knight is exchanged.

2 ...	Ke7
3 c4!	

3 ... c4 was now threatened.

3 ...	h6
4 Ke2	Rxd1
5 Rxd1	Rb8

We give here Alekhine's commentary on this position: "Black cannot exchange rooks, since after 5 ... Rd8 6 Rxd8 Kxd8 White wins as follows:

1st phase: 7 h4 followed by g2—g4 and g4—g5, against which Black has nothing better than ... h5, since the exchange of pawns will give the white knight the square h4.

2nd phase: b2—b3 followed by Kd3, Nc3 and Ke4.

3rd phase: the transfer of the knight to d3, which ties the black king to d6, in order to hold the twice-attacked e5 pawn.

4th phase: finally f2—f4, forcing the win of the g- or e-pawn, after which White wins easily.

By avoiding the exchange of rooks Black makes his opponent's task more difficult".

| 6 | Rd3 | Bh8 |
| 7 | a4! | |

White sets about creating weaknesses on the Q-side. Since 7 . . . a5 is not possible due to the loss of a pawn after 8 Rb3, the opening of the a-file is inevitable. This file will be occupied by the white rook, and this will become Black's second weakness.

7	. . .	Rc8
8	Rb3	Kd7
9	a5!	Kc6
10	axb6	axb6
11	Ra3	Bg7
12	Ra7	Rc7

Now after the exchange of rooks White could carry out his winning plan, but for this there is no necessity. At the moment his rook occupies an ideal position, and he has a quicker way to win.

13	Ra8!	Re7
14	Rc8+	Kd7
15	Rg8!	Kc6
16	h4	

Do not hurry! Black is deprived of the slightest counter-play, and so before the decisive offensive White 'packs in' the bishop at g7 by h2—h4 and g2—g4—g5.

16	. . .	Kc7
17	g4	Kc6
18	Kd3	Rd7+
19	Kc3	Rf7
20	b3	Kc7
21	Kd3	Rd7+

| 22 | Ke2 | Rf7 |
| 23 | Nc3! | |

The start of the concluding attack.

23	. . .	Re7
24	g5	hxg5
25	hxg5	Kc6
26	Kd3	Rd7+
27	Ke4	Rc7
28	Nb5	Re7
29	f3!	Kd7

29 . . . Kb7 loses to 30 Nd6+ and 31 Ne8, while if 29 . . . Rf7 30 Rc8+.

30	Rb8	Kc6
31	Rc8+	Kd7
32	Rc7+	Kd8
33	Rc6	Rb7
34	Rxe6	Resigns.

Karpov—Parma

Caracas, 1970

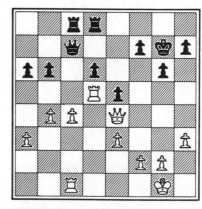

Black has a weak d-pawn, which can be finally nailed down by 1 Qd3 followed by e3—e4. This is probably what the majority of players would have done. But how then can Black be given a second weakness? After making a deep assessment of the position, Karpov takes what is at first sight a quite paradoxical decision: he relieves Black of his weakness at d6.

1 f4	Re8
2 fxe5!	

"2 f5 was also possible, but with the opponent having only one weakness (the pawn at d6) the win would have been more than difficult. But now, in addition to the weak e5 pawn, there are other advantages in my position, as for example control of the open file by the rooks and the possibility of combined play" (Karpov).

2 ...	dxe5
3 c5	Re6
4 Qd3	bxc5
5 bxc5	Qc6
6 Rb1	Qc7
7 Rf1	Rf8
8 Kh1	Qc6
9 Rb1	

"White does not have, and there cannot be, any clear-cut plan for realizing his spatial advantage, since his specific goals vary depending on the opponent's replies. The ideal for White would be to force the advance . . . f6, when, with the seventh rank weakened, he would gain the opportunity of establishing a rook at b6 and beginning a combined heavy-piece attack along the open files. However, Black's position is most probably still defensible, although his task is not an easy one" (Karpov).

9 ...	Qc7
10 e4	Rb8
11 Rf1	Rb7
12 Qc3	Rb5
13 a4	Rb8
14 Rc1	Rc8
15 Rb1	Kg8
16 Rbd1	Qe7
17 Rf1	Rc7
18 a5	Rec6

19 Rc1	f6

Parma succumbs to the opponent's positional pressure and weakens the seventh rank. Karpov skilfully exploits this error.

20 Qd2	Kf7
21 Kh2	Ke8
22 Rd6	Rd7
23 Rd1	Rcxd6
24 cxd6	Qe6
25 Qd3	Qa2
26 Qxa6	

White has won a pawn. The game is decided.

26 ...	Qc2
27 Qa8+	Kf7
28 Qd5+	Kg7
29 Rd2	Qc3
30 Ra2?!	h5!
31 Rd2!	

"There was the threat of a perpetual check after . . . h4. Yes, for many players 'taking a move back' is the most difficult thing of all. Now the rest is easier" (Karpov).

31 ...	h4
32 Rd1	Qc2
33 a6	Qa4
34 Qd3	g5
35 Rb1	f5
36 Rb7	g4
37 hxg4	fxg4
38 Qe2	Resigns.

Benko—Parma

Belgrade, 1964

(See next diagram)

White's bishop is much stronger than the enemy knight, which does not have

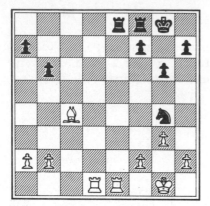

any strong points. Also actively placed are the white rooks, whereas the black rooks are merely carrying out defensive functions.

1 Bb3

Threatening to exchange on e8 followed by Rd7, which did not work immediately due to ... Ne5.

| 1 ... | Nf6 |
| 2 Kg2! | |

White begins the centralization of his king, not fearing the exchange of rooks on the e-file.

| 2 ... | Rxe1 |

Black could hardly have avoided this exchange for long.

| 3 Rxe1 | Re8 |
| 4 Rxe8+! | |

White has accurately worked out his possibilities in the ensuing minor piece ending. Contrary to the generally-accepted rule that a rook and bishop are stronger than a rook and knight, White exchanges rooks so as to centralize his king as quickly as possible. After 4 Rc1?! Re7! Black would have not allowed the white king into the centre, and would have had every chance of a

draw.

4 ...	Nxe8
5 Kf3	Kf8
6 Ke4	Nc7

Black has managed to check the opponent's first onslaught. The white king cannot break through on the Q-side. Now White's task is to create weaknesses in Black's K-side.

| 7 h4 | Ke7 |
| 8 f4 | h6 |

After 8 ... h5 White has the highly unpleasant 9 Ke5 followed by f4–f5.

9 Bc4!

A typical manoeuvre, which is repeatedly encountered in this ending. The black knight comes under the domination of the white bishop.

9 ...	Ne6
10 g4	Nc7
11 Ke5	

Black is in *zugzwang*. Further positional concessions are inevitable.

11 ...	f6+
12 Ke4	Kf8
13 h5!	

Capablanca's advice on the placing of pawns in endings with bishops (cf.p.110) is in the majority of cases correct, but it pays not to be dogmatic. In the given position it is more important to gain control of the key e5 square for the king — the 'manoeuvring pivot' for an attack both on Black's Q-side, and his K-side. It should be noted that the routine 13 g5 would have allowed 13 ... hxg5 14 hxg5 Ke7 with the threat of 15 ... fxg5 and 16 ... Ne6, when Black has excellent chances of a successful defence.

| 13 ... | g5 |

No better is 13 ... gxh5 14 gxh5 followed by 15 Kf5, when Black is in *zugzwang*.

14	fxg5	fxg5
15	Kf5	Kg7
16	Ke5	

The break-through of the white king to the Q-side is now inevitable.

16	...	Ne8
17	Be6	Nf6
18	b4!	

Do not hurry! Before the decisive invasion of the king it is useful to advance the Q-side pawns as far as possible.

| 18 | ... | Ne8 |
| 19 | b5! | |

Taking a concrete approach to the position, White places all his pawns on squares of the colour of his bishop.

19	...	Nf6
20	a4	Ne8
21	Bf5	Nf6
22	Ke6	Ne8
23	Be4!	

The black knight again comes under the domination of the bishop.

23	...	Nf6
24	Bf3	Ng8
25	Kd6	

Now to the Q-side!

25	...	Kf6
26	Kc6	Ke7
27	Kb7	Kd6
28	Kxa7	Kc5

29	Ka6	Nf6
30	Bc6!	Nxg4
31	a5	bxa5
32	b6	Ne5
33	Be8	Resigns.

Faibisovich—Westerinen

Vilnius, 1969

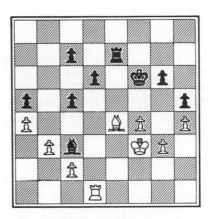

At first sight Black's pawn weaknesses — g6 and a5 — seem easily defended. But they can be subjected in turn to a combined attack, because it is easier for White to transfer his pieces, especially from wing to wing.

1 Rd5!

The white rook occupies the staging post from where it heads for g5, to tie down the opponent's forces to the defence of the weak g-pawn.

1	...	Rg7
2	Rg5	Bd2
3	Ke2	

The king makes for Black's second weakness — his a5 pawn.

3	...	Bc3
4	Kd3	Be1
5	Kc4	Kf7
6	Kb5	Bc3

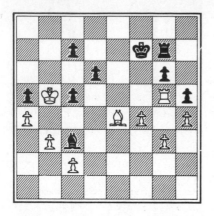

7 Rd5!

The white rook again occupies d5. White now threatens Rd3 and c2—c3, a plan which Black is powerless to oppose.

7 ...	Be1
8 Rd3	Kf6
9 c3	Re7
10 Bb7	Re2
11 Kxa5	Rc2
12 Kb5	Bxc3
13 a5	

Black has won back his pawn, but now White's passed pawn advances irresistibly. The game is decided.

13 ...	Be1
14 a6	c4

The best practical chance.

15 bxc4	Bf2
16 Ra3	c6+

If 16 ... Ba7, then 17 Bd5 followed by Kc6.

17 Kxc6	Rxc4+
18 Kxd6	Ba7
19 Bc6	Rb4
20 Kd7	Rb1
21 Ra5	Rb3
22 Rg5	

Again reminding Black of the weakness of his g6 pawn.

22 ...	Re3
23 Kc7	Re7+
24 Bd7	Bf2?
25 f5!	

The finish was:

25 ...	Re3
26 Rxg6+	Kf7
27 Be6+	Ke7
28 Rg7+	Kf6
29 Rf7+	Ke5
30 a7	Resigns.

This ending is a classic example of manoeuvring when there is an attack on two weaknesses.

Holzhausen—Nimzowitsch

Hannover, 1926

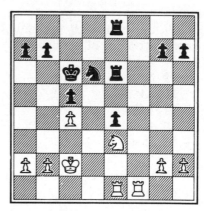

Even before Nimzowitsch many masters understood the principle of two weaknesses and were guided by it. But for a clear-cut and easily understood explanation of this principle we are undoubtedly indebted to Nimzowitsch.

1 ...	Rh6

"A move which arises from an exact

knowledge of the laws of alternation. The point is that sooner or later Black will have to resort to . . . a6 followed by . . . b5, which, with the white pieces fully committed to watching the e-pawn, will give Black chances of invading (by opening the a- or b-file). This would create the pivot necessary for the success of the alternating operation; what would be lacking, however, would be the essential 'two weaknesses', since the necessity for White to 'watch' the e4 pawn constitutes, of course, only one weakness. The manoeuvres in the game (1 . . . Rb6 etc.) have the aim of creating a 'second weakness', the presence of which will acquire decisive significance in the rook ending which later ensues" (Nimzowitsch).

2	h3	Rg6
3	Re2	a6
4	Rf4	b5
5	h3	Rg5
6	g4	Rge5
7	Kc3	a5
8	Ref2	a4
9	bxa4	bxc4
10	Rf8	R5e7
11	Rxe8	Rxe8
12	Nxc4	Nxc4
13	Kxc4	Ra8
14	Rf7	

If 14 Kb3, then 14 . . . Kd5.

14	. . .	Rxa4+
15	Kb3	Rb4+
16	Kc3	Rb7

"In this ending, as soon becomes clear, the K-side (the h3 and g4 pawns) is the decisive weakness" (Nimzowitsch).

17	Rf5	Ra7
18	Kc4	Ra4+
19	Kb3	Rd4
20	Re5	Kd6
21	Re8	Rd3+
22	Kc4	Rxh3
23	Rxe4	Ra3
24	Re2	Ra4+
25	Kb5	Rxg4
26	a4	Rb4+
27	Ka5	h5
28	Rh2	Kc6
29	Re2	Rg4
30	Re6+	Kd5
31	Re8	h4
32	Rd8+	Kc4
33	Kb6	h3
34	Rd1	Kb4
35	Rb1+	Kxa4
36	Kxc5	g5
37	Rh1	Rg3
38	Kd4	g4
39	Ke4	Rg2
40	Kf4	h2

White resigns.

CHAPTER 8

THE STRUGGLE FOR THE INITIATIVE

Every chess player knows how important it is to seize the initiative during a game. Nowadays one cannot hope for success without being prepared to battle for the initiative in a roughly equal position. It is no accident that World Champion Anatoly Karpov and his predecessor Bobby Fischer have demonstrated in many games their readiness at any moment to seize the initiative, not being afraid to take risks. For the sake of the initiative one sometimes has to disregard a possible deterioration in one's position. Courage, strength of will and judicious audacity are needed for a player to decide on a step which is frequently into the unknown. Just how difficult and dangerous this can be, especially in the endgame, will be shown by the following examples.

Schlechter—Lasker

Vienna, 1910

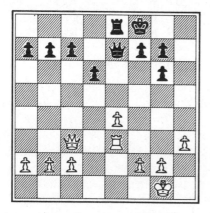

The position is level. The only active plan which might be suggested for White would be to try and exploit his pawn majority on the K-side. To do this he would have to remove the black pawn from the d-file, i.e. advance his Q-side pawns. But it is completely unclear which would be the more important: the advantages White would gain by advancing his pawns, or the dangers and weaknesses which would arise as a result of this.

1 Qb4

Schlechter does not wish to take the initiative.

1 ...   c6

Of course, not 1 ... b6 2 Qa4 a5, when Black's Q-dide pawns are markedly weakened and lose their flexibility.

2 Qa3	a6
3 Qb3	Rd8
4 c4	

So as not to allow ... d5. But the pawn at d6 is by no means a weakness.

4 ...	Rd7
5 Qd1	Qe5
6 Qg4	Ke8!
7 Qe2	Kd8

"Lasker gradually assumes the initiative and by extremely subtle play tries to gain minute advantages. First the king frees the rook from the defence of the Q-side pawns" (Tarrasch in his *Die Moderne Schachpartie*).

8 Qd2   Kc7

White has a pawn majority on the K-side, while Black has an extra pawn on the Q-side. The first signs of activity on Black's part have appeared. His king has transferred to the part of the board where he has every right to develop the initiative. But the simple advance of Black's pawns will merely lead to their exchange. It is necessary that White should weaken his position on the Q-side. It is this aim that is pursued by the appearance there of the black king. The king acts as a provocator, inducing White to throw his pawns forward. But to seize the initiative in a level position, without sacrificing anything in return, is impossible. The slightest attempt to play actively is often fraught with great danger.

| 9 a3 | Re7 |
| 10 b4 | |

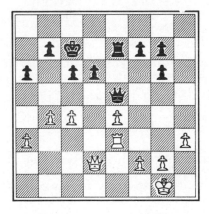

| 10 ... | b5!? |

"Very bold and energetic play, as one might expect from the great master. Although this move exposes the black king, at the same time the white a-pawn is made backward. Black thus hopes to create a passed pawn on the c-file" (Tarrasch).

| 11 cxb5 | axb5 |
| 12 g3 | g5 |

Lasker prevents f2—f4, and thus assures his queen of an excellent post in the centre. At the same time, however, the h5 square is exposed.

| 13 Kg2 | Re8 |

| 14 Qd1!? | |

Preparing a3—a4 or Qh5.

| 14 ... | f6 |

On 14 . . . Ra8 White has the unpleasant 15 Qh5.

| 15 Qb3?! | |

Schlechter is confused. He wants to play actively, but does not wish to weaken his position. 15 Qh5 would not have achieved anything due to 15 . . . Qe6, but he should have played 15 a4!? After missing this opportunity White has to switch to passive defence.

| 15 ... | Qe6 |
| 16 Qd1 | |

With exact play White should perhaps not lose the rook ending, but Black has an undisputed advantage.

| 16 ... | Rh8! |

Before attacking on the Q-side, Lasker reduces the value of White's extra pawn on the K-side.

| 17 g4 | Qc4 |
| 18 a4?! | |

Inconsistent. White has opted for passive defence, which is of course undesirable, but in principle is possible. Since earlier he avoided playing a3—a4 in a much more favourable situation, he should certainly not have done it now. Passive defence can be successful if the opponent's advantage is only very slight. In such play one must retain complete composure and ensure that the advantage does not grow to considerable proportions. To be considered was 18 Qf3 with the threat of 19 Rc3 and e4—e5. Here is Tarrasch's comment on this move:

"The opponent's steady strengthening of his position begins to frighten White, and he stakes everything on this move, sacrificing a pawn for an attack. But in fact, because of this advance he should have lost the game, even if it did give him certain chances. There was as yet no cause for desperation: all his weaknesses (a3, e4 and h3) were sufficiently defended by his rook, and if he had avoided the exchange of queens, he could have readily continued play."

18 . . .	Qxb4
19 axb5	Qxb5
20 Rb3	Qa6
21 Qd4	

Black is a pawn up with a sound position.

| 21 . . . | Re8 |
| 22 Rb1 | Re5! |

Defending against 23 Ra1.

23 Qb4	Qb5
24 Qe1	Qd3
25 Rb4	

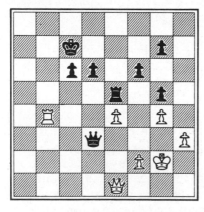

25 . . .   c5?

Fatigued by the hard struggle, Lasker plays carelessly and throws away the win. Black wins a pawn, but exposes his king too much. As shown by Tarrasch,

after 25 . . . Ra5! with the threat of 26 . . . Ra3 White would have been forced into a queen ending: 26 Rb3 Qxb3 27 Qxa5+ Kb7. Black would have had every chance of winning.

26 Ra4	c4
27 Qa1	Qxe4+
28 Kh2	Rb5

With the threat of 29 . . . Qe5+. Despite his two extra pawns, Black can hardly have any serious hopes of winning the game. The position of his king is too dangerous.

29 Qa2!	Qe5+
30 Kg1	Qe1+
31 Kh2	d5

By the queen checks Black has taken control of a5, and is now ready to meet 32 Ra7+ with 32 . . . Rb7

32 Ra8!

Threatening 33 Qa7+ and 34 Qc5+.

32 . . .   Qb4

So as to answer 33 Qa6 with a queen check at d6.

33 Kg2!

This cool king move renews White's threat.

33 . . .   Qc5

Black should have reconciled himself to the fact that after 33 . . . Rb8 34 Ra7+ Rb7 35 Ra8 the game could not be won.

34 Qa6!

White's attack is now irresistible. On 34 . . . Rb7 there follows 35 Qe6.

34 ...	Rb8
35 Ra7+	Kd8
36 Rxg7	Qb6
37 Qa3	Kc8

and, without waiting for the obvious 38 Qf8+, **Black resigned**. The game shows just how risky the struggle for the initiative can be in a level position.

By his uncompromising play Lasker almost won, but he lacked the strength to take the game to its logical conclusion.

Suetin—Bronstein

Moscow, 1968

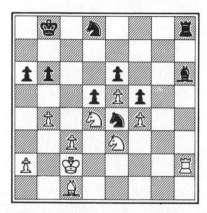

White has a spatial advantage, and a powerful knight at d4, attacking the weak e6 pawn. He has possibilities of active play involving c3—c4 or the sacrifice of a knight at f5. Black is required to defend accurately.

1 ...	b5!

Preventing c3—c4. Black could have approached the d5 pawn with his king by 1 . . . Kc7, after which the knight sacrifice at f5 would have promised White little, but then White could have fixed the b6 pawn by 2 a4 and followed up with c3—c4. For example: 1 . . . Kc7 2 a4! Bg7 3 Rxh8 Bxh8 4 c4 dxc4 5 Nxc4 Bg7 6 Be3, with

strong pressure. By the move in the game Bronstein sets his opponent a difficult problem: whether to allow the advance of the black king to the centre when a draw will be the most likely outcome, or whether to continue the struggle for the initiative by sacrificing a knight at f5.

2 Nexf5!?	

Suetin accepts the challenge.

2 ...	exf5
3 Nxf5	Bg7
4 Rg2!?	

4 Rxh8 Bxh8 5 Ne7 would have won White a third pawn, but hardly the game.

4 ...	Bf8
5 Ne3	

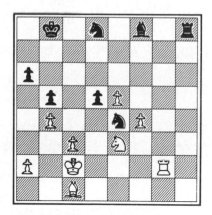

A crucial position. White is threatening to capture on d5, obtaining three pawns for his sacrificed piece. The pair of connected passed pawns at f4 and e5 are ready to sweep away everything in their path. In this difficult situation Bronstein finds a brilliant defensive plan, one of the chief links in which is the centralization of his king.

5 ...	Kb7!
6 Nxd5	Kc6
7 Ne3	Ne6!

Following his king, Black's entire army has thrown itself into the battle with the opponent's main forces. Now White achieves nothing by 8 f5 Nf4 9 Rg4 Rh2+.

8 Nd1!

Suetin continues to battle for the initiative. The white knight vacates the diagonal for the bishop, while defending the c-pawn.

8 ... Rh3!

Black consistently activates his forces.

9 Rg6

9 f5 can be met by 9 ...Ng7 10 Ne3 Ng3, blockading the passed pawns.

9 ...	Rh6
10 Rg8	Bg7!

Cutting off White's rook from his remaining pieces.

11 f5	Rh2+

Only now is Black's plan revealed. After 12 Kb1 Rh8 13 Rxh8 Bxh8 14 fxe6 Bxe5 his king eliminates the white e-pawn, and the game ends in a draw. Suetin chooses a different way, which meets with energetic resistance by Bronstein.

12 Kd3	N4c5+!

Obviously White had not expected this move.

13 bxc5	Nxc5+
14 Ke3	Bh6+
15 Kf3	Bxc1
16 Nf2!	

Suetin prevents the further central-

ization of the black king: 16 ... Kd5? 17 Rd8+, and 17 ... Kxe5 fails to 18 Ng4+.

16 ...	Rh4
17 e6?	

In his eagerness to win, White over-reaches himself. He should have forced a draw by 17 Rc8+ Kd5 18 Rd8+ Kxe5 19 Ng4+ Kxf5 20 Rd5+. Now the black king approaches the enemy passed pawns.

17 ...	Rf4+
18 Kg3	Kd6
19 Rf8	Be3
20 Ng4	

20 Nh3 or 20 Nd3 is very strongly met by 20 ... Rc4.

20 ...	Ne4+
21 Kh3	Rf3+
22 Kh4	Bg5+
23 Kh5	Rh3+
24 Kg6	Rh4!

White loses his knight, and his king, which has gone to the aid of his passed pawns, comes under a mating attack by the concerted action of the black pieces.

25 Nf2	Rh6+
26 Kg7	Nxf2
27 Ra8	Ng4
28 Rxa6+	Ke5
29 Rb6	Bf6+
30 Kf7	Kxf5
31 Rxb5+	Ne5+

White resigns.

He can defend against the mate only by giving up his rook.

Bronstein was awarded the prize for 'The most interesting ending'. Also commendable is Suetin's persistent striving for victory, right to the end.

Suetin—Gufeld

Tbilisi, 1969

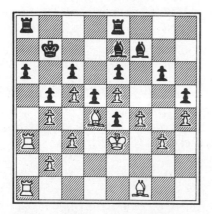

Not one pawn has yet been exchanged. White holds the initiative and a spatial advantage. He has the possibility of a pawn break both on the K-side (*g3—g4* after appropriate preparation), and on the Q-side (*b2—b3* and *c3—c4*). But Suetin immediately begins play on the Q-side.

1 c4!?

Unexpected and very interesting. White sets his opponent a difficult exchanging problem: he can capture on c4 with the b-pawn or d-pawn, or else not at all. Gufeld does not find the best reply.

1 ...   Bf8

1 ... bxc4 would have failed to 2 b3!, but better, as shown by Suetin in *Shakhmaty v SSSR* 1970 No. 4, was 1 ... dxc4!, when it is extremely difficult to pierce Black's position. Therefore the correct plan for White would have been 1 b3 followed by c3—c4, advantageously maintaining the tension on the Q-side. Of course, in a practical game it is often difficult to find the correct solution, especially in time trouble.

2 cxb5!?

Highly original and bold! White exploits a tactical possibility and carries out a combination, the consequences of which were not easy to assess. Of course, he could have played 2 b3 and then prepared g3—g4, when it is difficult to say how real his chances would have been. By the move in the game White risks losing his advantage, but he sharply complicates the play and sets his opponent difficult problems.

2 ...   axb5

2 ... cxb5 loses to 3 Bxb5! axb5 4 c6+.

3 Bxb5	Rxa3
4 Rxa3	cxb5
5 c6+	Kxc6
6 Ra6+	Kb7
7 Ra7+	Kc6
8 Rxf7	

The position has changed sharply, but the initiative is still with White. Here the game was adjourned, and Black sealed the strongest move.

8 ...   Bxb4!

Not 8 ... Ra8? 9 Rf6 Kd7 10 Bc5!, with an obvious advantage.

9 Rf6	Kd7
10 Rxg6	Rc8!

Forcing White to exchange rooks, since he cannot permit the counter-attack with 11 ... Rc2.

11 Rg7+	Ke8
12 Rg8+	Kd7
13 Rg7+	Ke8
14 Rg8+	Kd7

It is dangerous for Black to defend

against the checks by retreating his bishop, and anyway he has no reason to: he is perfectly happy with a draw.

15 Rxc8	Kxc8

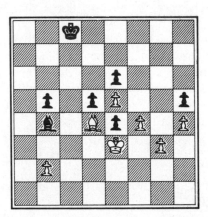

The position has greatly simplified, and one gains the impression that Black has achieved his desired draw. But even here Suetin finds a way to pour fuel on the fire.

16 g4!!

This move demanded exact calculation.

16 ...	hxg4
17 Kf2	Bd2
18 Kg3	e3?!

White's persistent attempts to extract a win bear fruit, as Black chooses a tempting but incorrect move. After 18 ... Kd7 19 Kxg4 Ke7 20 h5 Kf7 the game would have ended in a draw. The subsequent play is forced.

19 h5	e2
20 Bf2	e1=Q
21 Bxe1	Bxe1+
22 Kxg4	Bb4
23 h6	Bf8
24 h7	Bg7
25 Kg5!	d4!

25 ... Kd7 loses to 26 Kg6 Bh8 27 Kf7 followed by 28 f5.

26 Kg6	Bh8
27 f5	d3
28 fxe6	d2
29 e7	d1=Q
30 e8=Q+	Qd8

"Bad is 30 ... Kc7 31 Qxh8 Qg4+ 32 Kf6! Qh4+ 33 Kf7! Qh5+ 34 Kf8, when the white king escapes from perpetual check" (Suetin).

31 Qc6+	Kb8

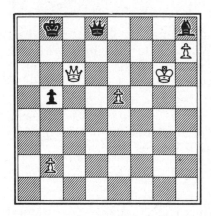

What amazing changes occur in this game! Who would have thought that a tedious blocked position with rooks and bishops would have led to something like this? Earlier White had merely an initiative, which for a long time he skilfully maintained, whereas now he has an obvious advantage, and the only question is how to realize it. It is well known that in the endgame the value of pawns increases. White now has two pawns for the bishop, and he can capture a third, Black's last, with check. But the essence of the position is that, with the disappearance of the b5 pawn the scope of Black's queen is widened, and his chances of perpetual check are increased. This means that White must play as if it were a pure queen ending, where the outcome is decided by king manoeuvres, and enemy pawns often serve as a screen against checks.

32 Kf7!

"After 32 Qxb5+ Ka8 33 b4 Qd2! Black's queen breaks out into the open, which gives him a draw" (Suetin).

32 ...   Ka7

33 Qd6+ was threatened.

33 Qd6!

"Again the only way. After 33 Qc5+ Kb7! 34 Qxb5+ Ka7 the black queen gives perpetual check" (Suetin). The variation can be continued with 35 Qc5+ Kb7 36 Qd6 Qg5, when Black has everything in order.

33 ...	**Qc8**
34 e6	**Qc2!**

Not 34 ... Qc4 35 b3!

35 e7!	**Qxh7+**
36 Ke8	**Bxb2**

Black has managed to eliminate two of the enemy pawns, but with the remaining pawn at e7 he is unable to cope.

37 Kd8	**Qh4!**
38 Kc8	**Qe4!**

Gufeld defends resourcefully. Now 39 Qd7+ Ka6 40 e8=Q allows Black perpetual check by 40 ... Qa8+ 41 Kc7 Qa7+ 42 Kd6 Qd4+.

39 Qc5+	**Ka6**
40 Qd6+	**Ka7**

40 ... Ka5 is stronger.

41 Kd8	**Qh4**

The position has been repeated. But Suetin nevertheless finds a manoeuvre which wins. The position of the queen must be improved, and then the king sent into the attack.

42 Qd7+	**Kb6**
43 Qe6+	**Kb7**
44 Qd5+	**Kb6**
45 Kd7!	**Qh7**
46 Qe6+	**Ka7**
47 Kc8!	**Qc2+**
48 Kd8!	**Kb7**
49 Qd7+	

Of course, not 49 e8=Q?? Qc7 mate.

49 ...	**Kb6**
50 Qd6+!	**Kb7**
51 e8=Q	

The hour of the white e-pawn has finally arrived.

51 ...	**Bf6+**

With a last trap: 52 Qxf6?? Qc7 mate.

52 Kd7	**Qh7+**
53 Ke6	**Qe4+**
54 Kf7	**Resigns.**

Suetin was awarded a special prize for the best endgame of the tournament.

Marshall—Lasker

New York, 1907

(See next diagram)

In his book *Chess Fundamentals* Capablanca comments as follows on this position:

"In this position it is Black's move. To a beginner the position may look like a draw, but the advanced player will realise immediately that there are great

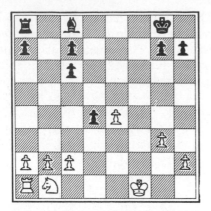

possibilities for Black to win, not only because he has the initiative, but because of White's undeveloped Q-side and the fact that a bishop in such a position is better than a knight. It will take some time for White to bring his rook and knight into the fray, and Black can utilise it to obtain an advantage. There are two courses open to him. The most evident, and the one that most players would take, is to advance the pawn to c5 and c4 immediately in conjunction with the bishop check at a6 and any other move that might be necessary with the black rook. The other, more subtle, course was taken by Black."

Capablanca goes on to explain that with his rook Black must all the time force White to defend something, when the activity of the white rook and knight is restricted, whereas the black rook and bishop retain complete freedom of action.

| 1 ... | Rb8 |
| 2 b3 | Rb5! |

Along the fifth rank the black rook can attack White's pawns both on the Q-side, and on the K-side.

| 3 c4 | |

On 3 Nd2 Black has the unpleasant 3 ... Rc5.

| 3 ... | Rh5 |
| 4 Kg1 | c5 |

Black's advantage assumes real proportions. The d-pawn has become a formidable force, the scope of the bishop has expanded, and the white knight is restricted by its own pawns.

| 5 Nd2 | Kf7 |
| 6 Rf1+? | |

Possibly the decisive mistake. At this point, in developing his initiative, Black was forced to allow his opponent a respite. Lasker would of course have been happy to play 5 ... Rh6, had he not been left with his king cut off after 6 Rf1. Marshall should have exploited the situation to create immediate counter-play. 6 a3! was correct. Now on 6 ... a5 White plays 7 Rb1 followed by b3—b4. In reply to 6 a3 Black can try to transfer his king to the centre by 6 ... Ke6, e.g. 7 b4 Ke5 8 bxc5 d3, or 7 Nf3 Kd6 8 b4 Bg4 with advantage to Black. But on 6 ... Ke6 quite in order is 7 Rf1!, with a stubborn battle in prospect.

| 6 ... | Ke7! |
| 7 a3 | Rh6! |

After operating very effectively along the fifth rank, the black rook switches to the sixth rank to attack White's Q-side.

| 8 h4 | |

8 b4 fails to 8 ... Ra6 9 Rf3 Bg4 10 Rb3 Bd1 11 Rb1 Bc2 12 Rc1 d3.

8 ...	Ra6
9 Ra1	Bg4!
10 Kf2	Ke6
11 a4	

11 Nf3 does not help: 11 ... Bxf3 12 Kxf3 Ke5 followed by ... Rf6+.

11	...	Ke5
12	Kg2	Rf6

White is completely helpless.

13	Re1	d3
14	Rf1	Kd4

The finish was:

15	Rxf6	gxf6
16	Kf2	c6
17	a5	a6

Zugzwang.

18	Nf1	Kxe4
19	Ke1	Be2
20	Nd2+	Ke3
21	Nb1	f5
22	Nd2	h5
23	Nb1	Kf3
24	Nc3	Kxg3
25	Na4	f4
26	Nxc5	f3
27	Ne4+	Kf4
28	Nd6	c5
29	b4	cxb4
30	c5	b3
31	Nc4	Kg3
32	Ne3	b2

White resigns.

Chigorin—Schlechter

Monte Carlo, 1902

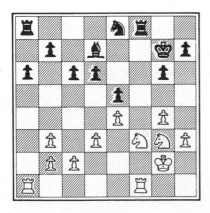

Material is level. The pawn formation is symmetric, neither side has any weaknesses, and neither player has gained a spatial advantage. It would seem that at any moment the players will begin peace negotiations. But the splendid Russian player used to agree to a draw only when all possibilities had been exhausted. Chigorin begins a persistent attempt to take the initiative.

1 d4!

To seize the initiative in a level position, without giving the opponent anything in return, is not possible. White creates in his formation an isolated e-pawn, obtaining in compensation lively piece play and an attack on the d6 pawn along the d-file.

1	...	exd4
2	Nxd4	Nc7
3	Rad1	Rxf1
4	Nxf1	Re8
5	Nf3	Rxe4

Practically forced, since 5 . . . Re6 6 Ng5 Rf6 7 e5 is obviously bad, while after 5 . . . d5 6 exd5 Nxd5 7 c4 Nb6 Black's pieces are badly placed.

6	Rxd6	Re7

As before, the position is level. But not without reason was Chigorin renowned for his ability to play with knights. The white cavalry embarks on an open attack, attempting to change the course of the battle.

7	Ne3!	c5

Vacating c6 for the bishop.

8	Ne5!	Be8
9	Nd5	Nxd5?

White's persistence bears fruit: Black

chooses the incorrect solution to an ex-changing problem. After 9 . . . Rxe5! 10 Nxc7 Bc6+ 11 Kf2 Kf7 (not *12 Nxa6 Ke7*) 12 Na8 Ke7 13 Rd1 a roughly level position is again reached.

10 Rxd5

White has a spatial advantage.

10 . . .   Kf6?!

It would have been preferable to go into the rook ending by 10 . . . b6 and 11 . . . Bf7, although even then White would have retained some advantage thanks to the activity of his rook and the weakness of Black's Q-side pawns.

11 g5+!	Ke6
12 c4	

Not 12 Rxc5? b6.

12 . . .	b6
13 Kf3	a5

Schlechter tries to activate his bishop by advancing this pawn to a4. It would have been better to transfer it to the long diagonal by . . . Bd7—c8—b7.

14 Kf4   a4

14 . . . Bd7 no longer works, since the pawn ending is lost for Black.

15 Rd8!

A brilliant refutation of the oppo-nent's plan. Against the threat of Rb8, winning material, Black has no satis-factory defence.

15 . . .	axb3
16 Rb8	Kd6
17 Rxb6+	Kc7
18 Rxb3	Bc6
19 Ra3!	

White must aim to exchange rooks, since the exchange of minor pieces is un-favourable for him.

19 . . .	Bb7
20 Ra5!	Kd6
21 Rb5!	

In three moves the white rook has switched from b3 to b5, and Black's position has immediately become hope-less.

21 . . .	Bg2
22 Rb6+	Kc7
23 Rf6!	

The final finesse. 23 . . . Bxh3 is met by 24 Rc6+, and otherwise 24 Rf7 is decisive.

23 . . .	Bb7
24 h4	

Do not hurry!

24 . . .	Ba8
25 Rf7	Kd6
26 Rxe7	Kxe7
27 Nd3	

After the transfer of the knight to e4, the white king breaks through to the K-side via e5.

27 . . .	Kd6
28 Nf2	Bg2
29 Ne4+	Kc6
30 Ke5	

The game concluded:

30 . . .	Bf1
31 Nd2	Bd3
32 Kf6	Kd6
33 Kg7	Ke5
34 Kxh7	Kf4
35 Nb3	Resigns.

Stein—Averbakh

Riga, 1970

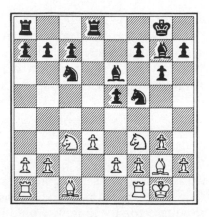

Only the queens and one pair of pawns have been exchanged, so the diagram position can hardly be called an ending. After possible exchanges the game will inevitably pass into an ending. Now much depends on who can seize the initiative. If Black had time to play . . . h6, his chances would not be worse. But it is White to move, and he rapidly builds up an initiative.

1 Ng5!	Bd7
2 Nge4!	

Threatening the unpleasant cavalry raids 3 Nd5 and 3 Nc5.

2 ...	Nfe7

Black tries to consolidate his position on the h1—a8 diagonal, but unpleasantness awaits him from another side.

3 Bg5!	

3 Nc5 would have been simply met by . . . Bc8 and then . . . b6. White's pieces attack a new weakness — at f6. It is curious that for the consolidation of his position Black is always short of one move.

3 ...	h6
4 Nf6+	Kh8

Perhaps 4 . . . Kf8 would have been preferable, bringing the king closer to the centre.

5 Nxd7	Rxd7
6 Be3	

White had another interesting possibility: 6 Bxe7!? Nxe7 (6 . . . Rxe7 7 Bxc6) 7 Bxb7 Rb8 8 Bf3 Rxb2 9 Na4 and 10 Rfc1, with a positional advantage.

6 ...	Rb8
7 Rfc1	Nd4
8 Kf1	c5
9 Rab1	b6
10 b4!	

The position gradually becomes more and more open, which of course favours' White.

10 ...	cxb4
11 Rxb4	Rc8
12 Rbb1	Rdc7
13 Bd2	Nef5
14 e3	Ne6
15 Nb5!	

Provoking a weakening of Black's Q-side.

15 ...	Rxc1+
16 Rxc1	Rxc1+
17 Bxc1	a6
18 Nc3	Nc5
19 Ke2	

The exchange of rooks has further increased White's advantage. It would appear that Black's position is already difficult to hold, and on top of everything he was in serious time trouble.

19 ...	Kg8

20	g4	Nd6
21	Bc6	Bf8
22	Nd5	f5

22 ... b5 is no better due to 23 Ba3 and 24 Nc7.

23	gxf5	gxf5
24	Nxb6	e4
25	d4	Nd3
26	Bd2	Nb5
27	Bb7	Nb4
28	a4	Nd6
29	Ba8	a5

Here **Black** overstepped the time limit. White has an easy win after 30 Bxb4 axb4 31 a5 Nb5 32 Bc6 Na7 33 Bd7.

Eingorn—Dolmatov

Tashkent, 1980

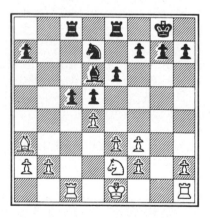

In this complex endgame Black has a slight advantage due to his superior pawn formation. 1 ... Bf8 suggests itself, but White replies 2 dxc5 Nxc5 3 Kd2, with approximate equality. Dolmatov avoids the routine bishop move, and finds a way to seize the initiative.

1 ...   e5!

Very timely and strong.

2	dxc5	Bxc5
3	Bxc5	Nxc5
4	Kd2	e4!

Only four moves have been made, and Black's advantage is clearly apparent. The ability to begin active play at the right time, using the minimum of preconditions, is an important endgame skill.

5	Nd4	Nd3
6	Rxc8	Rxc8
7	Ke2	g6!

Black makes a useful consolidating move, and at the same time opens an escape square for his king. It would have been wrong to go for the win of a pawn by 7 ... Rc1 8 Rxc1 Nxc1+ 9 Kd2 Nxa2 10 Nc6!, or 7 ... Nxb2 8 Rb1 Nd3 9 Rb7, when White has good compensation.

8	fxe4	dxe4
9	Rb1?!	

As shown by Dolmatov, White should have sought salvation in the knight ending after 9 f3!? Rc1 10 Rxc1 Nxc1+ 11 Kd2 exf3! 12 Nxf3 Nxa2 13 Ne5. In spite of being a pawn down, White has every chance of drawing, thanks to the active placing of his king and knight. But it was psychologically difficult for White to take such a decision.

9 ...	f5
10 h4?	

White loses the thread of the game and makes a second mistake. His previous move could to some extent have been justified by 10 a3 with the idea of f2—f3. But in fact White later plays f2—f4 and Kd2, when h2—h4 proves not only to be a loss of time, but also gives Black the possibility of taking his king to h5. It should be noted that 10 b4? was bad due to 10 ... Rc4, and if 11 a3 Rc3.

10 ...	Kg7
11 f4	Kh6!
12 Kd2	Kh5
13 b4	Kxh4!

A concrete approach to the position. 13 ... Rc4 was also good, answering 14 a3 with 14 ... Nxf4, but the move played is stronger.

14 Rh1+	Kg3
15 Rxh7	Nxb4
16 Rg7	

16 Rxa7 is met by 16 ... Nc6!

16 ...	Kf2
17 Rxg6	Rd8!

The point of Black's play. It transpires that White is helpless against the exchange sacrifice at d4.

18 Rh6	Rxd4+!
19 exd4	e3+
20 Kc3	Nd5+
21 Kc4	Nxf4
22 d5	e2
23 Rh1	

White loses quickly after 23 Rh2+ Ng2 24 Rh1 Ne3+ 25 Kc5 Nf1.

23 ...	e1=Q
24 Rxe1	Kxe1
25 d6	Kd2!

The most exact. Black retains control over d5.

| 26 Kd4 | |

26 d7 loses to 26 ... Ne6 27 Kd5 Nd8 28 Ke5 Kc3 29 Kxf5 Kb2 30 Ke5 Kxa2 31 Kd6 Kb3 32 Kc7 Nf7.

| 26 ... | Ne6+ |

27 Ke5	Nc5
28 Kxf5	Kc3
29 Kf6	a5
30 Ke5	a4

White resigns.

On 31 Kd5 a possible variation is 31 ... Nd7 32 Kc6 Nf6 33 Kb5 a3.

Kinderman–Speelman

Dortmund, 1981

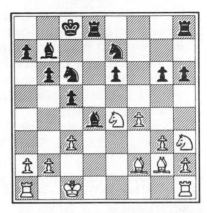

Although the queens have disappeared, the position is more of a middlegame one. It is as yet early to give it a definite assessment.

1 ...	Bxf2
2 Nhxf2	

The natural move, but a serious mistake. As shown by Speelman, annotating this game in Volume 31 of *Chess Informator*, 2 Nexf2! was correct. However paradoxical it may seem, the centralized knight should have been retreated, and the one on the edge of the board left in its place. This move nevertheless has a logical basis, since it makes it difficult for Black to develop an initiative, f4 being defended by the knight and 2 ...e5 3 Re1 leading to a very complicated game.

2 ...	e5!
3 fxe5	Nxe5

It has become clear that Black has seized the initiative. But the pawn formation is symmetric, and if White should be able to co-ordinate his forces the game will be completely level. The value of each move begins to grow immeasurably.

4 Re1	Nf5!

An excellent move. The difficulty of playing such positions is that there is an abundance of promising continuations, but normally only one of them is correct. 4 ... Rhf8 looks tempting, but, as shown by Speelman, after 5 Kc2 White succeeds in co-ordinating his forces. E.g. 5 ... Nc4 6 Rad1 Nd5 (6 ... Rxd1 7 Nxd1) 7 Rd3. After the move in the game Black meets 5 Kc2 with 5 ... Nc4!, while on 5 Bh3 he has the unpleasant 5 ... Nf3.

5 Nd6+

Probably the least evil.

5 ...	Nxd6
6 Bxb7+	Kxb7
7 Rxe5	

The position has simplified. If it were now White's move, after Kc2 a draw could be agreed. But by constant threats Speelman prevents White from making this single move separating him from equality.

7 ...	Rhf8!
8 Re2	Ne4!
9 Nd1	Rf1
10 Kc2	

White's king has come out to c2, but now his knight is pinned. How is Black to maintain his initiative? White hopes to free himself by 11 Rc1 followed by moving his knight off the back rank. In addition Black's knight is attacked.

10 ...	Nd6!
11 Rc1	Re8!

Here is the English grandmaster's solution. It becomes clear that 10 ... Nf6? 11 Rc1 Re8 would have led to equality after 12 Ne3 Rxc1+ 13 Kxc1 Ng4 14 Kd2, but now the analogous variation is not possible due to 13...Nc4.

12 Rxe8	Nxe8
13 Kd2	Rh1!

Accuracy to the end. After 13 ... Nd6?! 14 Rc2! White would have had saving chances, since 14 ... Rh1 can be met by 15 Kc1.

14 Ke2?!

White intends to continue the struggle a pawn down after 14 ... Rxh2+ 15 Nf2. The idea is correct, but incorrectly implemented. It was essential to play 14 Nf2! Rxh2 15 Ke3.

14 ...	Nd6!

Black wins a pawn in a much more

favourable situation. The outcome of the game is decided.

	15 h4	Nf5
	16 g4	

On 16 Kf3 Black wins by 16 ... Rf1+, and if 16 Kf2 h5! (Speelman).

	16 ...	Nxh4
	17 Rc2	Ng2
	18 Nf2	

18 Kf2 was better.

	18 ...	Re1+
	19 Kf3	Nh4+
	20 Kg3	g5
	21 Kh2	Kc6
	22 Nh1	Re3
	23 Rf2	Nf3+
	24 Kg2	Ne5
	25 Rf6+	Kd5
	26 Nf2	Re2

White resigns.

CHAPTER 9

SUPPRESSING THE OPPONENT'S COUNTER-PLAY

In his book *My System* Aron Nimzo-witsch put forward a new demand of positional play — the necessity for pro-phylaxis. He wrote: "We are in fact now concerned with the warding off of an evil, which has really never been under-stood as one, yet which can, and in general does, have a most disturbing effect on our game. The evil consists in this, that our pieces are out of, or in insufficient contact with their own strategically important points." In his other book *Chess Praxis* Nimzowitsch analyzes various forms of prophylaxis, and uses numerous examples to show how important it can be to make a timely move which suppresses the opponent's play.

In the endgame the contact of pieces with strategically important points has enormous importance. In this chapter we will be mainly considering the most obvious form of prophylaxis, involv-ing the suppressing of counter-play by the opponent which is directly threaten-ed, rather than in the process of genera-tion.

The demands of prophylaxis have much in common with the principle "do not hurry". Nimzowitsch expressed the idea that waiting moves are the start of any form of prophylaxis. The timely suppressing of the opponent's counter-play and the ability to employ waiting tactics are characteristic of all great masters of the endgame.

Ivkov—Hartoch

Raach, 1969

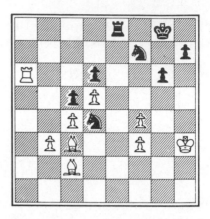

White is a pawn up and has the ad-vantage of the two bishops. But his black-squared bishop has to be exchang-ed for the knight at d4, after which Black acquires a strong passed pawn sup-ported by his rook. An interesting struggle is in prospect.

1 Bxd4	cxd4
2 b4!	

Ivkov allows the invasion of the enemy rook, since White does not achieve anything by 2 Be4 Rb8 3 Ra3.

2 ...	Re3
3 b5	Rxf3+
4 Kg4!	

A move which demanded deep calcu-lation and a precise evaluation of the position. After 4 Kg2 White would have won a piece, but Black would have been able to set up an unusual fortress. Here is a possible variation: 4 ... Rc3 5 Ba4 Rxc4 6 b6 Rb4 7 Bc6 d3 8 Kf3 Kg7 9 b7 Nd8 10 Ra4! Rb3 11 Ra8 Nxb7 12 Ra7 d2+ 13 Ke2 Kf6 14 Bxb7 Re3+! 15 Kxd2 Re7, and the advance of the h-pawn will cost

White his bishop.

| 4 ... | Rc3 |
| 5 b6 | |

With his king at g2 White would not have had this move.

5 ...	Rxc2
6 b7	Rb2
7 Ra8+	Kg7
8 b8=Q	Rxb8
9 Rxb8	Nh6+

Thus White has managed to win the exchange, but the game is not yet over. By the knight check Hartoch plans to set up an interesting fortress.

10 Kg5!!

For the Second time the Yugoslav grandmaster suppresses the opponent's counter-play by an exact king move. The natural 10 Kf3 leads to a draw: 10 ... Nf5 11 Ke4 h5 12 Rb7+ Kg8! But not 12 ... Kf6, when White plays his rook to h7, and Black is forced to 'tear' his h-pawn away from his g-pawn due to *zugzwang*.

10 ...	Nf7+
11 Kh4!	Nh6
12 Rb7+	Kf6
13 Kg3!	

Of course, not 13 Rxh7? d3!

| 13 ... | Nf5+ |

| 14 Kf3 | h5 |
| 15 Ke4 | |

Zugzwang!

15 ...	h4
16 Rh7	g5
17 fxg5+	Kxg5
18 Rf7	Ng3+
19 Kxd4	h3
20 Rf2	Kg4
21 c5	Nf5+
22 Rxf5!!	

White is on the alert. He again prevents the positional draw which was possible after 22 Ke4?! Ng3+ 23 Kd3 Nf5 24 c6 Ne7 25 c7 Kg3 26 Rf7 h2.

22 ...	Kxf5
23 c6!	h2
24 c7	H1=Q
25 c8=Q+	

Twenty-five moves ago it was impossible to foresee that the game would go virtually by force into a queen ending with White a pawn up.

25 ...	Kf4
26 Qf8+	Kg4
27 Qxd6	

White has a theoretically won ending.

27 ...	Qa1+
28 Kc5	Kf3
29 Qe6	Qa5+
30 Kc6	Qa6+
31 Kc7	Qa7+
32 Kd8	Qb8+
33 Ke7	Qc7+
34 Kf6	Kg2
35 d6	Qc3+
36 Kf7	Qf3+
37 Kg7	Qc3+
38 Kh7	Qc6
39 Qg4+	Kf1
40 Qf5+	Ke1
41 d7	Qd6
42 Qa5+	Resigns.

Timoshchenko—Makarichev

Moscow, 1979

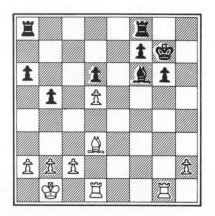

Black has the better chances in view of the weakness of the white h-pawn and the excellent strong point at e5 for the black bishop.

1 Rg4?

In *Shakhmaty v SSSR* 1979 No. 10 grandmaster Makarichev writes: "Black's plan is clear — pressure on the weak h2 pawn. Therefore White should first have played the prophylactic 1 h3! Rh8 2 Bf1, and only then Rg4 with the possibility of a2—a4. But White fails to sense the danger."

| 1 ... | Rh8 |
| 2 Rf1 | Ra7! |

Black prudently defends the seventh rank with his rook. He now threatens . . . Rxh2, which would not have worked earlier due to Rgf4.

| 3 Rf2 | Rh5! |

Black consistently engages in prophylaxis. By the threat to the d-pawn he provokes c2—c4, depriving White of counter-play with a2—a4.

| 4 c4 | bxc4 |

| 5 Bxc4 | Be5 |
| 6 Rgg2 | Rh4! |

"The last precise move. The rook occupies an ideal position and avoids the possible attack Be2" (Makarichev).

7 b3	a5
8 Bb5	Ra8
9 Kc2	Rah8
10 a3	Rh3

With the threat of 11 . . . Rc3+.

| 11 **Bd3** | Rxh2 |

11 . . . Rc8+ 12 Bc4 (*12 Kd2 Bc3+*) 12 . . . a4 would also have won.

12 b4	axb4
13 axb4	Rxg2
14 Rxg2	Rh2!

The most convincing. The bishop ending is hopeless for White.

15 Rxh2	Bxh2
16 Kb3	Kf6
17 Ka4	Ke5
18 Kb5	g5
19 Kc6	g4
20 b5	Bg1
21 Be2	

On 21 b6 there would have followed 21 . . . Bxb6 22 Kxb6 Kxd5 with an easy win.

21 ...	f5
22 Bd1	Bc5
23 Be2	Ke4
White resigns.	

Taimanov—Aronin

Moscow, 1949

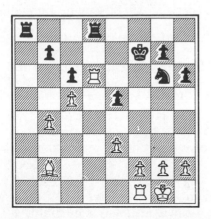

White is a pawn up, but the black rooks occupy open files, and his Q-side pawns may come under attack. Much depends on the next few moves, as to whether White can stabilize the position and retain his material advantage.

1 Rdd1!!

A strong but by no means obvious move, 1 f4 and 1 Rfd1 being the continuations which suggest themselves. This is what grandmaster Taimanov had to say regarding this in *Shakhmaty v SSSR* 1950 No. 1:
"First and foremost White must defend the first rank and not concede the d-file. The tempting 1 f4 would have been wrong due to 1 ... exf4 2 exf4 Ne7! 3 f5 Nd5, when 4 f6 fails to 4 ... Rxd6.
1 Rfd1 Rxd6 2 Rxd6 Ra4! would have led to great complications, e.g. 3 Rd7+ Ke6 4 Rxb7 Ra2 5 Bc3 Rc2 6 Be1 e4!, and in view of the threat of ... Ne5—d3 White must go in for the variation 7 f4 exf3 8 gxf3 Ne5 9 Bg3 Nxf3+ 10 Kf1 Nxh2+ 11 Bxh2 Rxh2 12 Rxg7 Kd5 with a draw. If after 2 ... Ra4 White plays 3 Bc3, Black has the very unpleasant reply 3 ... Ra3."

1 ...	Rxd1
2 Rxd1	Ra2
3 Rd2	

White has managed to parry the main threats and to keep his extra pawn.

| 3 ... | e4! |

Black again sets White difficult problems. He now threatens 4 ... Ne5 followed by ... Nc4.

| 4 f3! | |

By the use of tactics White extinguishes his opponent's burst of activity.

| 4 ... | exf3 |

Nothing is achieved by 4 ... Ne5 5 fxe4 Nc4 6 Rf2+ followed by Bd4.

| 5 Rf2! | |

Not 5 gxf3? Ne5.

| 5 ... | Nh4 |
| 6 g3! | |

Correctly solving the exchanging problem. After 6 gxf3?! g5! all White's pieces are awkwardly placed.

6 ...	Nf5
7 e4	Ne3
8 Rxf3+	Ke6
9 Bd4!	

Again suppressing the opponent's counter-play. "9 Bxg7 would have been a mistake due to 9 ... Rg2+ 10 Kh1 Re2, when in spite of White's two extra pawns he cannot win, e.g.:
(a) 11 h4 (or *11 Bc3 Nd1!*) 11 ... Re1+ 12 Kh2 Ng4+ 13 Kh3 h5.
(b) 11 h3 h5, and White cannot maintain his advantage: 12 Rf6+

(*12 Bd3 Nc2 13 Bc3 Rxe4*, or *12 Bc3 Nd1*) 12 ... Ke7 13 e5 Re1+ 14 Kh2 Re2+ 15 Kg1 Rg2+ 16 Kh1 Rxg3 17 Bf8+ Ke8 18 Bd6 Rxh3+ 19 Kg1 Nd5 20 Rf8+ Kd7 with a draw" (Taimanov).

9 ...	Ng4
10 Bxg7	Nxh2
11 Rf6+	

Before playing Rf2, White worsens the position of the enemy king.

11 ...	Ke7
12 Rf2	Rxf2
13 Kxf2	h5

The position has clarified, and White is a pawn up in a minor piece ending. Now, operating according to the principle of two weaknesses, he must combine the advance of his extra e-pawn with an attack on the h5 pawn with his king, and in some cases on the b7/c6 pawn pair.

14 Ke3	Ke6
15 Kf4	Ng4
16 Bd4!	

Note how the black knight constantly comes under the domination of the white bishop. If immediately 16 Kg5, after 16 ... Nf2 Black gains some counter-play.

16 ...	Nh2
17 Bf2!	Kf6

"After 17 ... Ng4 18 Bg1! Black ends up in an unusual *zugzwang* position:
(a) 18 ... Ne5 (*18 ... Kf6 19 Bd4+ Kg6 20 e5*) 19 Bd4 Nf7 (*19 ... Nd3+ 20 Kg5 Nxb4 21 Kxh5* is hopeless for Black) 20 Bg7!
(b) 18 ... Nf6 19 Bd4 Nh7 20 Bg7 Kf7 21 Be5 Ke6 22 Bd4, and Black has to allow the advance of the white king" (Taimanov).

18 Bg1	Nf1

Otherwise 19 Bd4+ wins immediately.

19 Bd4+	Kf7

"If 19 ... Ke6, then 20 Bc3 Kf7 (*20 ... Nh2 21 Kg5 Nf1 22 Be1 Ke5 23 Kxh5 Kxe4 24 g4* is hopeless for Black) 21 Be1 Kf6 22 e5+ Ke6 (on *22 ... Kg6* there would have followed *23 Bf2*, and then as in the game) 23 Kg5 Kxe5 24 Kxh5 Ne3 25 Kg5! Nd5 26 g4 Ke6 (*26 ... b6* fails to *27 cxb6 Nxb6 28 Kh6*, when the g-pawn advances irresistibly) 27 Kg6 Ne7+ 28 Kg7, and Black is defenceless against the following plan: White places his bishop at d2 and his pawn at g5, and then takes his king across to the Q-side" (Taimanov).

20 Bf2	Kg6

If 20 ... Ke6 21 Kg5, or 20 ... Kf6 21 Be1 followed by Bc3+.

21 e5	Nh2
22 Bd4!	Kf7
23 Kf5	Ke7
24 Be3	Ng4
25 Bf4	Nf2
26 e6	Nd3
27 Bd6+	Ke8
28 Kg6	

Black could have resigned at this point. The finish was:

28 ...	Nxb4
29 Kxh5	Nd5
30 g4	b5
31 cxb6	Nxb6
32 g5	Nd5
33 g6	c5
34 g7	Nf6+
35 Kg6	Ng8
36 Bxc5	Resigns.

Botvinnik—Alekhine

AVRO-Tournament, 1938

The pawn formation is symmetric, but Black's Q-side pawns are weak, and White's pieces are much better placed. In such a position, as in many others with a spatial advantage, the main thing is not to allow the opponent to free himself, and to deprive him of the slightest counter-play. Botvinnik copes brilliantly with this task.

1 ...	f6
2 Kf1	Rf7
3 Rc8+	Rf8
4 Rc3!	g5

There is nothing better. On any piece move, except 4 ... Rf7, there follows 5 Rc7!

5 Ne1!

The routine 5 Ke2 would have allowed Black to breathe more easily after 5 ... Re8+ and ... Kf7. By the knight manoeuvre White forces his opponent to undertake something, otherwise there follows Nc2—e3. But now any activity by Black is bound to create weaknesses.

5 ...	h5

Preparing to bring the king out via f7 to e6.

6 h4!

Timely and very strong. White attacks Black's pawns before his king can come to their help.

6 ...	Nd7

"Incidentally, Alekhine avoided 6 ... Kf7 since he was afraid of 7 hxg5 fxg5 8 Nf3 g4 9 Ne5+. To me this variation did not seem so convincing, and therefore on 6 ... Kf7 I was intending to continue 7 Nf3! g4 8 Ne1 Ke6 9 Nd3 Kf5 10 g3 (*10 f3* is also good) 10 ... Ke4 11 Nf4 when the position is hopeless for Black" (Botvinnik).

7 Rc7	Rf7
8 Nf3!	

By continuing the attack on g5 White provokes a further advance of the black pawns.

8 ...	g4
9 Ne1	

These knight manoeuvres have essentially decided the game.

9 ...	f5
10 Nd3	f4
11 f3	gxf3
12 gxf3	a5
13 a4	Kf8
14 Rc6	Ke7
15 Kf2	Rf5

Black has more than enough weaknesses, but White is not in a hurry to attack them.

16 b3!	Kd8
17 Ke2	Nb8

Black is tired of waiting, and he sets a little trap: 18 Rxb6? Kc7 19 R~Nc6. Had Black continued moving his king between e7 and d8, White would simply have strengthened his position by playing his king to c3 followed by b3—b4.

18	Rg6	Kc7
19	Ne5	Na6
20	Rg7+	Kc8
21	Nc6	Rf6
22	Ne7+	Kb8
23	Nxd5	

The first gain of material.

23	...	Rd6
24	Rg5	Nb4
25	Nxb4	axb4
26	Rxh5	Rc6

No better is 26 . . . Rxd4 27 Rf5. Now the rest is simple.

27	Rb5	Kc7
28	Rxb4	Rh6
29	Rb5	Rxh4
30	Kd3	Resigns.

"One of those games where there are no brilliant moves; all the moves seem very simple, but on the other hand not one of them can be excluded, since they are all closely connected. The difficulty of playing such games lies not in the complexity of the calculation, of course, but in correctly evaluating positions reached during calculation" (Botvinnik).

Brzozka—Bronstein

Mishkolts, 1963

(See next diagram)

"A dead draw" the reader will say, on glancing at this position. Indeed, such a result seems most probable. White has

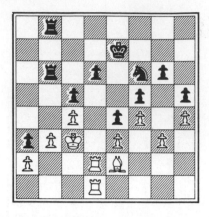

only to exercise a certain caution, and not allow the sacrifice of the black knight at b3 or a2. Black has no other active possibility (the pawn breaks . . . d5 and . . . g5 are too risky). For safety's sake White decided to place his rook at d5, nipping in the bud any pawn break in the centre, while after the exchange of knight for rook Black has nowhere to break through. In defending against his opponent's non-existent threats, White overdid it, and created the possibility for Black of real play.

1	Rd5	Ne8
2	R1d2	Nc7
3	Bd1	Na6
4	Bc2	Nb4
5	Bb1	Ra6!

Black's plan begins to take shape. Had the white rooks been at d2 and d1, the draw would have been obvious.

6	Rd1	Nxd5+
7	Rxd5	Rxb3+!!

A bolt from the blue.

8	Kxb3	Rb6+
9	Kc2	Rb2+
10	Kc1	Re2

In spite of his extra piece, White's position is difficult.

11	Rd1	Rxe3
12	Rg1	Rc3+
13	Bc2	Rxc4

The storm has died down. The white bishop is unable to oppose the three connected passed pawns in the centre. From his calm and placid drawing fortress White has been literally dragged into a tactical game, in which he has few saving chances.

14	Kd2	d5
15	Rb1	d4
16	Bd1	Rc3
17	Rb3	e3+
18	Ke2	Rc1
19	Rxa3	c4
20	Ra7+	Kd6

The black king comes to the aid of the pawns, and this decides matters.

21	Ba4	Rh1
22	Rd7+	Kc5
23	Rc7+	Kb4
24	a3+	Kc3
25	Bb5	Rh2+
26	Kf1	d3
27	Rxc4+	Kd2
28	Kg1	e2
29	Kxh2	e1=Q

White resigns.

Balashov—Szabo

Sochi, 1973

(See next diagram)

White is a pawn up and his bishop is stronger than the knight. In order to realize his advantage, he must create weaknesses in Black's position.

1	Be5	Rd3+!

In the event of the natural 1...Rc8

2 Re4! followed by 3 Rb4 b5 4 a4 Black would probably have lost. After 1 ... Rd3+ White has the problem of where to move his king. The centralizing 2 Ke4, as played in the game, suggests itself, but correct was 2 Ke2! followed by Rc1, depriving Black of counter-play. But it was very difficult to resist the temptation to obtain two connected passed pawns.

3	Ke4	Rd2!
4	Rc1?!	

It was not yet too late to go back with 4 Kf3!, but White follows the intended path.

3	...	Rxf2
4	Rc7+	Ke6
5	Rxb7	Re2+!

A very important moment. It is esseintial for Black to decentralize the white king and to centralize his own.

6	Kf3	Rxh2
7	Rb6+	Kd5!
8	Rxa6	Rh3+

While continuing to push back the white king, Black prepares the invasion of his own.

9	Kf2	Rh2+
10	Kg1	Rc2!

11 Rxg6

Black loses another pawn, and the white king is able to come into play after Rg2, but White can no longer win. With his limited forces the Hungarian grandmaster builds up an attack which obliges White to settle for a draw. All Black's pieces and his sole pawn take part in the attack, his army being led by the king itself.

11 . . .	Ke4!
12 Rg2	Rc1+
13 Kh2	Nh4
14 Rg7	

On 14 Re2+ the king goes via f3 to g4.

| 14 . . . | Nf3+ |
| 15 Kg2 | |

As shown by Szabo in *Shakhmatny Bulletin* 1974 No. 2, Black also has a draw after 15 Kh3 h5!, not allowing the white king to escape, e.g. 16 Rg2 Rh1+ 17 Kg3 h4+ 18 Kg4 Ne1! 19 Rd2 (also after *19 Re2+ Kd3 20 Rxe1 Rxe1 21 Kxh4 Rg1!* Black should not lose) 19 . . . Rg1+ 20 Kh3 Nf3! 21 Rg2 (*21 Re2? Kf5!*) 21 . . . Rh1+ 22 Kg4 Ne1!, creating a drawing mechanism. After the move chosen by Balashov a drawn rook ending is reached.

15 . . .	Nxe5
16 fxe5	Rc2+
17 Kh3	Rxb2
18 e6	Kf5
19 e7	Re2
Drawn.	

Euwe—Averbakh

Candidates Tournament
Zurich, 1953

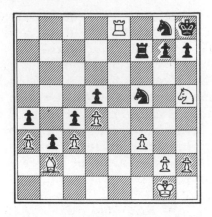

One is immediately struck by the unenviable position of the white bishop, shut in by its own pawns and forced to guard the enemy passed pawn. Black's Q-side pawns have seized a great amount of space, but in advancing so far have themselves become a target for attack by the opponent's pieces. The white rook has broken into the enemy rear, and the knight at h5 may be able to go via f4 and e6 to c5. But Black is able to neutralize the opponent's main threats, by exploiting the chronic defects in White's position.

| 1 . . . | Re7! |

Black forces the exchange of rooks, since otherwise he is threatening to win the bishop.

| 2 Rxe7 | Ngxe7 |
| 3 Kf2 | |

It was essential to parry the threat of 3 . . . Ne3, but now the black king is able to reach e6.

| 3 . . . | Kg8 |
| 4 g4? | |

An interesting point. Euwe continues the plan of transferring his knight to e6, but fails to take any precautionary measures against the opponent's counterplay. He should have gone promptly onto the defensive by Nf4, g2—g3, Ng2, Ne3, Nf1 and Nd2. In this case White would have had chances of saving the game, whereas now events develop almost by force.

4 ...	Nd6
5 Ke3	Nb5
6 f4	Nc8
7 f5	Ncd6
8 Nf4	

White has implemented his planned set-up, but his game is now lost.

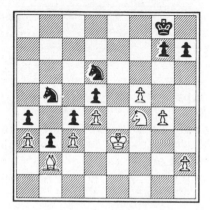

| 8 ... | Nxa3! |

"By positional play the maestro endeavours to secure and exploit true values; by means of a combination he aims to refute false values" (Lasker). The words of the great player are fully confirmed by the present example.

9 Bxa3	Nb5
10 Bc1	Nxc3
11 Ne2	Nb1!
White resigns.	

Boleslavsky—Averbakh

Candidates Tournament
Zurich, 1953

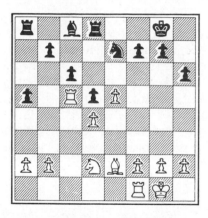

The normal plan in such positions is the minority attack by a2—a3 and b2—b4—b5, but that is with the white pawn at e3. Who is favoured by the advanced position of the pawn at e5? Most probably White, who, with his advantage in space, can combine play both on the Q-side and the K-side. True, Black may also acquire counter-play by the undermining ... f6 or ... b6 and ... c5. A complicated battle now commences.

1 Rc3

Vacating c5 for the knight.

| 1 ... | Rf8 |

Black prepares ... f6.

2 Re1!

Suppressing the opponent's counter-play. On 2 ... f6 White has the highly unpleasant 3 e6!

| 2 ... | g6 |

With the aim of erecting a defensive barrier on the K-side.

3 Bd3

White takes control of f5, so as to exchange off the black knight as soon as it appears there. In this closed position it is advantageous for each player to exchange bishop for knight.

3 ...	Bf5
4 Bf1!	

The side with a spatial advantage should agree only to very favourable exchanges.

4 ...	a4

A committing decision. If now White should succeed in provoking ... b5, the c6 pawn will be very weak, while Black has eliminated only temporarily the threat of the white knight penetrating to c5.

5 h3	Bd7
6 f4	h5

All Black's pawns are on squares of the same colour as his bishop, and it is well known that this is not the best arrangement in the endgame.

7 Nf3	Kg7
8 Kf2	Rh8
9 g3	Kf8
10 Kg2	Nf5
11 Bd3	Ng7
12 Ng5	Be6

Defending against a possible e5—e6.

13 Bc2!	Ke7
14 Ra3	Nf5

Black is prepared to allow the exchange of his knight for the bishop, merely to avoid playing ... b5. But after White's next move he is forced to drain the cup completely.

15 Nf3!	b5

Forced.

16 Rc3	Rac8
17 Bxf5!	Bxf5
18 Rec1	Bd7
19 Ne1	

In the tournament book Bronstein indicates the possibility of 19 e6! followed by Ne5, but Boleslavsky is not in a hurry to force matters. It only needs the white knight to penetrate to c5, and Black's position will immediately become hopeless.

19 ...	Rb8

20 Nd3?	

This natural move allows Black to save the game in amazing fashion. After Bronstein's suggestion of 20 Rc5! White was bound to win, e.g. 20 ... b4 21 Ra5!, or 20 ... Rhc8 21 Nd3 Bf5 22 Nb4. The game once again shows how carefully one must watch for counter-play by the opponent, even in won positions.

20 ...	b4!
21 Rc5	Bf5
22 Nf2	b3!
23 a3	

Nothing is achieved by 23 axb3 Rxb3, while after 23 Rxc6? a3!! it is Black who wins.

23 ...   Bc2!

It transpires that on 24 Rxc6 there follows 24 ... Rhc8 25 Rxc8 Rxc8, when White cannot defend his d-pawn, since 26 Kf3 fails to 26 ... Be4+.

24 Kf3

White would still have had some winning chances after 24 Nd1.

24 ...   Kd7
25 Ke3   Ra8
26 h4   Ra6
27 Nh3   Rb8
28 Ng5   Ke7

Drawn.

CHAPTER 10

POSITIONS WITH AN ISOLATED d-PAWN

Positions with an isolated pawn on the d-file arise in many openings. In the middlegame the side with the isolated pawn obtains compensation in the form of active piece play, but in the endgame the weakness of the isolated pawn is more noticeable. It is the methods of play in such positions that will be covered in this chapter.

Byelavyenets–Rauzer

Moscow, 1937

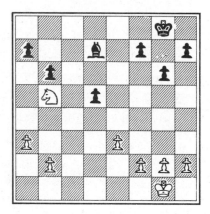

White has a strong knight against a bad bishop, with the opponent's d-pawn isolated. Is this ending won? Most probably the position is drawn (cf. the following example). What happened in this game? White's knight is attacked and must retreat to c3 or d4 (taking the a7 pawn is unfavourable). The knight stands very well at d4 in the middlegame, but in the endgame this is the square for the king. Therefore:

1 Nc3	Bc6
2 Kf1	Kf8
3 f3	

Forestalling . . . d4.

3 . . .	Ke7
4 Ke2	Ke6
5 Kd3	Ke5
6 f4+	Ke6
7 Kd4	Kd6
8 b4	Ke6

Black assumes that White will be unable to create any serious threats, and demonstratively moves only his king. Such tactics are acceptable, but only up to a certain point. It would not have done any harm to advance the f-pawn to f6, so as not to 'forget' to do it later. But how can White win? Black already has one weakness — the isolated pawn in the centre. What is needed is a second weakness, which can be created only on the K-side. Byelavyenets first strengthens his position to the maximum on the Q-side, by advancing his pawn to b5 and placing his knight at b4.

9 b5	Bb7
10 Na2	Kd6
11 Nb4	Ke6?

Here 11 . . . f6 was essential. Black calculated that after 12 Nc6 Bxc6 13 bxc6 Kd6 14 c7 Kxc7 15 Kxd5 f5! he would gain a draw, but he failed to take account of his opponent's reply.

12 g4!

Threatening by g4–g5 to fix the pawns at f7 and h7, while on 12 . . . h6 there follows 13 Nc6! Bxc6 14 bxc6 Kd6 15 c7 Kxc7 16 Kxd5, and the ending is won for White, since Black does not have . . . f5. Here is the

variation given by Byelavyenets: 16 ...
Kd7 17 e4 Kc7 18 e5 Kd7 19 f5
gxf5 20 gxf5 Kc7 21 e6 f6 22 h3
h5 23 h4 a6 24 a4 a5 25 Kc4 Kc6
26 e7 Kd7 27 Kb5, and wins.

| 12 ... | f5 |
| 13 g5 | |

The h7 pawn is fixed. Now White
must advance his h-pawn to h6, when
Black will be faced with the threat of a
knight sacrifice at h6 or f5, and hence
a second weakness will be created.

| 13 ... | Kd6 |
| 14 h3! | |

A concrete approach to the position.
"The more natural 14 h4 would have
been weaker due to 14 ... Ke6 15
Na2 Kd6 16 Nc3 Ke6 17 Ne2 Bc8
18 Ng3 Bd7 19 a4 Be8, when Black
succeeds in preventing h4—h5" (Byelavyenets).

| 14 ... | Ke6 |

Black moves his king to and fro as if
nothing has happened.

15 Na2	Kd6
16 Nc3	Ke6
17 h4	Kd6
18 Ne2	Bc8?

"The last saving chance was 18 ...
a6" (Byelavyenets).

| 19 Ng3 | Bd7 |
| 20 a4 | Ke6 |

There was no longer any defence
against h4—h5.

| 21 h5 | Be8 |
| 22 h6 | Kd6 |

23 Ne2

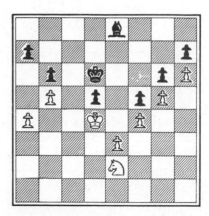

"Here the game was adjourned, and
adjudicated a win for White. He has
succeeded in implementing his plan completely, and Black, with three weak
pawns at a7, d5 and h7, is helpless,
for example:

(a) 23 ... Bd7 24 Nc3 Be6 25
Na2 Bf7 (Black cannot defend his d-
pawn with his bishop from b7, since
after, say, 25 ... Bc8 26 Nb4 Bb7
White wins by 27 Nd3 Bc8 28 Ne5,
when there is no defence against Nxg6)
26 Nb4 Be6 27 Nc6 a5 28 bxa6!
Kxc6 29 a7! (essential, since after
29 Ke5 Bc8! 30 a7 Bb7 31 Kf6 Kd6
32 Kg7 Ke7 33 Kxh7 Kf7 White has
no win) 29 ... Kb7 30 Ke5 Bd7 31
Kf6 Bxa4 32 Kg7 b5 33 Kxh7 b4
34 Kxg6 b3 35 h7 Be8+ 36 Kf6 b2
37 h8=Q b1=Q 38 a8=Q+ Kxa8 39
Qxe8+, and the queen ending is easily
won for White.

(b) 23 ... Bf7 (an unsuccessful
attempt to shut the knight in at a7) 24
Nc3 Be6 25 Na2 Bg8 26 Nb4 Bf7
27 Nc6 Be8 28 Nxa7 Bd7 29 Kd3
(Black is in zugzwang) 29 ... Kc7 30
Kc3 Kb7 (if 30 ... Kd6 31 Kd4,
and Black is forced to free the knight)
31 Kd4! Kxa7 32 Ke5, and White
wins.

The entire ending is a good example
of the battle between bishop and knight"
(Byelavyenets).

Flohr—Capablanca

Moscow, 1936

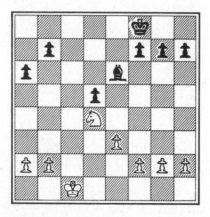

The position is virtually identical to the previous one, but the play develops rather differently.

1 ...	Ke7
2 Kd2	Kd6
3 Kc3	b6
4 f4	Bd7
5 Nf3	f6
6 Kd4	a5

In contrast to Rauzer, Capablanca thoughtfully places all his pawns on dark squares. In his book *Last Chess Lectures* Capablanca formulated the following rule: "When the opponent has a bishop, keep your pawns on squares of the same colour as this bishop. But if you have a bishop, then, irrespective of whether or not the opponent has a bishop, keep your pawns on squares of the opposite colour to that of your bishop".

7 Nd2	Bc8
8 Nb1	Be6
9 Nc3	Kc6
10 a3	h6
11 g3	

Black sticks to waiting tactics, and White also does not hurry. This manner of play led to Capablanca himself making a mistake.

11 ...	h5?!

With his last move White vacated g2. The Cuban grandmaster obviously thought that White was intending to play his knight to h4, advance f4—f5 and g3—g4, then transfer the knight to f4 and with the black king at c6 play Ne6, forcing a won pawn ending.

But the black bishop does not have to allow the knight to reach h4: with the knight at e1 it is sufficient to transfer the bishop to e4, to say nothing of the possible defence ...g5 with the knight at h4, to answer fxg5 with ...hxg5!? and Ng2 with ...g4! After the move in the game Black gets into serious difficulties.

12 b4	axb4
13 axb4	Kd6
14 b5	

Black has no good moves. 14 ... Bf7 is unpleasantly met by 15 f5.

14 ...	g6
15 Na4	Kc7
16 Nc3	Kd6
17 f5!	

Breaking up Black's pawn formation. Bad now is 17 ... Bxf5 18 Nxd5 Bd7 19 Nxf6 Bxb5 20 Nd5, and 20 ... Kc6 is not possible due to 21 Ne7+.

17 ...	gxf5
18 Ne2	Bd7

An inaccuracy. In anticipation of the pawn ending Black should have played 18 ... Bg8 19 Nf4 Bf7, provoking h2—h3, and only then attacked the b-pawn by ... Be8.

19 Nf4	Be8
20 Nxd5	Bxb5

| 21 Nxb6 | Bc6 |

On no account must the white knight be allowed to reach f4. Imagine that the knight stands at f4. In reply to ... Be8 there follows Nd5 winning a pawn, since the pawn ending after ... Ke6, Nc7+ and Nxe8 is won for White.

22 Nc4+	Ke6
23 Nb2	Bb5
24 Nd1	Be2
25 Nf2	Bf1

Now Flohr transposes into a pawn ending.

| 26 Nd3 | Bxd3 |
| 27 Kxd3 | Ke5! |

"27 ... Kd5 would have lost to 28 Kd2 Ke5 (or *28 ... Ke4 29 Ke2 Kd5 30 Kf3 Ke5 31 h3 Kd5 32 Kf4 Ke6 33 h4*; this is where the two reserve tempi on the K-side become important!) 29 Ke1! Kd5 30 Kf2! The king moves to e1 and f2 are given exclamation marks, since e2 cannot be occupied, e.g. 29 Ke2 Ke4 30 Kf2 h4 31 gxh4 f4 32 h5, and the e3 pawn is captured with check" (Bondarevsky). The game continued:

| 28 Ke2 | Ke4 |
| 29 h3 |

Or 29 Kf2 h4!

| 29 ... | Kd5! |
| 30 Kf3 | Ke5 |

In this position the players agreed a draw.

Karpov—Hort

Budapest, 1973

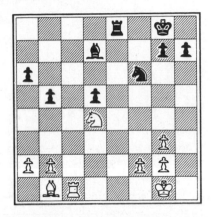

Were Black's Q-side pawns at a7 and b6, his position could be considered quite satisfactory. But in the given position, apart from the isolated d-pawn, Black has a complex of weaknesses on the Q-side, and in particular at c5.

1 f3

Karpov prepares to bring his king out at f2 followed by the invasion of his rook at c7.

1 ...	Rc8
2 Rxc8+	Bxc8
3 Kf2	Kf7
4 Ke3	Ke7
5 b4!

With the exchange of rooks the weakness of Black's Q-side has become even more appreciable. By this last move White consolidates his advantage.

| 5 ... | g6 |

Black is forced to reckon with the threat of g3—g4—g5. On 5 ... h6 White has the highly unpleasant 6 Bg6, while after 5 ... g5 6 Nf5+! Bxf5 7 Bxf5 Black cannot avoid loss of material.

| 6 g4! |

White intends to create a passed pawn

on the K-side, which will divert Black's forces away from the Q-side.

6	...	Nd7
7	f4	Nf8
8	g5	Kd6
9	Kf3	Ne6?!

Inviting a bishop ending, which White is happy to agree to. All Black's pawns are on squares of the colour of his bishop, and Karpov elegantly realizes his advantage.

10	Nxe6!	Bxe6
11	Ke3	Bg4
12	Bd3	Be6
13	Kd4	Bg4
14	Bc2	Be6
15	Bb3	Bf7
16	Bd1	Be6
17	Bf3	Bf7
18	Bg4	

Here **Black resigned**, since the only defence against 19 Bc8 is 18 ... Be6, but the pawn ending after 19 Bxe6 Kxe6 20 g4 Kd6 21 a3 is easily won for White.

Here we saw that the transition into the bishop ending proved fatal for Black, although in any case his position was lost. This ending shows how difficult it is for the weaker side to defend if, apart from the isolated d-pawn, there are also other weaknesses. Equally difficult is the problem of what to exchange in this type of ending.

Szabo—Korensky

Sochi, 1973

(See next diagram)

White has doubled b-pawns on the left side of the board, and it might be expected that the game will end in a draw.

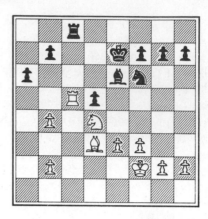

1	...	b6?!

There was no necessity for this weakening. 1 ... Kd8 was correct.

2	Rxc8	Bxc8
3	Ke2	Kd6
4	Kd2	g6?!

From previous examples we know that this move is undesirable. 4 ... h6 was better.

5	Kc3	Nd7
6	f4	

White begins playing actively on the K-side.

6	...	Nf8
7	Be2	Kc7
8	g4	h6
9	h3	Kd6
10	Bd3	Bb7?!

A further inaccuracy. The bishop lifts its control over the g4 pawn and retires to a passive position. Preferable was 10 ... f6 or the more energetic 10. . .g5!?, not allowing the K-side pawns to be fixed on white squares.

11	h4!	Bc8

Now 11 ... f6 no longer works due to 12 h5 gxh5 13 Nf5+.

12 g5	hxg5
13 hxg5	

White has achieved a great deal: he has firm control over the highly important central squares c5 and e5, he has the d4 square at his disposal, Black's K-side pawns are fixed on white squares, and the a6 pawn is weakened. But for a win these advantages would appear to be insufficient. Black is saved by the doubled b-pawns. Imagine that the white pawns were at b4 and a4. After a4—a5 it is unlikely that Black would be able to save the game: . . . b5 is obviously bad, while after the exchange of pawns on a5 the white king acquires an additional square for manoeuvring — b4.

13 . . .	Ne6?!

Black takes play into a bishop ending, in which the white king gains free access to d4. A highly committing decision. It would have been safer to continue the battle with two minor pieces.

14 Nxe6	Kxe6
15 Kd4	Kd6
16 Be2	a5
17 bxa5	bxa5
18 Bb5	Be6?

Black's last and decisive mistake. The bishop ending could have been saved only by exceptionally accurate play. In order to understand Korensky's mistake, we will first analyze the game continuation.

(See next diagram)

19 Be8	Ke7

Otherwise White penetrates with his king to e5, with an easy win.

20 Bc6!	Kd6
21 Bb7	

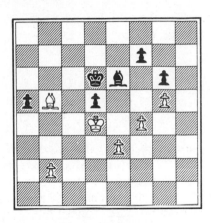

Black is in *zugzwang.*

21 . . .	f6
22 gxf6	Bf7
23 Bc8	

White's plan is to transfer his bishop to b3 and then play e3—e4.

23 . . .	Bg8
24 Bg4	Bf7
25 Bc8	Bg8
26 Bh3	Bf7
27 Bg4	Be8
28 Bf3	Bf7
29 Bd1	Ke6

29 . . . Be6 would also have failed to save Black.

30 Bb3	Kxf6
31 Bxd5	

White has won a pawn, and he now confidently converts his advantage into a win.

31 . . .	Be8
32 e4	g5
33 e5+	Kf5
34 fxg5	Kxg5
35 Kc5	Kf5
36 Bc6!	Bf7
37 Kd6	Bb3
38 Bd7+	Ke4
39 e6	Kd3

40	e7	Bf7
41	Ba4	Kc4
42	Kd7	

and within a few moves **Black resigned**.

In this game White first put his opponent in *zugzwang*, then transferred his bishop to b3 and by e3—e4 retained his extra pawn. In *Shakhmatny Bulletin* 1974 No. 2 Szabo showed that Black could have put up a successful defence. Correct was 18 . . . Bf5 or 18 . . . Bg4, not occupying e6 until White plays Be8. After 19 Be8 Be6 20 b3 (otherwise a *zugzwang* position cannot be obtained) 20 . . . Ke7 21 Bc6 Kd6 22 Bb7 f6 23 gxf6 Bf7 White wins a pawn, but he is no longer able to transfer his bishop to b3, and the game must end in a draw.

Polugayevsky—Mecking

Mar del Plata, 1971

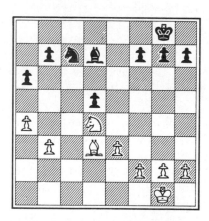

It is White to move, and Polygayevsky immediately fixes Black's Q-side pawns by

1 a5!

and we again encounter a typical ending, the principles of which have been analyzed in detail in previous examples.

1 . . .		Kf8?!

As was mentioned earlier, centralization of the king is hardly ever incorrect, it can only be inopportune. Black should have preferred 1 . . . Ne6, when if the knight moves from d4 he has 2. . .Nc5 with counter-play, while after 2 Nxe6 fxe6 3 f4 h6 he has good drawing chances.

2	Kf1	Ke7

2 . . . Ne6 is unpleasantly met by 3 Nxe6, when 3 . . . fxe6 is not possible due to the loss of the h-pawn. But 2 . . . h6 followed by 3 . . . Ne6 came into consideration.

3	Ke2	g6?!

This mistake is so 'popular' that there is no point in drawing attention to it each time.

4	Kd2	Ne6
5	Nxe6	

Polugayevsky takes play into a bishop ending, in which all Black's pawns are on squares of the colour of his bishop. As we have seen in previous examples, bishop endings are very difficult for the weaker side, if, apart from his isolated pawn, he has even just one more weakness. Nevertheless the decision of the Soviet player is highly committing, since Black gains the opportunity to unite his central pawns. White could have continued 5 Kc3, retaining all the advantages of his position. Annotating this game, grandmaster Timman gives the following interesting variations: 5 Kc3 Nc5 6 Be2! (*6 f3 Nxd3 7 Kxd3 Kd6 8 b4 g5!*, with drawing chances). By 6 Be2! Timman offers a pawn sacrifice: 6 . . . Ne4+ 7 Kb4 Nxf2 8 Kc5 Ne4+ (*8 . . . Kd8 9 Kxd5 Kc7 10 Ke5*) 9 Kb6 Nd6 10 Kc7 g5

114

(if *10 . . . f5*, then *11 Bf3 Be6 12 Ne2*)
11 Bf3 Be6   12 g4 followed by 13
Nf5+.

5 ...	fxe6

Of course, capturing on e6 with a
piece would be a blunder.

6 f4	e5!
7 g3	

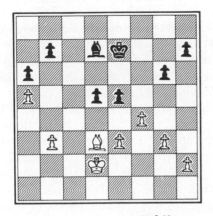

7 ...	Kd6?

This natural move, centralizing the
king, turns out to be a serious mistake.
Timman showed that Black could have
drawn by 7 . . . Bb5!, when White is
forced to retreat 8 Bc2, since in the
pawn ending Black gains a draw after
8 Bxb5 axb5   9 Kc3 Ke6, when on
10 Kb4? there follows 10 . . . d4!
After the retreat of the white bishop
Timman gives the variation 8 . . . Kd6
9 Kc3 Be2   10 Bb1! Bf1   11 Kb4 d4!
12 exd4 exd4   13 Be4 Kc7   14 Kc5
d3   15 Kd4 d2   16 Bf3 b6!

(See next diagram)

The Dutch grandmaster gives a detail-
ed analysis of this position: (a) 17 b4
bxa5   18 bxa5 Kd6   19 Kc3 Kc5,
regaining the pawn after 20 Kxd2 Kb4;
(b) 17 axb6+ Kxb6   18 Kc3 Kc5!   19
Kxd2 Kd4, and White, despite his extra

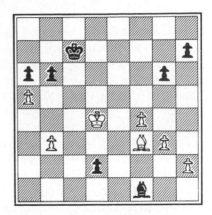

pawn, is unable to win; (c) 17 Kc3!
bxa5   18 Kxd2 Bb5   19 Bd1 Kd6
20 Kc3 Kd5!   21 Bc2 Bd7 intending
22 . . . Bf5, when Black is not in danger
of losing.
To be fair, it should be said that it was
hardly possible for Mecking to foresee all
these lengthy and complicated variations
at the board.

8 Kc3	Be6

It transpires that here it is not possible
to go into the pawn ending by 8 . . .
Bb5, since after 9 Bxb5 axb5   10 Kb4
d4 White has the capture 11 fxe5 with
check.

9 Kb4	exf4

In view of the threat of 10 fxe5+
Kxe5 11 Kc5, Black is forced to concede the centre. If 9 . . . d4, then 10
exd4 followed by h2—h4—h5.

10 gxf4	Bg4
11 Kc3	Bf3
12 Kd4	Bg2

Black keeps his bishop on the long
diagonal, in an attempt to prevent
e3—e4.

13 h4	Bf3
14 b4	Bh1

If the black bishop moves off the long diagonal, White wins by transferring his bishop to g2 and then advancing e3—e4 when the black bishop is at f7 or g8.

15	Be2	Bg2
16	Bg4	Be4
17	Bc8	Kc7
18	Be6	Kd6
19	Bg8	h6
20	Bf7	h5

Black is in *zugzwang*, but it is White to move.

21	Be8	Bc2
22	Bf7	Be4
23	f5!	

The decisive breakthrough.

23	...	Bxf5

After 23 . . . gxf5 a possible variation is 24 Bxh5 Ke6 25 Be2 Kd6 26 h5 Ke6 27 h6 Kf6 28 Bxa6! bxa6 29 b5, and one of the white pawns queens.

24	Bxd5	Bc8
25	e4	

Zugzwang.

25	...	Ke7
26	Ke5	g5
27	hxg5	h4
28	g6	h3
29	g7	h2
30	g8=Q	h1=Q
31	Qf7+	Kd8
32	Qf8+	Resigns.

Ribli—Pinter

Baille Herclane, 1982

White stands better. Although the most unpleasant pieces for Black — the white-squared bishops — have been exchanged, the advantage of the bishop over the knight is fairly appreciable. The black knight is well placed, but it cannot take part in the defence of the d-pawn, since the e7 square is easily controlled by the white bishop from a3. Thus Black is obliged to keep his rooks tied to the defence of his isolated pawn. With his next few moves Black takes his king to the aid of his rooks, and White attempts to prevent this.

1	g4!	Kf7
2	Ke2	Ke6
3	f4	f5?!

Black has prevented f4—f5+, but at a high price. The long diagonal has been opened for the white bishop, and targets have appeared for the white rooks on the g-file. 3 . . . g6 was more circumspect.

4	gxf5+!	Kxf5
5	Kf3	Ke6
6	h4!	Rf8

6 . . . g6 was bad because of 7 h5!

7	Kg4	g6?

Pinter decides to exploit the fact that the white king has moved to g4 and that 8 h5 is no longer very dangerous, since 8 ... gxh5 follows with check. But he has forgotten that the white king has moved away from the check that the d-pawn will announce when capturing on e4. To be fair, it must be said that playing such a position with Black is very difficult.

8 e4!

White's advantage becomes decisive.

| 8 ... | h5+ |

8 ... Rfd8 does not help due to 9 exd5+ Rxd5 10 Rxd5 Rxd5 11 Rxd5 Kxd5 12 f5.

9 Kg5!

This bold raid by the white king wins material.

9 ...	d4
10 Bxd4	Nd8
11 Bg7!	

Pretty, and very strong.

11 ...	Nf7+
12 Kxg6	Nh8+
13 Kh6	Nf7+
14 Kxh5	Resigns.

Averbakh—Keres

18th USSR Championship
Moscow, 1950

(See next diagram)

Black has chances of obtaining an outside passed pawn on the Q-side (with his pawn at a5 and the white pawn at a4, he can play ... b5 in a favourable situation). Black can also attempt to give his opponent an additional weakness on this part of the board.

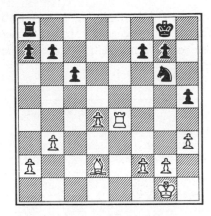

| 1 ... | f6 |

Black's initial task is to bring his king to the centre and securely blockade the d-pawn.

2 Kf1	Kf7
3 Ba5	b6
4 Bc3	Rd8
5 Bb2	Rd6
6 g4!?	

It is to White's advantage to simplify the position and reduce the number of pawns.

| 6 ... | hxg4 |
| 7 hxg4 | Re6?! |

After the exchange of rooks this type of ending is drawn, if the side with the isolated pawn does not have any additional weaknesses. In his book of selected games, Keres makes the following comment on this move:

"Not the best plan. Black wanted to facilitate the access of his king to the cherished d5 square, but, firstly, the exchange on e6 cannot be forced, and, secondly, even if it could be forced the simplification would only favour White. The ending after 8 Rxe6 Kxe6 9 Ke2 Kd5 10 Ke3 is advantageous to Black, but White has good chances of resisting. Therefore, if account is taken of the fact that the game was shortly to be

adjourned, better was 7. . .Nf8 followed by 8 . . . Ne6 and 9 . . . Rd5, which
in the end is what in fact happened
later."

8 f3

Here, and over the next few moves,
White wrongly avoids the exchange of
rooks.

8 . . .	Ne7
9 Bc1	Nd5
10 Bd2	Rd6!

"Black decided henceforth to avoid
the exchange of rooks" (Keres).

| 11 Ke2 | Rd8 |
| 12 Kf2 | Nc7! |

A strong move, provoking a weakening of White's Q-side and preparing to
bring the black king to the centre.

13 a4

The threat was 13 . . . Nb5, and if
14 Be3 Nd6, winning the exchange.

| 13 . . . | Ne6 |
| 14 Be3 | Rd5 |

"White's pieces are tied to the defence
of his d-pawn, and he is obliged to restrict himself to passive defence, practically only king moves being possible.

Black, on the other hand, has sufficient
time to prepare a break-through by
. . . b5. But this can be done only after
thorough preparation. Thus, for example, after 15 Ke2 it would be premature to advance 15 . . . b5 due to
16 a5 b4 (16 . . . a6 is slightly better)
17 a6!, when White unexpectedly obtains counter-play (17 . . . Nc7 18
Kd3 Nxa6 19 Kc4, or 17 . . . Ra5 18
d5 cxd5 19 Rxb4). Therefore Black
tries to strengthen his position to the
maximum, by transferring his king to d7,
when he will prepare . . . g6 and . . . a6,
and only at the appropriate moment
play . . . b5" (Keres).

| 15 Kg3 | Ke7 |
| 16 g5!? | |

Averbakh tries to catch his opponent
in a trap, but in doing so burns his boats
behind him. Objectively stronger was
16 Kf2 with chances of a draw, but it is
difficult to condemn White for taking
this risk. Had it succeeded he would have
immediately gained a draw, whereas
whether passive defence would have
saved the game is unclear.

16 . . .	f5
17 Re5	Kd6
18 Rxd5+	Kxd5
19 g6!	

19 . . .   a5!

Do not hurry! "The subtle trap set by White was that the pawn ending after 19 ... Nxd4 20 Bxd4! Kxd4 21 Kf4, which at first sight seems completely hopeless, is in fact drawn! The best continuation for Black is 21 ... b5! 22 axb5 cxb5, but even then White unexpectedly saves the game after 23 b4! Kc4 24 Kxf5 Kxb4. Let us examine this position in some detail:

(a) 25 Ke6 is the first move which comes to mind, so as to answer king moves with Kf7xg7—f6 and the advance of the g-pawn. But Black replies 25 ... a5!, when White's position becomes critical, e.g.:

(a1) 26 f4 a4 27 f5 a3 28 f6 gxf6! 29 g7 a2 30 g8=Q a1=Q 31 Qf8+ Kb3, with an easy win.

(a2) 26 Kf7 a4 27 Kxg7 a3 28 Kf7 a2 29 g7 a1=Q 30 g8=Q Qa2+, and it seems time for White to resign, but here, in this seemingly hopeless position, he is able to draw! 31 Kf8 Qxg8+ 32 Kxg8 Kc4 33 f4 Kd5 34 Kf7! If now 34 ... Ke4 35 Ke6 Kxf4 36 Kd5 with a draw, or 34 ... b4 35 f5 b3 36 f6 b2 37 Kg7 b1=Q 38 f7 with a theoretical draw. Amazing!

Perhaps in this variation Black should not exchange queens? However, after 30 ... Qa8+ 31 Kg7 Qxf3 we reach a queen ending in which it cannot be said with any confidence that the stronger side has a win.

(b) 25 f4! is undoubtedly stronger:

(b1) 25 ... Kc5 26 Ke6! b4 27 f5 b3 28 f6, or

(b2) 25 ... Kc3 26 Kg5! b4 27 f5 b3 28 f6 gxf6+ 29 Kxf6 b2 30 g7 b1=Q 31 g8=Q, and in neither case does White have any difficulty.

(b3) 25 ... a5!, and White's position again seems critical, since 26 Ke6 a4 27 f5 a3 28 f6 gxf6 etc. leads to a familiar won position for Black. But even here White has the saving 26 Ke4! a4 27 Kd3!, when his king arrives just in time, and it is Black who has to think

in terms of forcing a draw" (Keres).

We have given in full the analysis by the celebrated grandmaster, in order to demonstrate once again the care with which one must weigh up the consequences of an exchange leading to a pawn ending. Of course, the practical player would not be obliged to waste time on the calculation of such complicated variations, but on general grounds would make a more useful move, since in any case the d4 pawn is doomed.

20 Kh4	Nxd4?!

Here too Black should not have hurried over the capture of the pawn. He should have advanced his b-pawn to b4 and only then taken on d4. By the move played Keres allows White to activate his bishop.

21 Bh6!	Ne6
22 Be3	c5
23 Kh5	Ke5?

By 23 ... c4! Black could have won easily (24 bxc4+ Kxc4 25 Bxb6 Kb4 and 26 ... Kxa4), but he decided to try and win without giving his opponent the slightest chance. "But instead of making a simple and clear move, Black begins manoeuvring in the hope of gaining an even easier win in the opponent's time trouble. Such tactics are completely inappropriate, and lead to Black overlooking an important defensive possibility, which jeopardizes the win" (Keres). In this case Black should not have abused the principle "do not hurry".

True, in a practical game it is difficult for even a very strong player to find the golden mean.

24 Bc1	Nd4?!

As shown by Keres, he should have returned his king to d5, and if 25 Bb2 c4

26 bxc4+ Kxc4   27 Bxg7 Nxg7+   28
Kg5 Ne8!   29 Kxf5 Kd5 followed by
. . . b5.

25 Bh6   Kf6
26 Bg5+   Ke6

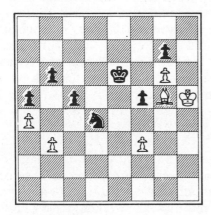

27 Bh6?

"The decisive mistake in time trouble.
White misses the excellent chance of 27
Bd8! During the game Black thought
that this move was not possible due to
27 . . . Nxb3 28 Bxb6? c4, but White

has another possibility: 28 Kg5! with
the threat of Bf6! The knight would
have had to return to d4, but after 28
. . . Nd4 29 Bxb6 Nxf3+ 30 Kf4 or
30 Kh5 White has good drawing chances.
28 . . . f4 is no better due to the simple
29 Kxf4.

But even so Black has a way to win.
On 27 Bd8 he plays 27 . . . Kd7! 28
Bf6 (if now *28 Bxb6 Nxb3 29 Kg5 c4*,
and wins) 28 . . . Ne6 29 Be5 Kc6
30 Bxg7 Nxg7+ 31 Kg5 Ne8 32 Kxf5
Kd6! 33 f4 Kd5 34 Kg5 Ke6 35 f5+
Ke5 etc., or 33 Kf4 Ke6 34 Ke4
Nd6+ 35 Kf4 Kf6 36 g7 Kxg7 37
Ke5 c4! etc.

Thus 27 Bd8! would not have saved
White, but Black would still have had a
lot to do" (Keres).

27 . . .   gxh6
28 Kxh6   Nc6!
29 g7   Ne7
30 Kh7   Kf7
31 Kh6   Kg8
32 f4   Kf7
White resigns.

CHAPTER 11

THE TWO BISHOPS

It is generally reckoned that in the majority of cases two bishops are stronger than two other minor pieces. But while in the middlegame the advantage of the two bishops is by no means always an important factor, in the endgame it is often decisive. Thanks to their long range, the bishops are excellent for supporting pawn advances which seize space and create weaknesses in the enemy position. In the end the stronger side frequently uses the principle of two weaknesses, and, by combining threats, breaks through on one of the wings.

Richter—Tarrasch

Nuremberg, 1888

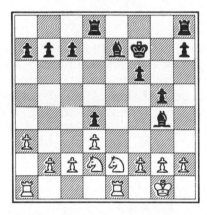

With two bishops against two knights Black has an undisputed advantage, in spite of the symmetric pawn formation.

$$1 \ldots \quad c5$$
$$2 \ Ng3?!$$

An aimless move. The only chance of a successful defence is to create strong points for the knights. In the given position c4 is a possible strong point, so

White should have played 2 a4 followed by the transfer of one knight to c4, and the other via c1 and b3 to d2. White's move could have been explained by a desire to set up the above formation by Ng3—f1—d2. But the further course of the game shows that he is not attempting to think schematically, but makes moves without any plan.

$$2 \ldots \quad h5!?$$

In his notes to one of Steinitz's games, Euwe writes:

"What is the advantage of a bishop over a knight? It is that it can influence the battle from afar, whereas the knight affects squares only in its immediate vicinity. How can the advantage of the bishop best be exploited? To do this the knight must be pushed back as much as possible, and then all the time prevented from coming into play. For this, pawns are the most suitable."

Later Euwe continues: "Of course, it is by no means always that a pawn advance leads to such a favourable position as in the given instance. But it can be considered that, if it has the result of weakening the opponent's pawns, then with the two bishops it must be considered favourable, since with the long-range bishops the resulting position can be better exploited than with the knights. On the other hand, it should be mentioned that knights are better at exploiting weak squares in the form of outposts from which they cannot be driven. Therefore the pawns should be advanced in such a way as to minimize the number of weak squares created. It is clear that for this aim the most suitable are rooks' pawns, since each move of a rook's pawn weakens only one square (the one alongside its new position), whereas a move by any other pawn simultaneously weakens two squares."

Euwe's remarks are fully applicable to the ending in question. After 1 ... c5 White could have immediately transformed c4 into an outpost.

3 f3?!

White quite unnecessarily weakens the e3 square.

3 ...	Bd7
4 Re2	

It was not yet too late for 4 a4.

4 ...	b5!

Black also starts an offensive on the Q-side.

5 Rae1	Bf8
6 Nge4	

Having missed the opportunity to establish a knight at c4, White is unable to set up a systematic defence.

6 ...	Rg8
7 Nb3	Rc8
8 Ned2	Bd6
9 Ne4	Bf8
10 Ned2	f5?!

Tarrasch plays purposefully, but too directly. He should have made one further prophylactic move, 10 ... Rg6, and only then set his pawns in motion.

11 Re5!?	Bd6
12 R5e2?	

The decisive mistake. Meanwhile, White had a chance to obtain counter-play after 12 Rd5! Rg6 (*12 ... Rc6? 13 Nxc5!*) 13 g4!

White removes all the barriers preventing his knight from occupying the outpost at e4. It is not easy for Black to counter this, e.g. 13 ... Rf6 (hardly good is *13 ... hxg4 14 fxg4*, when White obtains the additional square f3 for a knight) 14 gxf5 Bc6 15 Rxd6 Rxd6 16 Nxc5, and for the exchange White has fair compensation. 16 ... Bxf3? fails to 17 Nxf3 Rxc5 18 Nxg5+ Kg8 19 Ne4 Re5 20 Nf6+.

12 ...	Ra8

Black prepares the advance of his rook's pawn on the Q-side. To be considered was the exchange of one pair of rooks, so that the bishops should not be diverted by having to defend e6 and e7.

13 Na5	Rab8

Defending against 14 Nb7.

14 Nab3	h4
15 Kh1	Rg6
16 Kg1	Be6
17 Rf2	Ra8
18 Rfe2?	

White should not have allowed the advance of the a-pawn, although it is unlikely that 18 Na5 Bd5 would have affected the result.

18 ...	a5!

The Two Bishops

19	Nb1	a4
20	N3d2	c4
21	Nf1	Rc8
22	Kh1	c3
23	bxc3	dxc3
24	Ne3	b4

and within a few moves **White resigned.**

Tarrasch—Rubinstein

San Sebastian, 1912

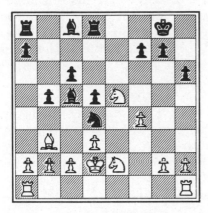

With his next move Black exchanges knights, and we again see a battle between two bishops and two other minor pieces.

	1 . . .	Nxe2

Of course, not 1 . . . Nxb3+, since after 2 axb3 Bb7 3 d4 the white knights acquire an excellent strong point at c5.

	2 Kxe2	Re8!

Before defending his c-pawn, Rubinstein sets his opponent a difficult problem, with which Tarrasch fails to cope. Black threatens 3 . . . f6, and so White is forced to move his king. The natural 3 Kd2 seems bad due to 3 . . . f6 4 Nxc6 Be3+ 5 Kc3 Be6, with a very strong attack. But even so White should

have played 3 Kd2!, and if 3 . . . f6 4 Nxc6 Be3+, then 5 Ke2!, and it is not clear that Black can gain any advantage from a discovered check. On 3 Kd2 Rubinstein would most likely have replied 3 . . . Bb7.

3	Kf1	Bb7
4	c3	f6

Otherwise White plays d3—d4 followed by Nd3.

5	Ng4	

No better is 5 Nf3 Be3 6 g3 Bc8.

5 . . .		h5
6	Nf2	Be3
7	Bd1	h4
8	g3	a5!

Black carries out a logical offensive with his rooks' pawns. This move prepares . . . b4, creating vulnerable points on White's Q-side. Black does not fear 9 Ng4 in view of 9 . . . b4.

9	Bf3	b4
10	Kg2	bxc3
11	bxc3	Ba6

Attacking the d-pawn. White is unable to avoid the creation of new weaknesses, since Black is threatening to invade with his rooks along the b-file. 12 Rhd1 is bad due to 12 . . . Rab8.

12 c4		

Now the d4 square is decisively weakened. Once it is occupied by the black bishop, the white knight will be completely helpless (one weakness), and Black can calmly set about winning the a2 pawn (the second weakness).

12 . . .		Rad8

123

With the threat of 13 . . . dxc4 14 Bxc6 Re6.

| 13 cxd5 | cxd5 |
| 14 Rhd1 | Re7! |

Played according to the principle "do not hurry!". Black transfers his bishop to d4 only when the white knight will come under its domination at g4. Before this there is no point in him lifting his control of c1. He now threatens . . . Rc7 followed by . . . Rc2.

15 Ng4	hxg3
16 hxg3	Bd4
17 Rac1	Rb7
18 Rc2	Kf7

Rubinstein does not forget about centralizing his king.

| 19 Nf2 | Rb2 |

Black exchanges one pair of rooks, to safeguard the advance of his king to the centre.

| 20 Rxb2 | Bxb2 |
| 21 Rd2 | |

21 d4 fails to 21 . . . Bc4.

21 . . .	Bd4
22 Nh3	Ke6
23 Rc2	Kd6
24 f5	

White tries to activate his knight, but Black finds a convincing rejoinder.

| 24 . . . | Rc8! |
| 25 Bd1 | |

25 Rd2 is decisively met by 25...Rc3.

25 . . .	Rxc2+
26 Bxc2	Ke5
27 g4	Be3!

Domination! The white knight has no moves. 28 Nf2 is bad due to 28 . . . Bxf2 29 Kxf2 Kf4.

| 28 Kf3 | Kd4 |

First d4 was occupied by Black's bishop, and now his king uses it as a spring-board for transferring to the Q-side.

| 29 Bb3 | Bb7?! |

Here Black could have ignored the principle "do not hurry", and won by 29 . . . Bxd3 30 Bxd5 Bf1 31 Nf2 Bxf2 32 Kxf2 Kxd5 33 Kxf1 Kc4.

| 30 Ke2 | Ba6 |
| 31 Bc2 | Bb5 |

Threatening the advance of the a-pawn to a3.

| 32 a4 | Bd7 |
| 33 Kf3 | Kc3! |

After a concrete evaluation of the position, Rubinstein goes for the exchange of bishops.

| 34 Kxe3 | d4+! |

An important link in Black's plan. If immediately 34 . . . Kxc2 35 Kd4, with counter-play.

| 35 Ke2 | |

35 Ke4 is hopeless due to 35 . . . Bc6+.

35 . . .	Kxc2
36 Nf4	Bxa4
37 Ne6	Bb3!
38 Nxd4+	Kb2
39 Nb5	a4
40 Ke3	a3
41 Nxa3	Kxa3

42 Kd4   Kb4
White resigns.

Michel—Tartakover

Marienbad, 1925

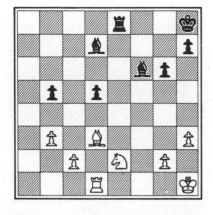

Black has two bishops, but there are no weaknesses in White's position and he has the more compact pawn formation. This suggests a draw as the likely result, but to achieve this White must play systematically, and in particular create a strong point for his knight.

1 Kg1   Kg7
2 Kf1

Why not the natural 2 Kf2? After all, 2 ... Bh4+ is not dangerous in view of the simple 3 Kg1, when White threatens both 4 Nd4 and 4 Ra1.

2 ...   Bc6
3 Ng1

The knight is transferred to f3, where it occupies an insecure position — it can be driven away by the g-pawn. A good strong point for the knight would be d4, and here it would have been quite sensible to play 3 c3 with a probable

draw. Perhaps White wanted to obtain winning chances and so he provoked the advance of the g-pawn, which weakens Black's control of f5? Although rather risky, such tactics are perfectly possible.

3 ...   g5!?

Black begins advancing his K-side pawns.

4 Nf3   h5
5 Be2?

An incomprehensible move. White as though taunts his opponent: "Do what you want, all the same the game will end in a draw". But such passive tactics are very dangerous against two bishops. After 5 Bf5 White would have had everything in order.

5 ...   Re4!
6 Bd3   Rf4!
7 Ke2   g4
8 hxg4   hxg4
9 Nh2   g3

Forced, unfortunately. Of course, Black would have preferred not to free the knight.

10 Nf3   d4
11 Rf1   b4

All White's pawns are fixed on white squares, and in the event of the knight being exchanged for the black-squared bishop, Black will win the ending.

12 Nd2!

Against passive play by White, Black could have strengthened his position by transferring his king to the centre, his rook to the h-file, and his bishop via e5 and f4 to e3.

12 ...   Rh4

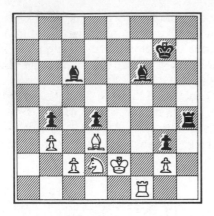

13 Nf3?

It transpires that White made his previous move without any intention of playing actively, and yet he had an interesting possibility to do so: 13 Rf3! The exchange sacrifice has to be accepted, since after 13 ... Be5 14 Rf5 Bb8 15 Nf3 Rh2 16 Kf1 White is out of danger. Thus there could have followed 13 ... Bxf3+ 14 Kxf3 Be5 15 Be4! Rf4+ (if *15 ... Kf6*, then all the same *16 Ke2*, and if *16 ... Bf4 17 Nf3*) 16 Ke2 Rf2+ 17 Kd3, when White sets up a strong and possibly impregnable defence. Having missed this possibility, White quickly succumbs to an exchange sacrifice, but this time by Black.

13 ...	Rh8
14 Kd2?	

This allows a decisive blow. True, after 14 Ke1 Rh5 followed by the transfer of the black king to the centre White would have had a difficult position.

14 ...	Rh2!
15 Nxh2	gxh2
16 Rh1	Be5
17 Bf1	Be4!

A picturesque position. White has only king moves left.

18 Kd1	Kf6
19 Kd2	Kg5
20 Kd1	Kg4
White resigns.	

Averbakh—Botvinnik

22nd USSR Championship
Moscow, 1955

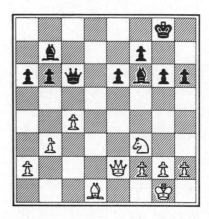

Here the pawn formation is not symmetric, and Black's K-side pawns can easily advance, cramping White's position. White has no way of opposing Black's plan. Play on the Q-side will merely create weaknesses, so he can only watch the unfolding of events.

1 ...	e5
2 Ne1	e4
3 Nc2	

Averbakh defends logically. By the advance of his e-pawn Black has weakened his control of d5. It is this square that the white knight aims for, since in the event of its exchange for Black's white-squared bishop, even with the loss of a pawn an ending is reached with opposite-coloured bishops and their characteristic drawing tendencies.

3 ...	Qd6
4 Ne3	Qd4

The queen has taken up an ideal position, and White will be forced to exchange it. It will then be possible for the black king to advance into the centre.

| 5 Nd5 | Bg5! |

Of course, neither now, nor subsequently is Black tempted into winning a pawn after the exchange on d5. It is interesting to follow how Botvinnik manoeuvres with his black-squared bishop.

6 g3	f5
7 h4	Bd8
8 Bc2	Kf7
9 Qd1	Qxd1+
10 Bxd1	Ke6
11 Nf4+	Kf6
12 Kf1	g5
13 hxg5	hxg5
14 Nd5+	Ke5
15 a4	Kd4

Black has achieved a great deal: his king occupies a dominating position in the centre, and his K-side pawns cramp White. But how is he to win the game? White's position is held together by the knight at d5. Undermining its strong point by . . . b5 is ineffective in view of the considerable reduction in the number of pawns. To Black's aid comes a pawn sacrifice enabling his king to break through on the Q-side, which first of all he blocks.

| 16 Be2 | Bc8 |
| 17 Kg2 | |

White should also have played his king across to the Q-side, but for this he would have had to anticipate Black's plan..

17 . . .	Bd7
18 Kf1	Be8
19 Kg1	Bf7

| 20 Kg2 | a5! |

Only now does Black reveal his idea. White was ready to meet 20 . . . b5, on which there could have followed 21 axb5 axb5 22 Nb4 with the threat of Nc6, and Black's plan caught him unawares. There is no way of preventing . . . f4.

21 Kf1	f4!
22 gxf4	gxf4
23 Nxf4	

Forced, in view of the threat of 23 . . . f3 24 Bd1 Bxd5 25 cxd5 Kc3.

23 . . .	Kc3
24 Bd1	Kd2
25 Bg4	Kc2

The black king has broken through to White's Q-side pawns. It is true that he now succeeds in exchanging bishops and winning the e4 pawn, after which there is little material left on the board. Black's rook's pawn nevertheless decides the game. It is interesting to follow the battle between bishop and knight, in which the bishop is clearly dominant.

26 Be6	Bxe6
27 Nxe6	Be7!
28 Nd4+	Kc3
29 Nf5	Bf8!
30 Ng3	Kxb3
31 Ke2	Kxa4
32 Nxe4	Kb3
33 Kd3	a4
34 Nd2+	Kb2
35 c5	b5!
36 c6	Bd6
37 Ne4	Bb8
38 Nc3	a3
39 f4	Bxf4

White resigns.

Englisch—Steinitz

London, 1883

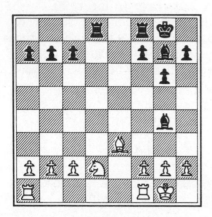

Black's bishops rake the board, and he threatens 1 ... Bxb2 2 Rab1 Bd4, winning a pawn. White is forced to weaken his position.

1 c3

There is hardly anything better. 1 Rab1 is very unpleasantly met by 1 ... Bf5.

1 ...	Rfe8
2 Nb3	b6!

Beginning a consistent plan to restrict the mobility of White's minor pieces.

3 h3	Be6
4 Rfd1	c5

Black's Q-side pawns neutralize the white bishop and deprive the knight of d4.

5 Bg5	f6
6 Bf4	Kf7

It is useful to centralize the king.

7 f3	g5

The black pawns squeeze White's position on both wings.

8 Rxd8	Rxd8
9 Be3	h6
10 Re1	f5
11 f4	Bf6
12 g3	

Having gained space on the K-side, Black switches play to the Q-side.

12 ...	a5!
13 Nc1	a4
14 a3	Bc4
15 Kf2	gxf4

A concrete solution to the problem. 15 ... Rd5 followed by ... b5—b4 was also very strong.

16 Bxf4	Bg5!

After the exchange of bishops the helplessness of the white knight becomes apparent. The invasion of the rook at d2 is now threatened.

17 Bxg5	hxg5
18 Ke3	Kf6
19 h4	

This loses quickly, but the position was already untenable.

19 ...	gxh4
20 gxh4	Re8+
21 Kf2	Rxe1
22 Kxe1	Ke5
23 Ne2	Bxe2
24 Kxe2	Kf4
25 c4	Kg4
26 Ke3	f4+!

After 26 ... Kxh4?? 27 Kf4 it is White who wins.

27 Ke4	f3
28 Ke3	Kg3

White resigns.

Blackburne—Lasker

London, 1892

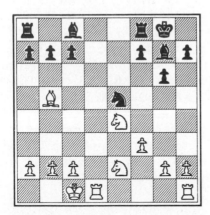

The pawn formation is as in the previous example. White has a weakness at e3, but for the moment it cannot be approached. Lasker begins a systematic restriction of the white pieces.

1 ...	a6
2 Bd3	f5!

Black does not exchange his knight for the white bishop, but erects a line of pawns in its path. When there are two bishops and a knight against two knights and a bishop, the exchange of the lone knight frequently eases the defender's task.

3 N4c3	Be6
4 Kb1	Rfd8
5 Nf4	Bf7
6 Be2	Nc6

Black takes control of d4, which in case of necessity can be occupied by either knight or bishop.

7 Rxd8+	Rxd8
8 Rd1	Re8!

In the given position the exchange of any pieces favours White, who is short of space. Now Black threatens 9 ... g5,

10 ... Bxc3 and 11 ... Rxe2.

9 Bf1	b5!
10 Nd3	Bd4
11 Ne2	Bb6
12 b3	Kg7!

There is no reason to hurry. The centralization of the king is always useful.

13 c3	Kf6
14 Kc2	Ne7

The time has come to aim for e3.

15 Nec1	Nd5
16 Kb2	

The white pieces are extremely cramped, and there is nothing to prevent Black from continuing to strengthen his position. But Lasker chooses the shortest path — a combinational one.

16 ...	b4!
17 Nxb4	

Forced. After 17 cxb4 Black wins by 17 ... Bd4+ 18 Ka3 Ne3.

17 ...	Ne3
18 Re1	Nc4+
19 Bxc4	Rxe1

Black has won the exchange. The rest is straightforward.

20 Bxa6	Rg1
21 g3	Rg2+
22 Ka3	Rxh2
23 Ne2	Rg2
24 Nc2	g5
25 Bd3	h5
26 Kb4	Bf2
27 a4	c5+
28 Kb5	Bxb3
29 a5	c4
30 Bxc4	Bxc2

31	a6	Bd1
32	Nd4	Bxd4
33	cxd4	Bxf3
34	d5	Be2
35	Bxe2	Rxe2
36	a7	Ra2

White resigns.

Kotov–Florian

Moscow, 1949

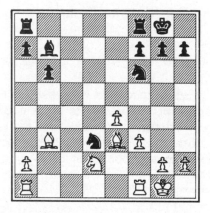

The position is an open one. White has the two bishops, but there are no weaknesses in Black's position, and his advanced knight at d3 seriously restricts the opponent's play. White must first deploy his pieces well, and then deal with the annoying knight. Which white piece stands worst? The knight at d2! Kotov finds an excellent post for it — at f5.

| 1 | Nc4! | Ba6?! |

Black does nothing to oppose White's plan. To be considered was 1 ... Rfd8. Black probably did not like the fact that after 2 Bg5 h6 3 Bxf6 gxf6 4 Ne3 his pawns would be broken up. But at the same time White would have been deprived of his splendid bishop, which would have allowed Black to put up a stubborn defence.

2	Nd6	Rad8
3	Nf5	Rd7
4	Bg5	Nh5
5	Rfd1	h6
6	Be3	Rfd8

White's pieces have taken up excellent posts. It is now time for him to turn his attention to the knight at d3. How can it be driven away? Kotov approaches this question differently: let the knight remain where it is, but dislodge its support — the pawn controlling c5, where the knight has an alternative and no less comfortable post.

| 7 | Ba4! | |

"Such moves are often more difficult to find than lengthy, forcing combinations. However, their effect is just as strong as that of many sacrifices" (Kotov).

| 7 ... | | b5 |

Practically forced, since on 7 ... Rc7 White has the highly unpleasant 8 Rd2 followed by Rad1.

8	Bb3	Nhf4
9	Rd2	Ne6
10	Rad1	b4
11	Bd5	

The knight is forced to retreat, and it has no strong point.

| 11 ... | | Ndc5 |
| 12 | Nd4! | |

Forcing further concessions by Black, in view of the threats of 13 Nc6 and 13 Nxe6 fxe6 14 Bxe6+.

12 ...		Nxd4
13	Rxd4	Rb8
14	Rb1	Nd3
15	Rb3	

This leads to gain of material.

15 ...   Rc7?

An oversight in a lost position.

16 Rbxd3   Bxd3
17 Bf4!

Black was hoping for 17 Rxd3, which is also good enough to win, but the move in the game forces the win of a piece.

Black resigns.

Kotov–Katyetov

Moscow, 1946

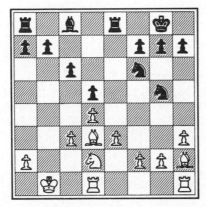

The white bishops are strong, especially the black-squared one which has no opponent. White's superior centre enables him to prepare f2–f3 and e3–e4 or c3–c4. But Black has no weaknesses, and the advance of the white pawns may lead to the creation of strong points for his knights. Kotov chooses a different plan, in which the leading role is played by the bishop at h2. White gives Black weaknesses on the Q-side, exploiting the half-open b-file, the black-squared bishop and the a-pawn, without undertaking any activity in the centre.

1 Kc2   Nge4

2 Nxe4   Nxe4
3 Rhf1   Bd7
4 Rb1   b6

The first weakening.

5 f3   Ng5
6 Kd2   f5

Black would like to play 6 ... Ne6 followed by ... c5, but on 6 ... Ne6 there follows 7 e4!

7 a4!   Nf7
8 a5   b5

The aim is achieved: a complex of black squares on the Q-side has been weakened. But how is White to exploit this weakening, since he has no knight? This mission is assigned to the white king. So that its journey should be a safe one, in accordance with the principle of two weaknesses White must strike a blow on the other side of the board, to create vulnerable points there and divert the enemy forces.

9 Rf2   h5
10 h4   Re7
11 Bf4   g6?!
12 g4!

Black's last move assisted White's plan to a considerable extent. There is now the threat of an attack on the black king.

12 ...   Kh7
13 gxh5   gxh5
14 Rg2   Rg8
15 Rxg8   Kxg8
16 Kc2   Kh7
17 Rg1

White controls all the key points of the position. Now it is the turn of his king.

17 ...   Re8

18 Kb3	Rc8
19 Kb4!	

The white king boldly advances. By a desperate pawn sacrifice Black tries to halt its advance, but he comes under attack by the white bishops.

19 ...	c5+
20 dxc5	a6
21 e4!	dxe4
22 fxe4	Rc6
23 exf5	Rf6
24 Rg6	Resigns.

Shereshevsky—Yuferov

Minsk, 1971

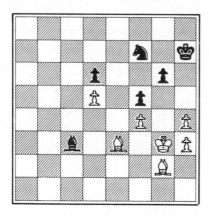

This game was played in the last round of the Sokolsky Memorial Tournament. Only a win would earn the author of these lines the title of USSR Master of Sport. Shortly before the time control, in a difficult position, Black was able to land a clever tactical blow, as a result of which the game went into an ending where a win for White seemed improbable. I thought that the position was a clear draw. Indeed, how can White improve it? The threat of h4—h5 is easily parried, and if the white king moves across to the Q-side, Black attacks the pawns at f4 or h4 with his bishop. But when analyzing the adjourned position, my trainer Isaak Boleslavsky found that White had serious winning chances. A brilliant analyst and a grandmaster of world class, Boleslavsky appreciated very well the potential of the two bishops. In spite of the fact that the play was essentially confined to one wing and that there was very little material, he found a latent plan of playing for a win. It cannot be ruled out that, had Black realized the danger facing him, he could have found a defence. But it was evident that my opponent also considered the position to be drawn.

1 Bf2

Defending against 1 ... Be1+.

1 ...	Kg7?!

Black sticks to waiting tactics, since it is not apparent how White can refute them. It would have been stronger to transfer the knight via d8 and b7 to c5.

2 Bf3	Kh6

Defending against h4—h5.

3 Be2

Now it is not easy for the black knight to break out, but so what? After all, Black has something akin to a fortress. But the two bishops seem able to break up any fortress, even the most solid.

3 ...	Bd2
4 Kf3	Kh7

Having improved his position, White begins to carry out his plan.

5 Bd4	Nh6
6 Bb5	Be1

7 h5!

The point of Boleslavsky's plan. By returning his extra pawn, White breaks up the opponent's pawns, after which the two bishops go to work.

7 ...	gxh5
8 Bc8!	h4
9 Bd7	Kg6
10 Be6	Nf7
11 Bb6	

Black is completely tied up. The only way to avoid loss of material is to move the king between f6 and g6, but then the white king makes a decisive attack on the d6 pawn. The move in the game merely hastens the end.

11 ...	Bb4
12 Bf2	Nd8
13 Bc8!	Bc3
14 Bxh4	

The rest is less difficult. By the march of his king to the Q-side White concludes the game.

14 ...	Bf6
15 Bf2	Nf7
.16 Ke2	Nh6
17 Be6	Kh5
18 Be1	Be7
19 Bc3	Kg6
20 Kd3	Bh4

21 Bb4	Be7
22 Kc4	Kh5
23 Bc3	Bh4
24 Kb5	Bg3
25 Bd2	Kh4
26 Kc6	Resigns.

Gheorghiu—Olafsson

Athens, 1969

White has a mobile pawn centre and two strong bishops, but the closed nature of the position and the existence of a strong point at c4 for the knight allow Black to put up a stubborn defence. White will naturally aim to open up the position and create scope for his bishops.

1 f3	Nd6
2 Bc3	

2 e4 would be a serious positional mistake due to 2 ... f5!, when Black gains control of the key squares in the centre.

2 ...	Bb7
3 g4!	

White carefully prepares an advance in the centre.

3 ...	f5?!

One of those cases where the threat is stronger than its execution. Black prevents e3—e4 by placing his K-side pawns on squares of the colour of his bishop, but in doing so he weakens catastrophically the dark squares in the centre. Preferable was 3 . . . f6, and if 4 e4, then 4 . . . Nc4 followed by . . . e5.

4 h3	Kf7
5 Kf2	Bd5
6 Bd3	Bb7
7 Be1!	Bd5
8 Kg2	Bc4?!

After this move the opening up of the position can be prevented only at the cost of loss of material. By 8 . . . g6 Black would have weakened his position still further, but he would have maintained material equality.

9 Bc2	Bd5
10 gxf5!	exf5
11 Bg3	Nc4
12 Kf2	Nd2

12 . . . g6 would have been answered by 13 e4, when the two connected passed pawns in the centre quickly decide matters.

| 13 Bxf5 | Bxf3 |
| 14 Bc8 | |

The Rumanian grandmaster wins a pawn, and with it the game.

14 . . .	Bd5
15 Ke2	Ne4
16 Be5	g5
17 Bxa6	Bc4+
18 Kf3	Nf6
19 Bxf6!	

The exchange of the black-squared bishop for the knight is the quickest way to win.

19 . . .	Kxf6
20 Bc8	Bd5+
21 e4	Bf7
22 e5+	Resigns.

Flohr—Botvinnik

Moscow, 1933

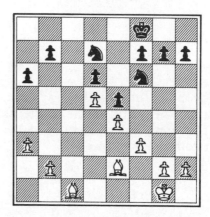

The pawn formation is symmetric and fairly blocked. A stubborn battle is in prospect, and it is difficult to predict whether or not White will succeed in advantageously opening up the game.

1 Kf2	Ke7
2 Be3	Kd8
3 Ke1	Kc7
4 Kd2	Nc5
5 b4	

The first clash takes place on the Q-side. White evicts the knight from c5, but in doing so weakens his control of a4.

| 5 . . . | Ncd7?! |

Seriously to be considered was 5 . . . Na4 followed by . . . b5, creating a strong point for the knights.

| | 6 g3?! |

This move could have been delayed. 6 a4 looks stronger, preventing Black from establishing a knight at a4. Besides, the advance of rooks' pawns is always unpleasant for the side battling against two bishops.

6 ...	Nb6
7 Kc2	Nbd7?!

Again the knight should have been played to a4.

8 a4!	Nb6
9 a5	

On the Q-side the black knights are now rather cramped.

9 ...	Nbd7
10 Bc1	Kd8
11 Bb2	Ne8
12 Kd2	Nc7
13 Ke3	Ke7
14 Bf1	Nb5
15 h4!	Nc7
16 Bh3	Ne8

White has regrouped his forces for an attack on the K-side, and Black has prepared a defence. There is no point in waiting any longer.

17 f4

Already threatening 18 Bxd7 and 19 fxe5.

17 ...	f6
18 Bf5	

It is essential to provoke weakenings.

18 ...	g6
19 Bh3	h6!

"The point of Black's entire defensive set-up. White's main threat is f4—f5 followed by fxg6 and g3—g4, creating a passed pawn on the h-file. Therefore on f4—f5 Black must be ready to reply

... g5. But without 19 ... h6 this cannot be played, since on 19 ... Ng7 20 f5 g5 21 hxg5 fxg5 there would follow 22 f6+, when White wins. Therefore Black adds an extra defence to g5, so that on 21 hxg5 he can recapture with the h-pawn" (Botvinnik).

20 Bc1	Ng7
21 fxe5	dxe5

Bad is 21 ... Nxe5 22 Bc8, or 21 ... fxe5 22 Kf3 h5 23 Bg5+.

22 Kf3	h5
23 Be3	Kd6
24 Bh6	Ne8
25 g4	hxg4+
26 Bxg4	Nc7
27 Be3	Nb5
28 Ke2	Nc7
29 Kd3!	

Zugzwang. 29 ... Nb5 is not possible, since after 30 Be6 Ke7 31 Bc5+ Nxc5 32 bxc5 Black's 32 ... Nd4 is without check.

29 ...	f5
30 exf5	gxf5
31 Bxf5	

The passed h-pawn and the chronic weakness of Black's Q-side promise White a quick win.

31 ...	Nxd5
32 Bd2	N7f6
33 Kc4	Kc6
34 Bg6	b5+
35 Kd3	Ne7
36 Be4+	Ned5

No better is 36 ... Nxe4 37 Kxe4 Kd6 38 h5 Ke6 39 h6 Kf6 40 h7 Kg7 41 Kxe5.

37 Bg5	Nh5
38 Bf3	Ng3

39 Bd2!

Suppressing the opponent's counter-play. After 39 h5? Nxh5! and ...Nxb4+ Black has drawing chances.

39 ...	Kd6
40 Bg4	

Aiming for c8.

40 ...	Nf6
41 Bc8	Kc6
42 Be1!	

Do not hurry!

42 ...	e4+
43 Kd4	Ngh5
44 Bf5	Kd6
45 Bd2	Resigns.

Lasker–Chigorin

Hastings, 1895

White's strong pawn centre and two bishops give him the advantage. After 1 f5 the position is opened to his advantage, and the bishops obtain scope. But the move made by Lasker on general grounds

1 Rag1?

allows Black to block the position.

1 ...	c4!
2 Bc2	f5!

In just two moves the character of the position has changed. The white bishops are deprived of their mobility, and the knights have acquired some convenient posts, in particular at d5.

3 Bc1	Rf7
4 Ba3	Rc6
5 Bc5	Ra6!

White provokes the advance of Black's Q-side pawns, hoping to open up the position on that part of the board. Indeed, after 5 ...a5 6 Ba4! b5 7 Bc2 followed by a2–a4 White activates his pieces. Instead of this, Chigorin himself provokes

6 a4

which restricts still further the opponent's white-squared bishop. 6 Ra1 or 6 a3 is unfavourable, since then 6...b6 7 Bb4 Nc6 leads to the exchange of the black-squared bishop.

6 ...	Nc6
7 Rb1	Rd7
8 Rgg1	Nge7
9 Rb2	Nd5
10 Kd2	Ra5
11 Rgb1	

White does not fear either 11 ... Rxc5, since the knight at d5 has no favourable retreat, or 11 ...Nxf4, on which there follows 12 Rxb7 (*12 Bb4* is also quite good).

11 ...	b6
12 Ba3	g6
13 Rb5	Ra6!

The correct solution to an exchanging

problem. After 13 ... Rxb5 14 axb5 the a-file is opened to Black's disadvantage. Chigorin realizes that the imprisonment of his rook at a6 is only temporary, since the white rook at b5 is badly placed and will be forced to leave its post.

14 Bc1	Nd8
15 Ra1	Nf7
16 Rbb1	Nd6?!

Black provokes f2—f3, missing the favourable opportunity of 16 ... g5! 17 fxg5 Nxg5 18 Bb2 Ne4+ 19 Bxe4 fxe4, leaving White with a bad bishop against a strong knight.

17 f3	Nf7?!

Black has obviously noticed his oversight, and attempts to repair the mistake, but White has time to regroup his forces and open up the position. Black should have played 17 ... Rf7, preventing a possible e3—e4.

18 Ra3!

Lasker does not prevent ... g5, rightly assuming that in an open game only he will have winning chances.

18 ...	g5?

It was not yet too late to return the knight to d6.

19 Ke2!

Much stronger than 19 fxg5 Nxg5 20 Ke2 Rg7, and if 21 e4 fxe4 22 fxe4 Nf6, when Black has everything in order.

19 ...	gxf4
20 e4!	Nf6
21 Bxf4!	

21 exf5 was also possible, but after 21 ... e5! 22 dxe5 Nxe5 23 Bxf4 Nd3 Black would acquire counter-play.

21 ...	Nh5
22 Be3?	

Now Black again blocks the position. After 22 Rg1+ Kf8 23 Bc1 followed by Ba3 White would have developed a very strong attack.

22 ...	f4!
23 Bf2	Ra5?

Black should have immediately blocked the centre by 23 ... e5!, since 24 Rg1+ Kf8 25 dxe5 Nxe5 26 Rg5 is refuted by 26 ... Rd2+!

24 Rg1+	Kf8
25 Raa1?	

White returns the compliment. After 25 e5! Black has a difficult game. In his notes to this game Chigorin writes: "If 25 e5 b5 26 Bxh7, then 26 ... Nxe5! 27 Rg8+ Kf7 28 dxe5 b4! 29 cxb4 Rxe5+ 30 Kf1 Nf6, and by returning the piece Black obtains a probably won position". These variations are interesting, but what is Black to do if instead of 26 Bxh7 White plays Raa1 or Rga1?

25 ...	e5!

Erecting a new defensive barrier.

26 Rab1	Ng7
27 Rb4	Rc7
28 Bb1	Ne6
29 Rd1?!	

Played according to the principle "do not hurry". But, as we know, such tactics should not be abused. After 29 Ba2! b5 (29 ... Nd6 30 dxe5 Rxe5 31 Bd4) 30 Rxb5 the position is opened up on the Q-side, and White retains the advantage. Lasker, evidently assuming that he will have time for Ba2, gives extra support to his centre, but underestimates his opponent's latent counterplay.

29 ...   Ned8!

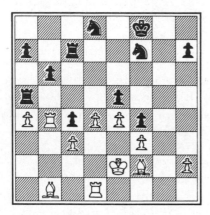

30 Rd2?

White fails to sense the danger. He had the possibility of opening the centre by 30 dxe5!, when, as shown by grandmaster Vasyukov in the book *Mikhail Chigorin*, after 30 ... Nc6 31 e6! (but not *31 Rb5 Rxb5 32 axb5 Ncxe5 33 Rd5 Ke7!*) 31 ... Nfe5 32 Bc2 Nd3 33 Rb5 the chances are with White. By the move played Lasker prepares Ba2, erroneously assuming that

30 ...   Nc6!

is impossible. This knight move would also have followed on 30 Ba2, but not 30 ... b5?, which is what Lasker was afraid of when defending a2 with his rook.

31 Rb5

A sad necessity. It transpires that 31 Rxc4 is met by 31 ... Nd6 (not *31 ... Nxd4+ 32 Rdxd4!*), when White loses the exchange.

31 ...   Rxa4
32 dxe5   Nfxe5

Black is a pawn up with a won position.

33 Bh4   Rg7
34 Kf2   Rg6
35 Rdd5   Ra1
36 Bd8   Nd3+
37 Bxd3

Otherwise ... Ncb4 is decisive.

37 ...   cxd3
38 Rxd3   Rag1
39 Rf5+   Kg8
40 Bg5   R6xg5
White resigns.

This game is a good illustration of the strengths and weaknesses of two bishops in a battle against knights. The frequent mistakes can be explained by the tension of a crucial encounter between two outstanding players upholding their creative conceptions.

In recent times opening theory has made great advances. To make an assessment of any opening without linking it to the middlegame is unthinkable, but more and more often the assessment of a particular variation depends on the prospects of the two sides in the endgame.

At the end of the seventies the Averbakh Variation of the King's Indian Defence began a period of rapid development. A considerable influence was made by some games in which an endgame was tested where White had the advantage of the two bishops. Now the opinion of the specialists is unanimous — White has a big advantage. Few players with Black are willing to defend this ending, and King's Indian players have had to find new paths, which has assisted the progress of theory. The initial game, in which Black encountered difficulties, was **Polugayevsky—Uhlmann**, Amsterdam, 1970.

1 c4	Nf6
2 Nc3	g6
3 e4	d6
4 d4	Bg7
5 Be2	0—0
6 Bg5	c5
7 d5	e6

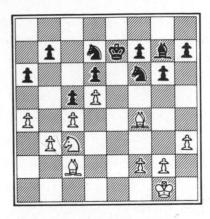

This line has now been discarded, Black preferring to try his luck with the sharp pawn sacrifice 7 . . . h6 8 Bf4 e6 9 dxe6 Bxe6 10 Bxd6 Re8.

8 Qd2!	exd5
9 exd5	Re8
10 Nf3	Bg4

Games in which Black did not develop his bishop here also confirmed White's advantage.

11 0—0	Nbd7
12 h3	Bxf3
13 Bxf3	a6
14 a4	Qe7

Knowing beforehand the further course of the game, one could suggest here the ugly 14 . . . a5, which despite all its drawbacks blocks the Q-side, and makes the coming ending more acceptable for Black.

15 Rae1	Qf8
16 Bd1	Rxe1
17 Rxe1	Re8
18 Rxe8	Qxe8
19 Bc2	Nb6
20 b3	Nbd7
21 Bf4	Qe7
22 Qe2!	Kf8
23 Qxe7+	Kxe7

(See next diagram)

We have an ending with a symmetric pawn formation and the advantage of two bishops for White. The plan for exploiting this advantage is now well known. The way for the bishops must be paved by the pawns.

24 a5!

As in previous positions, the envelopment of the opponent's position begins from the wings. Were Black himself to succeed in playing . . . a5, White's winning chances would be sharply reduced.

24 . . .	h5
25 Bd2	Ne8
26 g3	

White unhurriedly strengthens his position, preparing an offensive on both wings.

26 . . .	Bd4
27 Kg2	Ng7
28 f4	Nf5
29 Nd1	Nh6
30 Kf3	f5

Black's desire to block the K-side is perfectly understandable.

31 Bd3	Kd8
32 Ne3	Ke7
33 Nc2	Bb2
34 Ke3	Nf6
35 Ne1	

Black is deprived of the slightest counter-play, and Polugayevsky skilfully combines the strengthening of his position with action according to the principle "do not hurry".

35 ...	Bd4+
36 Kf3	Bb2
37 Ng2!	Nd7
38 Nh4	Kf6
39 Ke3	Nf7
40 Bc2	Ba1
41 Ke2	Bb2
42 Be1	Ba1

42 ... Nh6 was preferable, temporarily preventing the inevitable opening of the position.

43 g4!

The bishops break free, smashing all obstacles in their path.

43 ...	hxg4
44 hxg4	fxg4
45 Nxg6	Kg7
46 Nh4!	Kf8
47 Bf5	Nf6
48 Bc8	Nd8
49 Nf5	Nh5
50 Bd2	Bd4
51 Nxd4	Resigns.

In subsequent games Uhlmann successfully employed this variation, but this time from the white side.

Uhlmann—Gligoric

Hastings 1970/71

(See next diagram)

The position resembles the previous one, like two peas in a pod.

1 a5!	Ne8
2 Bd2	h5
3 Kf1	Bd4

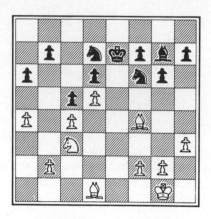

4 b3	Ng7
5 Bc2	Ne8
6 Ne2	Bb2
7 f3	Ng7
8 Kf2	Bf6
9 Nc3	Bd4+
10 Ke2	f5
11 f4!	

Events develop along familiar lines.

| 11 ... | Ne8 |
| 12 Bd3 | Bxc3 |

In many instances two knights battle against two bishops better than do a bishop and knight, by occupying strong points created in the opening up of the position. Therefore it is difficult to condemn Gligoric for this exchange.

13 Bxc3	Nef6
14 Be1	Kf7
15 Ke3	Ke7
16 Bc2	Kf7
17 b4!	

The start!

17 ...	cxb4
18 Bxb4	Nc5
19 Kd4	Nfd7

The black knights have become established at c5, so White sets about opening up the K-side.

| 20 | Bd1! | Ke7 |
| 21 | g4! | |

The continuation!

21	...	hxg4
22	hxg4	Kf6
23	Ke3	b6

Waiting tactics would not have saved Black. 23 ... Kf7 loses to 24 gxf5 gxf5 25 Bh5+ Ke7 26 Bg6 Kf6 27 Bh7! Ne4 28 Ba3, with the threat of Bb2+ (Maric).

| 24 | gxf5 | gxf5 |

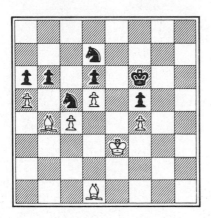

25 Bxc5!

The end! One advantage of the two bishops is that it is not difficult to exchange one for a knight in a favourable situation.

| 25 | ... | Nxc5 |

The other captures were no better. 25 ... bxc5 26 Ba4 Nb8 27 Kf3 Kg6 28 Kg3 Kh5 29 Be8+ Kh6 30 Kh4, or 25 ... dxc5 26 Ba4 Ke7 27 Bxd7 Kxd7 28 axb6, and wins.

26	axb6	a5
27	Bc2	Ke7
28	Kd2!	Kd8
29	Bxf5	Na4

30	b7	Kc7
31	Bc8	Nc5
32	f5	Ne4+
33	Kc2	Kb8
34	Kb3	Nd2+
35	Ka4	Nxc4
36	f6	Ne5
37	Kxa5	Resigns.

Uhlmann—Andersson

Skopje Olympiad, 1972

The black knights are badly placed, a factor which Uhlmann exploits to begin immediate play on the Q-side.

1	b4!	cxb4
2	Na4	Ngf6
3	Nb6!	

Preventing a black knight from reaching the strong point c5 via d7.

| 3 | ... | Bd8? |

A serious mistake. It was essential to ensure the knight access to c5 by 3 ... b3! 4 Bxb3 Ne4.

| 4 | Bxb4 | Bxb6 |
| 5 | axb6 | Kf8 |

5 ... Nd7 6 Ba4 Nef6 7 Bxd6 Nxb6 is more tenacious, although after

8 Bb3 White is close to a win.

6 c5!!

The white pawns finally "break the ground" for the bishops on the Q-side.

6 ... Nd7

As shown by Uhlmann, annotating this game in Volume 14 of *Chess Informator*, on 6 ... Nxd5 White would have won by 7 c6! Nxb6 8 cxb7 Nd7 9 Ba4, or 7 ... Nxb4 8 c7!, when the pawn queens.

7 c6!   bxc6
8 b7!   cxd5

No better is 8 ... c5 9 Ba4 Nb8 10 Ba5 Ke7 11 Bxe8 Kxe8 12 Bc7 (Uhlmann).

9 Ba4   Nb8

Or 9 ... Nef6 10 Bc3! Ke7 11 Bxf6+.

10 Bxe8   Kxe8
11 Bxd6   Resigns.

CHAPTER 12

THE 3–2 QUEEN-SIDE PAWN MAJORITY

In many openings — the Caro–Kann Defence, Nimzo–Indian Defence, Sicilian Defence, French Defence, Queen's Pawn Opening and others — a pawn formation of the type shown in the following diagram can arise.

The two sides' plans normally follow from the pawn formation: the four pawns advance against the three on the K-side, and the three against the two on the Q-side, although cases of a minority attack are also possible. Formerly it was considered more favourable to have the extra pawn on the Q-side, since it is easier to set up a passed pawn there. Modern-day practice has not confirmed this unshakeable principle of the Steinitz theory.

Everything depends on the specific features of the position.

In the majority of cases control of the only open d-file confers an advantage, irrespective of the number of pawns on the wings.

Yates—Alekhine

The Hague, 1921

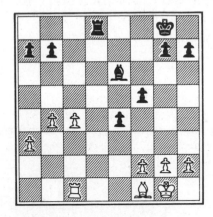

Here is what Alekhine had to say regarding this position:

"The ending in this game is noteworthy in the sense that White's celebrated Q-side pawn majority proves to be completely illusory. Regarding this I must remark that one of the most characteristic prejudices of modern theory is the widely-held opinion that such a pawn majority is important in itself — without any evaluation of the pawns which comprise this majority, or of the placing of the pieces. In the given position Black has the following compensation:

(1) Great freedom for his king in comparison with the white king.

(2) Dominating position of the rook on the only open file.

Used correctly, these two advantages should provide the basis for a win."

1 g3	Kf7
2 c5	Kf6

Were White able to exchange the bishops, he would gain a draw. After Black has played . . . f4, following a preparatory . . . g5, his bishop will play an important role in the attack on the white king.

3 Bc4	Bc8!
4 a4?!	

White should have hastened with his king to e1, although even in this case he has a difficult game.

4 ...	g5
5 b5?!	f4
6 Kf1	

Too late. By invading the second rank with his rook, Black creates an attack on the white king.

6 ...	Rd2!
7 gxf4	gxf4
8 Ke1	Rb2
9 Be2	

Defending against 9 ... Bg4. In the event of 9 Rd1 Bg4 10 Rd6+ Ke7 11 Rd4 Bf3 12 Bd5 Rb1+ 13 Kd2 e3+ 14 fxe3 Rd1+ 15 Kc3 Rxd4 16 Kxd4 Bxd5 17 Kxd5 fxe3 the black pawn queens.

9 ...	Ke5!
10 c6	bxc6
11 Rxc6	

After 11 bxc6 f3 12 Bd1 or 12 Bf1 Black wins by 12 ... e3.

11 ...	Be6
12 Bd1	Rb1
13 Rc5+	Kd4
14 Rc2	e3
15 fxe3+	fxe3
16 Rc6	Bg4
17 Rd6+	Ke5
18 h3	Bh5!
White resigns.	

There is no defence against ... e2.

Marshall—Capablanca

USA, 1909

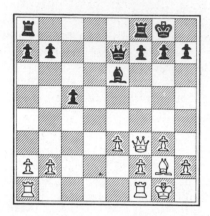

The diagram position is not an endgame one, but play soon goes into an ending where Black seizes control of the d-file, which in fact decides the outcome.

1 Rfc1?

White should have begun a battle for the d-file and advanced his K-side pawns. Therefore 1 Rfd1 or 1 e4 was quite appropriate, with a roughly equal game.

1 ...	Rab8
2 Qe4?	

With the threat of exchanging bishops after Bh3. Again White deviates from the correct path.

2 ...	Qc7!

A simple move, yet at the same time difficult to find. It is not so easy voluntarily to place the queen opposite an enemy rook. But this move is part of a plan to provoke White into opening up the game on the Q-side, which can only favour Black.

3 Rc3?

Of course, it is difficult to admit one's mistake. At the given moment there would not have been anything particularly terrible in store for White after the correct 3 Rd1! But after the move played his position begins to deteriorate, the reason being that Black seizes control of the d-file.

3	...	b5
4	a3	c4
5	Bf3	Rfd8
6	Rd1	Rxd1+
7	Bxd1	Rd8

"Black now dominates the entire board" (Lasker).

8	Bf3	g6
9	Qc6	Qe5

Capablanca does not object to an endgame, but only in a different version.

10	Qe4	Qxe4

Now the b5 pawn is not hanging.

11	Bxe4	Rd1+!

The white king must be decentralized.

12	Kg2	a5
13	Rc2	b4
14	axb4	axb4
15	Bf3	Rb1

White's game is hopeless.

16	Be2	b3
17	Rd2	

Not 17 Rc3 due to 17 ... Rxb2 18 Bxc4 Rc2.

17	...	Rc1!
18	Bd1	c3
19	bxc3	b2

Black wins a piece, and the realization of his advantage does not present any great difficulty.

20	Rxb2	Rxd1
21	Rc2	Bf5
22	Rb2	Rc1
23	Rb3	Be4+
24	Kh3	Rc2
25	f4	h5
26	g4	hxg4+
27	Kxg4	Rxh2
28	Rb4	f5+
29	Kg3	Re2
30	Rc4	Rxe3+
31	Kh4	Kg7
32	Rc7+	Kf6
33	Rd7	Bg2
34	Rd6+	Kg7

White resigns.

Didishko—Maryasin

Minsk, 1980

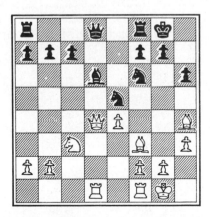

White's pieces are exerting unpleasant pressure on the opponent's position. Black chooses a forcing variation, involving a transition into an endgame.

1	...	g5
2	Bg3	Nxf3+
3	gxf3	Bxg3
4	fxg3	Qxd4+
5	Rxd4	Rfd8

6 Rfd1	Rxd4
7 Rxd4	Re8

In spite of the numerous exchanges, Black's position remains difficult.

8 Kf2	Re6

Played in the hope of obtaining counter-play on the Q-side. Passive defence by 8 ... Kf8 9 Nb5 c6 10 Nd6 Rd8 was also uninviting for Black.

9 f4	Rb6
10 Rd2	gxf4
11 gxf4	Rb4
12 Ke3	Kf8
13 b3!	

White is not in a hurry to take positive action, and first strengthens his position.

13 ...	c6
14 Rd8+	

This invasion by the white rook leads to gain of material, whereas 14 e5 would have afforded Black additional counter-chances after 14 ... Nh5.

14 ...	Ke7
15 Rh8	a5
16 Rxh6	a4
17 bxa4	Nd7
18 Rh5!	

Preventing 18 ... Nc5.

18 ...	Nb6
19 a5	Na4
20 Ne2	Rb2
21 Nd4	Rxa2
22 Nf5+	Kd7
23 Rh7	Ke6
24 Rh6+	Kd7

If 24 ... f6, then 25 e5!

25 Rf6	Ra3+

26 Kd4	Nb2

and **Black resigned**, without waiting for the obvious 27 Rxf7+.

Smyslov–Szabo

Hastings, 1954

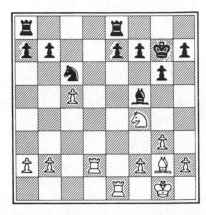

White's Q-side pawns have gained space, and all his pieces are ready to support their advance. In addition the d-file is under White's control.

1 a3	g5?

Black fails to battle for the only open file, and ends up in a very difficult position. "Black does not yet sense the danger, and chooses an ineffective method of defence. He should have tried 21 ... Rad8, so as after 22 Bxc6 bxc6 23 Rxd8 Rxd8 24 Rxe7 g5 to gain counter-play at the cost of a pawn" (Smyslov).

2 Nd5	Red8
3 Red1	Bg4
4 f3	Be6
5 b4	

White advances his pawns further, avoiding the positional trap 5 Nc7? Bb3!

5 ...	h6
6 Kf2	Rd7

146

Black resourcefully exploits White's last move (now 7 Nf4 is not possible, since the rook takes on d2 with check) and successfully contests the d-file, but it is too late.

7 Nc3	Rxd2+
8 Rxd2	Rd8
9 Rxd8	Nxd8
10 f4	gxf4
11 gxf4	Bb3

In order to stop the white pawns, Black tries to bring his king across and vacates e6 for it, but he runs into another misfortune.

12 Ke3	Kf6
13 b5	e5

The intended 13 . . . Ke6 would not have worked, since, as shown by Smyslov, White then has a pretty win: 14 c6 Kd6 15 b6!, while if 14 . . . bxc6 15 bxc6 Kd6 16 Nb5+.

14 Ne4+	Ke6
15 c6	

Exploiting the tactical features of the position.

15 . . .	exf4+
16 Kxf4	bxc6
17 Nc5+	Kd6
18 Nxb3	

White has won a piece, and the rest is not difficult.

18 . . .	cxb5
19 h4	Nc6
20 Bxc6	

The quickest way to win.

20 . . .	Kxc6
21 Kg4!	b4
22 axb4	Kb5
23 Nd4+	Resigns.

Bronstein—Rantanen

Tallinn, 1975

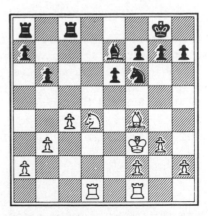

White has a spatial advantage, better placed pieces, a centralized king, and control of the only open d-file.

1 g4!

The doubling of rooks on the d-file suggests itself, but Bronstein, after a subtle evaluation of the position, begins advancing his K-side pawns. White's idea is not to carry out a minority attack, but to push back the opponent's firmly established pieces on the K-side and gain control of the invasion squares on the d-file, thereby creating the preconditions for a pawn advance on the Q-side, where White has a quantitative majority.

1 . . .	a6

Black vacates a7 for his rook, and hopes for possible counter-play by . . .b5.

2 g5	Ne8

White has chosen a very favourable moment for the advance of his g-pawn. Black's K-side is now paralyzed, and for the moment his extra pawn on this part of the board is of no significance at all.

3 a4	Ra7
4 h4	

147

In order to free his bishop from having to defend the g5 pawn.

4 ...   Rb7?!

Black persists in his desire to obtain counter-play on the Q-side, where he is clearly weaker. He should have gone totally onto the defensive. To be considered was 4 ... Kf8, transferring the king to e7 after ... Bc5, and thus covering White's invasion squares on the d-file.

5 Rd3

White sets about doubling rooks on the d-file.

5 ...   Rc5

With the threat of 6 ... e5.

6 Re1   Rd7?!

This allows White, by using tactical motifs, to seize control of the d-file.

7 Red1!   g6

If 7 ... e5   8 Nf5 Rxd3   9 Rxd3 Kf8, then 10 Be3 with an overwhelming positional advantage.

8 Ne2!

The d-file is completely in White's hands.

8 ...   Rxd3+
9 Rxd3   b5

This merely accelerates Black's inevitable defeat.

10 cxb5   axb5
11 Rd7   Kf8
12 a5   Rc6
13 Rb7   b4

14 Rb8!   Bc5
15 Ng3

After 16 Ne4 loss of material is inevitable, and so **Black resigned**.

Larsen—Spassky

Lugano Olympiad, 1968

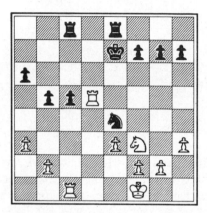

Black's position is preferable: his Q-side pawns have advanced, whereas White's on the K-side are not yet ready to move. The centralized black king has greater scope than White's. But White controls the important d-file. With his next move Spassky begins a battle for the only open file.

1 ...   Rcd8
2 Rh5?!

Larsen plans to attack with his pawn minority. After the correct 2 Rcd1 the position would have been approximately level.

2 ...   h6
3 b4   c4
4 a4?

(See next diagram)

It was this position that Larsen was aiming for. He should have exchanged

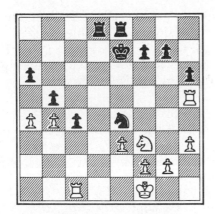

one pair of rooks by 4 Re5+ and blocked the d-file by Nd4.

| 4 ... | Kf6! |
| 5 axb5 | g6! |

A brilliant manoeuvre. Black sacrifices a K-side pawn, shutting the white rook out of play for a long time. He will then attack on the Q-side with superior forces.

| 6 Rxh6 | axb5 |
| 7 Nd4? | |

This loses. After 7 Rh4 Rd3 8 Rf4+ Kg7 9 Nd4 Nd2+ 10 Ke2 Nb3 11 Rd1 Nxd4+ 12 Rxd4 Rb3 Black would have obtained two connected passed pawns, but the outcome of the game would still have been unclear.

| 7 ... | Nd2+ |
| 8 Kg1 | |

The king cannot stand on the e-file due to 8 ... Rxd4.

8 ...	Nb3
9 Nxb3	cxb3
10 Rb1	

10 Rh4 is too late due to 10 ... b2 11 Rb1 Rd2 12 Rd4 Rxd4 13 exd4 Re2.

| 10 ... | Re4! |

Black again exploits the unfortunate position of the rook at h6.

| 11 g3 | |

Not 11 Rxb3 Kg7.

| 11 ... | Rxb4 |
| 12 Rh4 | |

The rook has finally broken free, but it is too late.

12 ...	Rxh4
13 gxh4	Rd3
14 Kg2	Ke5

White resigns.

Levenfish—Flohr

Moscow, 1936

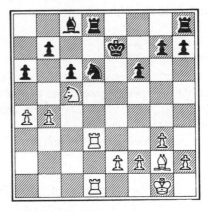

After White plays a4—a5 Black's Q-side pawns will be paralyzed. The open d-file is in White's possession, and his minor pieces are better placed than his opponent's.

1 Re3+	Kf7
2 Red3	Ke7
3 f4!	

It is time to set about realizing the

K-side pawn majority. At the same time a way for the king to the centre is opened.

3	...	Nc4
4	Kf2	Rxd3
5	Rxd3	Rd8
6	Rxd8	Kxd8

With the exchange of rooks the position has simplified, and White's advantage has become obvious.

7 Be4!

The knight has to be driven from its strong position at c4. To this aim the bishop is transferred to d3, at the same time provoking a fresh weakening of the opponent's K-side.

| 7 | ... | h6 |
| 8 | Bd3 | Nb6 |

After 8 ... Nb2 9 a5 the exchange on d3 is little consolation.

9 e4

Black has no way of opposing the advance of the white pawns in the centre.

9	...	Na8
10	Ke3	Nc7
11	a5	

11 ... b6 was threatened.

11	...	Ke7
12	Bc4	Kd6
13	Kd4	Ne8
14	e5+	fxe5
15	fxe5+	Ke7
16	h4!	

Good technique. According to the rules of the endgame the king and knight should have changed places. But Levenfish puts his opponent in *zugzwang*,

forcing him to weaken d6 for the decisive invasion by the white knight. 16 ... g5 fails to 17 hxg5 hxg5 18 Ne4, and after 18 ... g4 the white king goes across to f4 and wins the pawn.

| 16 | ... | Nc7 |
| 17 | Ne4 | Be6 |

Otherwise the white king breaks through at b6.

18	Nd6	Bxc4
19	Kxc4	Ke6
20	Nxb7	

Black resigned in view of the obvious 20 ... Kxe5 21 Kc5 Nd5 22 Nd8 Ke4 23 Nxc6 Nc3 24 Nb8 Kf3 25 Nxa6 Kxg3 26 Nc7.

In all the endings examined in this chapter, control of the d-file was a decisive factor. It is true that one comes across endings (usually with just one pair of rooks) where this does not give any real advantage, but these are merely exceptions which confirm the rule.

In conclusion we will examine an example in which the side with the initiative achieves success by play on the wing where the opponent has a pawn majority. Here, with rooks on the board, he has a bishop against a knight, which is in itself an advantage when there is play on both wings.

Kasparov—Vukic

European Team Championship
Skara, 1980

(See next diagram)

An experienced player will immediately be aware that the position has arisen from a Caro—Kann Defence. Black controls the d-file, but this is of no significance, since there are not, and cannot be,

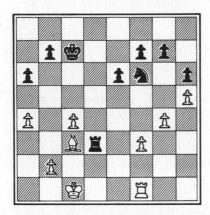

any invasion squares on it. On the other hand, Black's pawn structure on the K-side, where he has a numerical superiority, is completely fixed by the three white pawns, and the difference in strength between the white bishop and black knight is so great that the position can be assessed as won for White.

1 ...	Kc6
2 Kc2	Rd7
3 a5!	

In the plan of creating a passed pawn on the Q-side, this move seems illogical. But Kasparov makes a concrete assessment of the position, and finds a plan based on exploiting the difference in strength of the bishop and knight. This aim is best served by a minority attack

with f3—f4 and g4—g5. At the same time he suppresses Black's only chance of counter-play — the attempt to create a strong point for his knight at d5. Black was planning to carry out the counter-blow . . . b5 at a convenient moment, and to set up the defensive formation . . . Ne8, . . . f6 and . . . Nc7. Kasparov radically forestalls Black's plan of removing the c4 pawn's control of d5.

| 3 ... | Ne8 |
| 4 Re1! | |

White again denies his opponent counter-play. It is not at all in his interests to allow . . . f6.

| 4 ... | Rd6 |
| 5 f4! | Nf6? |

The decisive mistake in a difficult position. 5 . . . f6 was bad due to 6 Bb4, while on 5 . . . Kd7 there would have followed 6 g5. Now White takes play into a pawn ending.

| 6 Bxf6 | gxf6 |
| 7 Rd1 | Resigns. |

After the exchange of rooks Black has no satisfactory defence against g4—g5.

CHAPTER 13

COMPLEX ENDINGS

In the previous chapters we have been analyzing examples where one specific principle of endgame play was most clearly revealed. In the present chapter the reader will meet endings where the players make use of a variety of methods and principles. Along with examples of impeccable endgame technique, we will also be considering endings where there are highly instructive mistakes by both sides.

Factor—Rubinstein

Lodz, 1916

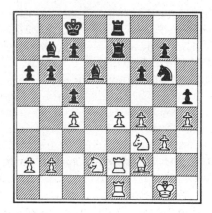

The position has arisen from the exchange variation of the Ruy Lopez. White has an extra pawn on the K-side, while Black has the two bishops. In such positions White usually plays on the K-side and in the centre, while Black creates counter-chances on the Q-side. But in the given position the pawn at e4 is not a strength, but a weakness, since it is securely fixed and under direct attack by the black pieces. In addition, White has a 'hole' at g4. On the other hand, Black has no prospect of active play on the Q-side, so Rubinstein decides

to block the Q-side and to begin play on the opposite wing. In the first instance Black needs his knight at g4, but it can be transferred via h8—f7—h6 only when White does not have the possibility of playing e4—e5.

| 1 ... | a5 |
| 2 a4 | |

There was no necessity for this.

2 ...	Kd7
3 Kf1	Bc6
4 b3	Kc8

Black is in no hurry to take positive action. By manoeuvring with his king he dulls White's vigilance, and begins gradually strengthening his position. He must first safeguard the retreat of his bishop from d6 in the event of e4—e5, and this can only be achieved by ... c6. This means that the white-squared bishop must make way for the pawn. Black's ideal set-up would be: knight at g4 and bishop at g6 or h7, but for the moment this is not a reality.

5 Re3	Bd7
6 Kg2	c6
7 Nb1	Bc7
8 Nc3	Nh8!

The right moment! White cannot play 9 e5, since after 9 ... fxe5 10 fxe5 Nf7 he loses a pawn. Black has taken all the precautionary measures well in advance.

9 Rd3	Nf7
10 Red1	Bg4
11 R1d2	Nh6
12 Bg1	Bb8!

Suppressing the opponent's counter-play. Black prepares the transfer of his bishop to g6 via e6 and f7, and fore-stalls the possibility of Nd5, which could have followed on 12 ... Be6.

13	Bf2	Be6
14	Rd1	Bf7
15	Bg1	Bg6
16	Nd2	Nf7

Do not hurry! Black has planned to play his knight to g4 and his bishop to h7, followed by ... g5, but he decides to manoeuvre a little more, so as to hinder his opponent's orientation.

17	Re1	Bh7
18	Kf3	Nh6
19	Bf2	Ng4
20	Bg1	g5!

The start of the attack. The tempo of the play changes sharply, as Black is transformed and becomes very active.

21	Re2	gxf4
22	gxf4	Rg8
23	Re1	Reg7
24	Ne2	

Defending against 24 ... Nh6 followed by ... Rg4.

24 ...		f5!

A fresh blow, which decides the game. White cannot play 25 e5 due to 25 ... Bxe5 26 fxe5 Nxe5+ 27 Ke3 f4+.

25	exf5	Bxf5
26	Ne4	Bxe4+
27	Kxe4	Re8+
28	Kf3	Rf7

The f4 pawn cannot be defended.

29	Rdd1	Ref8
30	Rf1	Bxf4

31	Nxf4	Rxf4+
32	Ke2	Rxf1
33	Rxf1	Rxf1
34	Kxf1	Nh6,

and within a few moves White resigned.

Najdorf—Stahlberg

Candidates Tournament
Zurich, 1953

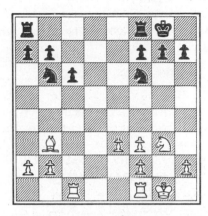

The position is roughly level. The advance of White's K-side pawns is hindered by his doubled f-pawns, while on the Q-side it is not easy for Black to advance his pawns. White has a good bishop, but the black knights may prove stronger due to the presence of the doubled pawns. A prolonged struggle for the accumulation of small advantages is in prospect.

1	Nf5	Rad8
2	Rfd1	Nc8?!

Black defends d6, voluntarily withdrawing his knight to a passive position. A more natural plan would be 2 ... Nbd5 or 2 ... Nfd5 followed by ... g6 and the advance of the king to e7. Had White wanted to drive the knight from its centralized position by e3–e4, this would have left him with a weakness — at f4.

3 Kf1	Rfe8
4 Ke2	Kf8
5 Rxd8	Rxd8
6 Rg1	Ne8?

Playing with fire. All Black's pieces are now on the back rank. Not wishing to weaken his position, Stahlberg cedes his opponent more and more space. After the correct 6 ... g6 the position would have remained level.

7 Rg4

The rook advances for the decisive offensive.

7 ...   Ne7?

An incorrect approach to the exchanging problem. It is easier to defend with two knights than with one, which in addition is badly placed at e8. Even here 7 ... g6 was not yet too late.

8 Nxe7	Kxe7
9 Re4+	Kf8
10 Ra4	a6
11 Rf4	f6?

This finally ruins Black's game. After 11 ... Nf6 things would not yet have been hopeless, although after 12 Rf5 followed by the advance of the f- and e-pawns White would have retained a marked advantage. Now the white squares on Black's K-side are decisively weakened.

12 Rh4	h6
13 Rh5!	

Paralyzing the opponent's pawns along the rank.

13 ...	Nc7
14 f4	Ke7
15 Rc5	Rd6
16 Rc1?!	

A slip, which could have had serious consequences. 16 f5 was correct.

16 ...   b6?

A mistake in reply. The correct 16 ... f5! would have improved things considerably for Black.

17 f5!	c5
18 f4	Rc6

A belated attempt at activity on the Q-side.

19 a4	b5
20 Bc2!	

So as to answer 20 ... c4 with 21 Be4 Rb6 22 b3!

20 ...	Ne8
21 Be4	Rc7
22 Bd5	c4
23 e4	Nd6
24 axb5	axb5
25 Ke3	Ra7
26 Rg1	Kf8
27 Kd4	

White centralizes his king, not allowing the opponent's into the centre.

27 ...	Rc7
28 Rc1!	

Preventing the slightest attempt at counter-play. On the natural 28 Ra1 there could have followed 28 ... b4! 29 Ra8+ Ke7 30 Rg8 c3 31 Rxg7+ (*31 bxc3 Nb5+*) 31 ... Kd8 32 Rxc7 cxb2!

28 ...	Nb7
29 Ra1	Nc5
30 Ra8+	Ke7
31 e5!	

White finds the quickest way to win,

having accurately worked out all the variations.

| 31 ... | Nb3+ |
| 32 Kc3 | Nc1 |

On 32 ... Rc5 there could have followed 33 Ra7+ Kf8 34 Rf7+ Ke8 35 Be6 fxe5 36 Rxg7 Nd4 37 Kb4 Nxe6 38 fxe6, with a won rook ending.

33 Rg8	Ne2+
34 Kd2	Nxf4
35 Rxg7+	Kd8
36 exf6!	Rd7
37 Rxd7+	Kxd7
38 Bc6+!	Resigns.

A splendid creative achievement by the Argentinian grandmaster!

Lasker—Pillsbury

Paris, 1900

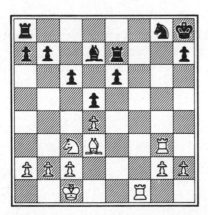

Black has weak pawns at e6 and h7, and his king is badly placed. Lasker carries out an interesting knight manoeuvre, to attack both Black's weaknesses.

1 Nb1

A pretty way of realizing his advantage, but evidently not the strongest. Black's defence would have been difficult after the natural 1 Rg5!, e.g. 1 ... Rae8 (*1 ... Rg7 2 Rxg7 Kxg7 3 Bxh7*) 2 Rh5 h6 3 Ne2 Kg7 4 Nf4 Rf8 5 Rf3, with an overwhelming advantage.

| 1 ... | Rae8 |
| 2 Nd2 | e5 |

Practically forced. If Black allows the white knight to occupy e5, his position becomes hopeless.

| 3 dxe5 | Rxe5 |
| 4 Nf3 | Re3? |

This loses a pawn. After 4 ... R5e7 5 Ng5 Be6 White has the advantage, but no forced win is apparent (*6 Re1 Bd7*).

5 Ng5	Rxg3
6 hxg3	h6
7 Nf7+	Kg7
8 Nd6	Re7
9 Nxb7	

White has won a pawn. The realization of the advantage should not be too difficult due to Black's numerous weaknesses on the Q-side.

9 ...	Nf6
10 Nc5	Bg4
11 Rf4!	

White defends against 11 ... Nh5, and switches his rook for an attack on the opponent's Q-side.

11 ...	Bc8
12 Ra4	Ng4
13 Ba6?!	

The natural 13 Kd2! was stronger, the move demanding a rather lengthy, although not difficult, calculation of variations: 13 ... Ne3 14 Rb4 Nxg2 15 Rb8 Bh3 (*15 ... Bg4 16 Rb7 Kf6 17 Rxe7 Kxe7 18 Bf1 Bf3 19 Be2*) 16 Rb7 Kf6 17 Rxe7 Kxe7 18 Ke2 Kd6 19 Nb7+! (*19 b4 d4!*) 19 ... Kc7 20 Na5 c5 21 Kf2 Kb6 22 b4!, and wins. The move in the game allows Black to evict the white rook from the Q-side and to obtain some counter-play.

| 13 ... | Bf5 |
| 14 Rf4 | |

Not 14 Bb7 Re2.

14 ...	Ne3
15 c3	Kg6
16 Rf2	Be4!

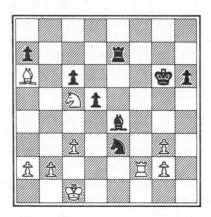

The black pieces have come markedly to life.

17 b3?!

A difficult move to find, and one which was unanimously praised by all the commentators. White plans to exchange the K-side pawns (two for one!), so as to then attack Black's weakened Q-side with all his forces. 17 b3 is an important step in White's plan, preparing the transfer of his king via b2 to the Q-side, and to some extent follows the principle of "do not hurry". But in the given position more energetic measures were required. 17 Bb7! was correct,

when Black would appear to have nothing better than 17 ... Rc7. Then by 18 a4 White could have forced Black onto the defensive after 18 ... Nc4.

| 17 ... | Bxg2 |
| 18 Bd3+ | Kg5?! |

Actively played. The cool 18 ... Kg7 was also perfectly possible, when it is not altogether clear how White is to demonstrate the correctness of his plan.

19 Rf8

Lasker begins an attack on the h6 pawn.

19 ...	Kg4
20 Rg8+	Kf3
21 Rg6	Ng4
22 Bf5	h5
23 Rg5	Re1+

On 23 ... Re2 White has the unpleasant 24 Bg6!

| 24 Kb2 | Rh1? |

This defensive move is the decisive mistake. 24 ... Nf2! was correct, when the threats of 25 ... Nd1+ and 25 ... Ne4 give Black excellent counterplay, e.g. 25 Bg6 Nd1+ 26 Ka3 (*26 Kc2 Ne3+*) 26 ... Nxc3 27 Bxh5+ Ke3, and Black at least equalizes.

| 25 Bg6! | Kxg3 |
| 26 Bxh5 | |

White has achieved his aim. With the exchange of bishop for knight Black is deprived of any counter-play.

26 ...	Bh3
27 Bxg4	Bxg4
28 Rg6	Rh2+
29 Ka3	Rc2!
30 Nd3!	

Lasker avoids a clever trap: 30 Rxc6? Rxc3! 31 Ne4+ dxe4 32 Rxc3+ Kf2, with a draw.

30 ...	Kh4

There is nothing better. 31 Ne5 was threatened.

31 Ne5	Bf5
32 Rxc6	

White is a pawn up with a positional advantage.

32 ...	Kg3
33 Rc5	Rd2
34 Nc6	Kf4
35 Nb4	d4
36 cxd4	Rxd4
37 Ra5	Rd7
38 Nc6	

38 Nd5+ would have immediately concluded the game.

38 ...	Be4
39 Nxa7	Rd2
40 Nb5	Rd5
41 Kb4	Bd3
42 Nc7	Rxa5
43 Kxa5	Ke5
44 Kb4	Kd6
45 Nb5+	Kc6
46 a4	Kb6
47 Na3	Be2
48 Nc4+	Ka6
49 Kc3	Bd1
50 Nb2	Bh5
51 b4	Be8
52 Kb3	Bc6
53 Kc4	Bd7
54 Kc5	Bg4
55 Nc4	Bd1
56 b5+	Ka7
57 a5	Bf3
58 Ne5	Bg2
59 Nc6+	Ka8
60 Kb6	Bh3

61 Nb4	Bg2
62 Na6	Bf3
63 Nc7+	Kb8
64 a6	Resigns.

Fischer–Reshevsky

USA, 1963

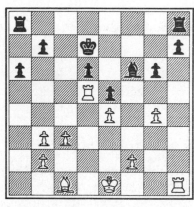

White has a clearly superior bishop, a spatial advantage, and a better pawn formation, while Black's d-pawn is very weak. With his next move Fischer fixes the h7 pawn, giving Black a further weakness.

1 g5!	Be7
2 Ke2	

White improves the positions of all his pieces.

2 ...	Raf8
3 Be3	Rc8
4 b4	

White's pressure grows with every move. He threatens both b4–b5, and also the simple strengthening of his position by 4 Kd3 followed by c3–c4. Black therefore decides to upset his opponent's plans, even at a cost of weakening his own position.

4 ...   b5

At the sides of the board Black has weak backward pawns, while 'adorning' the centre is his d6 pawn. But three weaknesses are too many, and later Fischer allows Black to rid himself of one, while attacking in turn the weaknesses which are far from each other — the pawns at h7 and a6.

5 Rdd1!

Instantly changing the target of attack.

5 ...   Ke6
6 Ra1   Rc6
7 Rh3!   Bf8
8 Rah1   Rc7
9 Rh4!

Zugzwang! White provokes ... d5. Rook moves along the seventh rank are not possible due to Ra1, while after 9 ... Rc4 19 f3 an analogous situation arises a move later.

9 ...   d5

This leads to a decisive opening of lines.

10 Ra1!

The final finesse. The rook must be lured onto the sixth rank, diverting it from the h7 pawn.

10 ...   Rc6
11 exd5+   Kxd5
12 Rd1+   Ke6
13 Rd8

If Black's rook were at c7, he would have 13 ... Bg7.

13 ...   Kf5
14 Ra8   Re6
15 Rh3!

Forcing the win of a pawn by the threat of 16 Rf3+. Black is not helped by 15 ... Kg4 16 Rg3+ Kh5 17 Rf3 Bg7 18 Rxh8 Bxh8 19 Rf8 Bg7 20 Rf7.

15 ...   Bg7
16 Rxh8   Bxh8
17 Rxh7   Re8
18 Rf7+

Winning control of e4.

18 ...   Kg4
19 f3+   Kg3
20 Kd3

Consistent, but even stronger was 20 Kf1 with mating threats.

20 ...   e4+
21 fxe4   Rd8+
22 Bd4   Kg4
23 Rf1!   Be5
24 Ke3   Bc7
25 Rg1+   Kh4
26 Kf3   Rd7
27 e5   Rf7+
28 Ke4   Rf5
29 e6   Bd8
30 Bf6!   Bxf6
31 gxf6   Rxf6
32 Kd5   Rf2
33 Re1   Resigns.

Smyslov–Simagin

19th USSR Championship
Moscow, 1951

(See next diagram)

The white pieces are more actively placed, but the win is still far off. It is interesting to follow how, by moves which are simple but are often difficult to find, Smyslov consolidates and then increases his advantage.

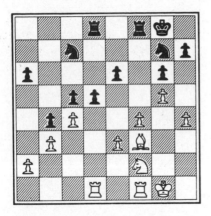

1 Ng4!

The knight takes control of the weak e5 and f6 squares in Black's position. The threat is 2 Nf6+, winning the d5 pawn.

1 ...   Nf5
2 Kf2!

Very strong. White renews the threat of winning the central pawn. It transpires that 2 ... Nxh4 is bad due to 3 Nf6+ followed by Rh1.

2 ...   dxc4

2 ...d4 is no better due to 3 e4 followed by h4—h5. White's pressure grows with every move.

3 bxc4   a5

Black tries to create counter-play by advancing his pawns on the Q-side, where he has a numerical superiority.

4 Nf6+   Kg7
5 Nd7!

Smyslov rejects the possibility of a K-side attack, preferring to exchange his h-pawn for the black c-pawn. He reckons that in this case he will gain a number of other advantages: he will have control of

the only open file, his king and knight will be much more active, and, very important, Black will be deprived of the slightest chance of counter-play.

5 ...   Rf7

On 5 ... Rfe8 White has the unpleasant 6 h5.

6 Nxc5   Rxd1
7 Rxd1   Nxh4
8 Nd7!

An excellent move. White does not prevent the exchange of knight for bishop, since it is much more important to forestall the possible counter ... e5.

8 ...   Nxf3

Otherwise White will withdraw his bishop.

9 Kxf3

The position has clarified, and White's advantage has grown markedly.

9 ...   Nd5!?

Clever, but insufficient.

10 Nc5!?

White ignores the opponent's offer to go into a rook ending. After 10 cxd5 Rxd7 11 d6 Kf7 followed by 12 ...Rd8 and 13 ...Rb8 Black would gain counter-play.

10 ...   Nc7
11 Ke4!

Again preventing ... e5.

11 ...   h6

There is no other possibility of counter-play.

12	Rd6	hxg5
13	fxg5	Kf8
14	Rc6!	

Smyslov again avoids going into a rook ending, but continues to play for a squeeze on his opponent's position.

14	...	Ke8
15	Ke5!	

By his previous move White tied down the enemy rook, and now comes the decisive invasion of the white king.

15	...	Kd8
16	Rb6!	

Each move by White deserves an exclamation mark, although they seem simple. The immediate 16 Kd6 would have been premature due to 16 ... Ne8+ 17 Kxe6 Re7+, but now c6 is vacated for the white king.

16	...	Kc8
17	Kd6	Rf2
18	Kc6!	

Do not hurry! 18 Rb7 would not have worked due to 18 ... Na6!

18	...	Rc2
19	Rb7	Ne8
20	Ra7	Kb8
21	Re7	Resigns.

Smyslov–Matanovic

Monte Carlo, 1967

(See next diagram)

At first sight the position seems roughly level. Black is threatening ... Rb8, and 1 Bc6 is met by 1 ... Rd8 with a probable draw. But Smyslov again succeeds in demonstrating that in

the endgame a rook and bishop are normally stronger than a rook and knight. By a veiled manoeuvre White ensures the invasion of his rook at d7, after which his advantage assumes real proportions.

1	Rc1!	Kd7
2	Bc6+	Kc8

After 2 ... Kd6 or 2 ... Ke7 White has the very unpleasant 3 Ba4.

| 3 | Ra1! | |

Following the principle "do not hurry", White forces the black pawn to move to a6, where it restricts the knight still further, and only then carries out the invasion.

3	...	a6
4	Rd1!	

The aim is achieved. Black is unable to prevent 5 Rd7, since 4 ... Rd8 loses to 5 Bb7+.

4	...	Rf8
5	Rd7	Kb8
6	e5	Ka7!

By this clever manoeuvre Black frees his king. Now 7 Rxc7+ allows 7 ... Kb6, equalizing.

7 Be4	Kb6

Now it is time for the white king to come into play. Of course, not 8 Bxh7 Nd5.

8 Kg2	h6
9 Kg3	f6

Otherwise the advance of the white king to h5 will decide the game.

10 exf6	Rxf6
11 Kg4	Rf8
12 Rh7	Rd8
13 Rxh6	Kb5
14 Rh7	Nd5
15 Rb7+	Kc6
16 Rg7	

Before exchanging his b-pawn for the g-pawn, White, operating according to the principle "do not hurry", improves the position of his rook.

16 ...	Kb5
17 Kxg5	Kxb4
18 h4	

Both sides have obtained an outside passed pawn, and in such cases a bishop is much stronger than a knight.

18 ...	Nxe3
19 h5	Rf8
20 h6	Nf5
21 Rb7+	Kc5
22 h7	Nd6
23 Rc7+	Kd4
24 Bg6!	

Domination.

24 ...	Nf5
25 Rf7	Resigns.

Geller—Shcherbakov

22nd USSR Championship
Moscow, 1955

As a rule, in the endgame a queen and knight are stronger than a queen and bishop. This is the case when the knight occupies a strong point of the opposite colour to the bishop and in the immediate vicinity of the enemy king, and creates the threat of a mating attack. The present ending is an exception. The only square that can become a strong point for the black knight is f5 after the preparatory . . . h5. But as soon as the knight tries to go to f5 via e7, White begins an attack with his queen and bishop on the weak c-pawn. Therefore Black is forced to stick to passive, waiting tactics, whereas White has the possibility of combining pressure on the weak black a- and c-pawns with play for an attack on the opponent's king.

1 ...	Qc6
2 Qc2	Qb6

Black defends against the threat of 3 Qc4 followed by 4 Ba7.

3 Be5	Qc6
4 Bb2	Qd6
5 Qc4	Kf8
6 h4	

A useful prophylactic move. White creates the potential threat of h4—h5, and vacates h2 for his king.

6 ...	h5
7 Qe4	Kf7
8 Ba3	Nb4
9 Qc4+	Kf8
10 Bc1!	

Geller transfers the bishop onto the c1—h6 diagonal, where it has many excellent posts.

10 ...	Qd1+?

Black fails to withstand the tension. He should have returned his knight to d5, controlling e3.

11 Kh2	Qd5

A sad necessity. If 11 ... Qd6, then 12 Bf4 Qc6 13 Be3.

12 Qxd5!	

The simplest way of realizing the advantage. In the resulting minor piece ending the bishop is much stronger than the knight. White's king is closer to the centre than Black's, and White's K-side pawn majority allows him to create an outside passed pawn.

12 ...	Nxd5
13 Ba3!	

The black knight must be diverted away from the centre, to ensure the approach of the white king.

13 ...	Nb4
14 Kg2	Ke7
15 Kf3	a5
16 Ke4	Kd6
17 f3	

Geller sets about creating a passed pawn on the K-side.

17 ...	Nd5
18 g4	hxg4
19 fxg4	Nc3+
20 Kf4	Nb5

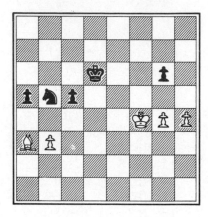

21 h5!

The most energetic and convincing way of realizing the advantage.

21 ...	Nd4
22 h6	Ne6+
23 Ke4	Ng5+
24 Kd3	Ke5
25 Bxc5	

25 Bc1 would also have won.

25 ...	Nh7
26 Be3	g5

Black resigned, without waiting for the obvious 27 Bd2.

Spassky—Karpov

Montreal, 1979

(See next diagram)

Black's pieces are excellently placed, and he has a more promising pawn formation than his opponent. He now has to

162

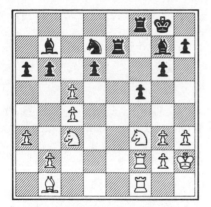

solve an exchanging problem.

1 ...	bxc5!

"The strongest of the three possible continuations. After the plausible 1 ... dxc5 White develops pressure on the d-file. Then the exchange on c3 would not be dangerous for him, and he could even go after the pawn at b6. 1 ... Nxc5 looks sensible, since ... Bxc3 is then a strong threat, but after 2 Nd5 Bxd5 3 cxd5 I thought it doubtful that Black would be able to win." (Karpov).

2 Rd1

If 2 Nd5, then 2 ... Bxd5 3 cxd5 Rb8 with a big and possibly decisive positional advantage.

2 ...	Bxc3!
3 bxc3	Rf6!
4 Rfd2	

"How should Black proceed further? After the apparently natural 4 ... Bxf3 5 gxf3 Ree6 the white king moves across to f2, and then White himself can prepare an invasion on the b-file. The immediate 4 ... Ne5 is also possible, but then 5 Ng1 Rd7 6 Ne2, and all the time the capture on c4 is not possible because of the pin Ba2. After looking deeply into the position, I came

to the conclusion that it was necessary to activate my rook straight away." (Karpov).

4 ...	Re3!
5 Ng1	

As shown by the World Champion, after 5 Rxd6 Rxd6 6 Rxd6 Bxf3 7 gxf3 Ne5 8 f4 Nf3+ 9 Kg2 Rxc3 10 Rd5 Nd4 11 Rxc5 Rb3 12 Rd5 Rb2+ Black wins easily.

5 ...	Kf7!

This pawn sacrifice is part of Black's plan.

6 Rxd6	Rxd6
7 Rxd6	Ke7
8 Rd3	Re1

White's game is lost.

9 Ba2

After 9 Bc2 Black wins by 9 ... Ne5 and 10 ... Nxc4.

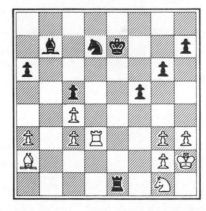

9 ...	Rc1!

"Perhaps one of the most exact moves in the game. So as to use the full power of the black bishop, the rook heads for c2." (Karpov). The World Champion's entire play is imbued with a striving for complete harmony, whereas the white pieces scattered around the board are lacking in co-ordination.

10	Nf3	Bxf3!
11	Rxf3	Ne5
12	Re3	Kf6
13	Bb3	a5

White is in complete *zugzwang*.

14	Ba4	Nxc4
15	Re8	Rxc3
16	Rc8	Ne3
17	Bb5	c4

17 ... Rc2 18 Bc6 Nf1+ 19 Kg1 Nxg3 and 20 ... f4 was more exact.

18	Kg1	Rc2
19	Bc6	c3
20	Bf3	g5
21	g4	f4

White resigns.

Botvinnik—Konstantinopolsky

Sverdlovsk, 1943

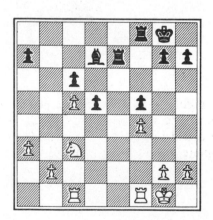

White's knight is significantly stronger than the enemy bishop, and his pawn formation is more compact. He plans active play on the Q-side (the pawn break *b4—b5* after suitable preparation), whereas Black must try to activate his bishop. Therefore White's main task is to deprive Black of counter-play and to blockade the d5 pawn.

1 Rfe1

It is to White's advantage to exchange rooks, since in the minor piece ending his king will be much more active than the opponent's.

1 ...   Rfe8

After 1 ... Rxe1+ 2 Rxe1 d4 3 Ne2 Black could have lost a pawn, but gained some counter-play, after 3 ... Rb8 4 b4 d3 5 Nc3 a5 6 bxa5 Rb3 7 Nb1! If instead 4 Nxd4, then after 4 ... Rxb2 5 Re7 Rb7 the advantage is with White, but nothing decisive is apparent. After missing this possibility which, though rather risky, was the most unpleasant for White, Black gradually ends up in a bind.

2	Rxe7	Rxe7
3	Kf2	Kf7
4	Rd1!	

It is time to take the d-pawn under control. 4 Re1? would have been a mistake due to 4 ... Rxe1 5 Kxe1 d4! followed by the centralization of the king. White must seize the e-file in such a way that the d-pawn is unable to advance.

4	...	Re8
5	Rd2!	h6
6	Re2	Rb8
7	Ke3	

The blockading square is best occupied by the king, the knight being needed for the preparation of b4—b5.

7	...	Rb3
8	Kd4	Kf6
9	Na2	

White follows his plan.

9 ...	Rb8
10 b4	g5
11 g3	gxf4
12 gxf4	a6
13 Nc3	Rg8
14 a4	Rg4
15 Rf2	

Black has slightly activated his forces, but it is too late — White is all ready for the decisive break.

15 ...	Be6
16 b5	

This same move would have followed on 15 ... Be8.

16 ...	axb5
17 axb5	cxb5
18 Nxb5	Rg1
19 Nc3!	Kf7
20 Rb2!	Rf1
21 Ne2!	

Do not hurry! After 21 Ke5 Re1+ 22 Kd6 Black would have gained counter-play by 22 ... d4.

21 ...	Re1
22 Ke5	d4

This pawn sacrifice merely delays the inevitable.

23 Kxd4	Kg6
24 Nc3	Kh5
25 Re2	Rxe2
26 Nxe2	Kg4
27 Ke5	Bc8
28 Nd4	h5
29 Nxf5!	

In conclusion — a tactical blow. If 29 ... Bxf5 30 h3+, winning.

29 ...	Bd7

30 Ng7	Ba4
31 f5	Kg5
32 Ne6+	Resigns.

Goldin—Korzubov

Dushanbe, 1980

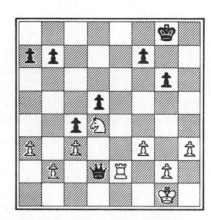

In spite of Black's material advantage, it is very difficult for him to break up the opponent's fortress. If he advances his pawns by ... a5 and ... b5—b4, White's defences hold if he exchanges on b4 and plays Rc2. Only play on both wings can give Black winning chances.

1 ...	Qc1+
2 Kf2	f5!

A highly important move, which has to be made immediately. If White were to succeed in playing g2—g3 and f3—f4, the game would most probably end in a draw.

3 Kg3

3 g3 would have been met not by 3 ... Qh1 4 f4! with a probable draw, but 3 ... f4!, exposing the white king.

3 ...	Qg5+!
4 Kh2	f4

165

The first stage of Black's plan is complete: White's K-side pawns have been fixed. The next stage is a Q-side pawn offensive.

5 Re8+	Kf7
6 Re2	a6
7 Ne6	Qh4
8 Nd4	b5
9 Kg1	Qf6
10 Kh2	Qb6
11 Re5	

The pawn ending after 11 Re6 Qxe6 12 Nxe6 Kxe6 13 g4 a5 followed by ...d4 is hopeless for White.

11 ...	Qb7
12 Kh1	Qd7
13 Kg1	a5
14 Kh2	Qd6
15 Re2	b4
16 axb4	axb4

This concludes the second part of Black's plan. Now he must take his queen into White's rearguard.

17 Kh1	Qa6
18 Kh2	

White loses immediately after 18 cxb4? Qa1+ 19 Kh2 Qd1.

18 ...	Qa1
19 Rc2	Qe1

The king must now be brought to a4. Before advancing his king, Black, operating according to the principle "do not hurry", manoeuvres with his queen, trying to avoid revealing his plans to his opponent.

20 Re2	Qd1
21 Rf2	Qa1
22 Rc2	Kf6
23 Nc6	Qd1
24 Nd4	

After 24 Nxb4? Kg5 White is in *zugzwang*, since 25 Rf2 is bad due to 25 ...d4 26 cxd4 Qe1.

24 ...	Qd3
25 Rc1	Qe3
26 Rc2	Qe1
27 Re2	Qb1
28 Rd2	Qa1
29 Rc2	

The series of manoeuvres has not brought any tangible result, and Black sets about transferring his king to the Q-side.

29 ...	Ke7
30 Re2+	Kd7
31 Rc2?	

After this Black is able to carry out his plan. Interesting complications would have arisen after 31 Re5!, e.g.:

(a) 31 ... Qxb2 32 Rxd5+ Kc7 33 Rc5+ (*33 ... Kb6 34 Rb5+ Ka6 35 Rxb4 Qxc3 36 Nc6 also promises Black little*) 34 Rxc4 bxc3 (or *34 ... b3 35 Nxb3*) 35 Rxc3, with a draw.

(b) 31 ... bxc3 32 Rxd5+ Kc8 33 bxc3 Qxc3 is Black's best chance, when much depends upon whether the position after 34 Nb5 Qb4 35 Nd6+ Kc7 36 Nxc4 Qxc4 37 Re5 is a win or a draw.

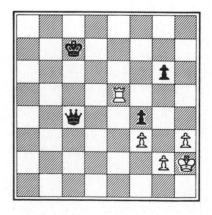

The winning plan can be as follows: Black places his g-pawn at g5, his queen at c1 and his king at d5. Suppose that, with his rook at e1, it is White to move:

(i) The rook moves to e8. Black advances his king to d3, plays ...Qe3!, and then proceeds with his king to f2, after which at some point the ...g4 break is decisive.

(ii) The rook keeps on the fourth rank. Black achieves the following position with White to move: rook at e4, black king at c5, queen at a1. White is forced to allow the black king to reach d3.

Thus by playing 31 Re5! White would not have attained a theoretically drawn position, but would have retained drawing chances. He is not obliged to give up his knight for the pawn immediately.

But after the insipid move in the game White quickly ends up in a lost position. The "do not hurry" tactics have played their part: White has been uable to switch from passive defence to active play.

31 ...	Kc8
32 Ne6	Kb7
33 Nd4	Kb6
34 Ne6	Kb5
35 Nd4+	Ka4

Black has carried out his plan in full, and White is in *zugzwang*. To any knight move Black replies 36 ...Kb3, and if 37 Nd4+ Ka2 followed by 38 ...b3, and 39 ...Qxb2, winning. If White plays 36 Nc6 Kb3 37 Nxb4, then 37 ...d4 is decisive.

36 g3

White is forced to expose his king.

| 36 ... | g5! |

Of course, not 36 ...fxg3+? 37 Kxg3, when the white king breaks out to the centre.

37 g4	Qe1
38 Kg2	Qg3+
39 Kf1	Qxh3+
40 Kf2	Qh2+

Black has captured the h-pawn, but it is still by no means easy to win the game. In order to breach White's position he has to sacrifice his queen for the rook.

| 41 Ke1 | Qh1+! |
| 42 Kf2! | |

42 Ke2 loses to 42 ...Qg1 43 Kd2 Qf1.

42 ...	Qd1
43 Re2	Qd3?!
44 Rc2	

(See next diagram)

| 44 ... | Qxc2+? |

Fatigued by the tense struggle, Korzubov makes it much harder for himself to win. The idea of the queen sacrifice at c2 is correct, but it should be made with the white king at g2. This can be achieved by a study-like manoeuvre, making repeated use of *zugzwang*:

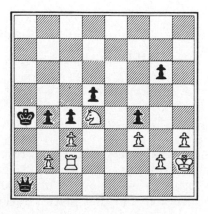

44 ... Qd1! 45 Re2 Qc1! 46 Rc2 Qa1 47 Kg2 (any knight move is decisively met by *47 ... Kb3*, while on *47 Ke2* Black wins by *47 ... Qg1*) 47 ... Qe1! 48 Re2 Qc1! 49 Rc2 Qxc2+! 50 Nxc2 bxc3 51 bxc3 Kb3 with an easy win. After the move played the battle flares up anew.

45	Nxc2	bxc3
46	bxc3	Kb3
47	Nb4!	

The only move, the alternatives being hopeless:
(a) 47 Nd4+ Kxc3 48 Ne2+ Kd2 49 Nxf4 gxf4 50 g5 c3 51 g6 c2 52 g7 c1=Q 53 g8=Q Qe1+ 54 Kg2 Qe2+ and 55 ... Qxf3.
(b) 47 Ne1 Kxc3 48 Ke2 d4 49 Kd1 d3 50 Ng2 Kd4 51 Kd2 c3+ 52 Kd1 d2! 53 Kc2 Kc4 54 Nxf4 gxf4 55 g5 Kd5.

47	...	d4
48	cxd4	Kxb4
49	Ke2	

Here is where it becomes significant that the king is at f2, and not g2.

49	...	c3
50	d5	Kb3
51	d6	c2
52	d7	c1=Q
53	d8=Q	Qe3+

54	Kd1	Qxf3+
55	Kd2?	

A new phase of the struggle has begun — a queen ending where Black is a pawn up. Queen endings are mainly a battle of the kings. Black's plan includes taking his king to f3, and therefore White should have kept his king at e1, f1 and f2. Here he should have retreated to e1, and the outcome would have been not altogether clear. After the move played Black cuts the white king off from the K-side, and the win becomes merely a question of time.

55	...	Qe3+!

After 55 ... Qxg4?! White would have had every chance of giving perpetual check.

56	Kd1	Qe5
57	Kd2	Kc4
58	Qc8+	Qc5
59	Qa6+	Kd5
60	Qb7+	Ke5
61	Qg7+	Ke4
62	Qh7+	Kf3
63	Qh3+	Kf2
64	Qh2+	Kf1
65	Qh5	Qd5+
66	Kc1	Kg2

White resigns.

The f-pawn will queen.

Eliskases—Flohr

Semmering, 1937

(See next diagram)

The black pieces occupy more comfortable positions, and the a2 pawn may prove a weakness. White has to play accurately, so that Black's initiative

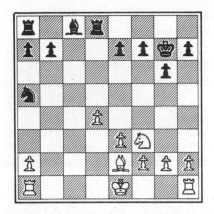

| 5 | Bxf3 | Rac8 |
| 6 | Rd2 | e5! |

The positional blows follow one after another.

| 7 | d5 | Nc4 |
| 8 | Re2 | Nd6 |

The blockade is complete. From being roughly level the position has been transformed into one which is won for Black. But the win is still far off.

9	Rb1	Rc4
10	g3	Rdc8
11	Bg2	

Now Black has many tempting possibilities: . . . b5, . . . Rc2 or . . . f6 followed by the transfer of the king to e7. Flohr takes a different, and interesting decision: he exchanges rooks. One cannot help being struck by the confidence of the grandmaster in the correctness of his evaluation of the position. After all, if the resulting minor piece ending should not prove to be won for Black, the exchange of his rooks, excellently deployed on the only open file, will have thrown away the win.

11	. . .	Rc1+!?
12	Rxc1	Rxc1+
13	Re1	Rxe1+
14	Kxe1	f5!

The base of White's central pawn chain has to be weakened.

| 15 | f3 | |

After 15 exf5 gxf5 the d5 pawn would in time be lost, while on 15 f4 Black has a simple reply: 15 . . . Kf6.

15	. . .	fxe4
16	fxe4	b5
17	Kd2	a5

should not be transformed into a solid positional advantage. Possibly he should have castled long, so as to co-ordinate his rooks and bring his king closer to the defence of his a-pawn.

For example: 1 0—0—0!? Be6 2 Kb1 Nc4 3 Nd2 Rac8 4 Nxc4 Bxc4 5 Bxc4 Rxc4 6 Rc1 Rb4+ 7 Ka1 e5 8 dxc5 Rd2 9 Rb1, or 2 . . . Rac8 3 Nd2 Bf5+ 4 e4 Bd7 5 Rc1, with chances of equalizing. White chooses K-side castling, and takes his king away from the centre.

| 1 | 0—0 | Be6 |
| 2 | e4? | |

And this pseudo-active move is a serious positional mistake. To be considered was 2 Nd2 Rac8 3 Rfc1, restraining Black's offensive.

| 2 | . . . | Bg4! |
| 3 | Rfd1? | |

There was no point in stopping half-way. 3 d5 was more correct.

| 3 | . . . | e6! |

Flohr skilfully exploits his opponent's errors. First he restrains White's pawn centre, and then embarks on a complete blockade of it.

| 4 | Kf1 | Bxf3! |

18 Kd3	Kf6
19 Bf3	Ke7
20 h4?	

In the end this leads to a weakening of White's position on the K-side. The immediate 20 Bd1 followed by 21 a4 was better, as suggested by Euwe.

20 ...	h6!

Not allowing White to fix the pawns at h7 and g6 and obtain counter-play after g3—g4—g5. Now on 21 g4 there follows 21 ...g5, restricting the white bishop still further.

21 Bd1	Kd8
22 a4	

Following the change in the K-side pawn structure, this move is not as good as it was earlier.

22 ...	bxa4?!

22 ...b4! is stronger. Euwe gives the following variation: 23 Bb3 Kc7 24 Bd1 Kb6 25 Bc2 (25 *Bb3 Nb7 26 Kc4 Nc5 27 Bc2 h5*) 25 ...Nb7 26 Kc4 Nc5 27 g4 g5 28 h5 b3 29 Bb1 b2 30 Kc3 Nxa4+ 31 Kb3 Nc5+ 32 Kxb2 Nd7 and 33 ...Nf6. The difference in the position of the white h-pawn leads to a win for Black.

23 Bxa4	Kc7
24 Bc2	Kb6
25 Kc3	Kb5
26 Kb3	Kc5
27 Ka4	

White makes a desperate attempt to obtain counter-play. On 27 Kc3 there would have followed 27 ...a4!

27 ...	Nc4
28 Bb3?	

"The decisive mistake. The correct continuation was 28 Bb1 Nd2 29 Bd3, not allowing the knight to attack the K-side pawns." (Averbakh).

28 ...	Nd2
29 Bc2	Nf1
30 Kxa5	

30 g4 Ne3 would not have changed anything.

30 ...	Nxg3
31 Ka4	Nh5
32 Kb3	Kd4!

Now precise calculation is required.

33 Kb4	Nf6
34 d6	g5
35 hxg5	hxg5
36 Kb5	g4
37 Bd1	g3
38 Bf3	Ke3
39 Bh1	Kf2
40 Kc6	g2
41 Bxg2	Kxg2
42 d7	Nxd7
43 Kxd7	Kf3

White resigns.

We give the following game in full, since the exchange of queens takes place as early as the ninth move, and the subsequent play follows the typical principles of endgame strategy.

Shereshevsky—Veremeichik

Minsk, 1978

1 d4	Nf6
2 Bg5	c5
3 Nc3!?	Qa5
4 Bxf6	gxf6
5 e3	f5
6 Qh5	cxd4
7 exd4	Qb6

8	0–0–0	Qh6+
9	Qxh6	Bxh6+
10	Kb1	d6

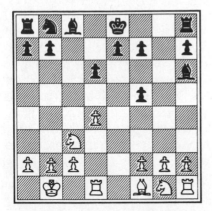

A complex endgame position has been reached. Black's K-side pawn formation is compromised, but he has the two bishops. White must play thoughtfully and consistently, otherwise he may gradually be saddled with even the inferior game. First he must restrict the scope of the black bishops, and then think about creating weaknesses in the opponent's position.

11 g3!

With the idea of developing the bishop at g2 and of setting up the pawn column h2/g3/f4, restricting the opponent's black-squared bishop. 11 ...f4 fails to 12 Nd5.

| 11 ... | Bd7 |

Black plans to exchange the white-squared bishops, but he merely aids the development of White's game.

12	Bg2	Bc6
13	d5!	Bd7
14	f4	

Now the possible targets for attack take shape — the pawns at f5 and e7, while the black bishops have no particu-

lar prospects.

14 ...	Bg7
15 Nge2	h5
16 h4	

White leaves himself with a backward pawn at g3, but it is easily defended. At the same time the black h5 pawn also becomes vulnerable.

16 ...	Na6
17 Rhe1	Nc7
18 Nd4	Kf8
19 Re3	Bf6
20 Bh3	Bxd4

After this exchange Black is doomed to passive defence. After 20 ...e6 White could have made the piece sacrifice 21 dxe6 fxe6 22 Nxf5!? Bxc3 23 Rxd6, although, of course, he would not have been obliged to do so. Nevertheless, this continuation would have given Black counter-chances in a tactical struggle, whereas, without his black-squared bishop, his position will gradually deteriorate against correct play by White.

21 Rxd4 Re8

White must again form a plan. Black has weak pawns at h5, f5 and e7 on the K-side. But these weaknesses are close to one another and are not difficult to defend. Therefore, following the principle of two weaknesses, White must also create some vulnerable targets on the Q-side. But first he should improve the placing of his pieces and tie Black down on the K-side. To do this he centralizes his king and transfers his knight to e3, after which his rooks gain the opportunity to attack the opponent's Q-side.

22 Kc1!	Kg7
23 Kd2	Kf6
24 Ke1	Rc8

25 Bf1	Ne8
26 Rd2	

Preparing the transfer of the knight to e3.

26 ...	Ng7
27 Nd1	Rhe8
28 Ra3	a6

It would have been better to avoid this weakening and play 28 . . . Ra8.

29 Rb3	Rc7

After 29 . . . b5 White has the unpleasant 30 a4.

30 Rb6	

Now the pawn at b7 is fixed.

30 ...	Rd8
31 Be2	Kg6
32 Ne3	Ne8
33 Rd4	Nf6
34 Bd3	Rg8

Black is completely tied down, and can only watch as White improves his position. Being short of time, White is not in a hurry to take positive action.

35 Ke2	Ra8?!
36 Rdb4	Ra7?!

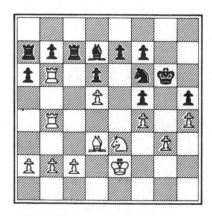

This rook will for a long time be shut out of play. White has a clear procedure for realizing his advantage: (1) fix Black's Q-side by a2—a4—a5; (2) exchange the black rook at c7 by Rc4; (3) with his bishop at d3 and knight at e3, tying Black's pieces to the defence of the f5 pawn, transfer the king to d4; (4) advance c2—c4—c5, after which Black's position will begin to collapse.

White mentally outlined this plan, but then, fearing the possibility of time trouble, decided to act according to the principle "do not hurry" and to repeat the position once or twice.

37 Rd4?	

But this principle should be employed only when the player is confident that such tactics will lead to a deterioration in the opponent's position and to a favourable outcome. During the game White was convinced that there was altogether nothing that Black could do, and he overlooked a latent possibility of counter-play.

37 ...	Bb5!

An unpleasant surprise. It transpires that the f5 pawn is immune, while after 38 Bxb5 axb5 39 a3 Rc5 the black pieces break free. White does not wish to play 38 c4, since this square is earmarked for his rook, and so he decides on an exchange sacrifice.

38 Rxb5!?	axb5
39 Nxf5	Ra4
40 b4	Rxa2
41 Kf3?!	

Again abusing the principle of "do not hurry". The immediate 41 Nxe7++ was simpler and better, but time trouble and a sharp change of situation can put many players out of their stride. Fortunately for White, 41. . .Ng4 fails to 42 Nxd6+!

f5 (or *42 . . . Kb6 43 Nxf7+ Kg7 44 Ne5*) 43 Nxf5! (but not *43 Bxf5+? Kf6 44 Ne8+ Kxf5 43 Nxc7 Rxc2*), but he should not have allowed Black a wide choice of continuations by playing 41 Kf3. This was clearly irrational.

41 . . .	Rc3
42 Nxe7++	Kg7
43 Nf5+	Kf8
44 Ke2	

White has no right to give up his c2 pawn, since it and the bishop at d3 are the base of his entire position.

44 . . .	Rc8?!

Black again selects a comparatively passive plan, transferring his rook to d8 to defend the d-pawn. Much more unpleasant for White would have been an attempt at counter-attack. A possible variation would be:

44 . . . Rc7 (so that *Nxd6* should not be with gain of tempo) 45 Kd2 Ra1 46 Bxb5 Rg1 47 Bd3 Ng4 48 b5! Nf2 49 b6 Rc5 50 Nxd6 Nxd3 51 Nxb7 Rc8 52 d6!, and White must win. But Black has other possibilities. Instead of 47 . . . Ng4 he can play 47 . . . Rg2+ 48 Ke1 Ng4 49 b5 with a very sharp game.

In choosing passive tactics, Black had possibly not guessed at White's idea. At first sight, Black's set-up does not seem at all bad: one rook is transferred to the defence, the second will attack at g1, and the knight can go via e8 to g7.

45 Kd2	Rd8

All the same the b5 pawn cannot be saved. White was threatening 46 Nxd6 Rd8 47 Nxb5, when 47 . . . Nxd5 is not possible due to 48 Bc4.

46 Bxb5	Ra1
47 Kc3	Re1

The immediate 47 . . . Rg1 is more logical.

48 Bd3	Ne8
49 Kc4!	

Now we see White's plan. His king goes onto the attack, shattering Black's defences.

49 . . .	Ng7
50 Kb5	Nxf5
51 Bxf5	Ke7

51 . . . Re3 is obviously too slow.

52 Kb6	Kf6

With the idea of answering 53 Bd3 with 53 . . . Re7.

53 Kc7!

The king lands the decisive blow, worthily crowning its lengthy journey.

53 . . .	Rg8
54 Bd3	Re7+
55 Kxd6	Rc8

With the threat of 56 . . . Rcc7.

56 Rc4	Rd8+
57 Kc5	Rc7+
58 Kb6	Rcd7
59 Rc7	

The simplest.

59 . . .	Rxd5
60 Kxb7	Rxd3

Despair.

61 cxd3	Rxd3
62 b5	Rxg3
63 b6	Rb3
64 Rc5	Rb4
65 Kc7	Resigns.

Rubinstein—Tackacs

Budapest, 1926

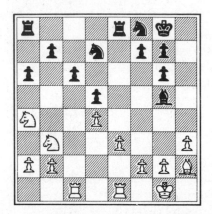

The position has been reached from the Carlsbad Variation of the Queen's Gambit. The pawn formation is characteristic for the carrying out of the so-called minority attack, by which White advances his Q-side pawns to a4 and b5 to create weaknesses in his opponent's pawn formation. But Black has succeeded in exchanging the white-squared bishops, which in this position is to his advantage, and White's pawn attack can be met by the direct . . . b5 (with the white pawn at b4) followed by the transfer of the knight to c4. Therefore there is no point in White forcing events. He must attempt to break up the opponent's defences and worsen the placing of the black pieces, and only then seek a possible breakthrough.

1 . . .	Ne6
2 Na5	Ra7?

Such moves are made only *in extremis*. Black's position is inferior, and he should have decided on 2 . . . b5 3 Nc3 Rac8, aiming for . . . c5. In this case, despite his obvious pawn weaknesses, Black's pieces would have occupied active positions, and White's task would have been markedly more difficult. From the purely practical view-

point, better chances were offered by the cunning 2 . . . Nxd4?!, and if 3 exd4 Bd2!, when it is Black who wins. But White, of course, is not obliged to take on d4; he can simply play 3 Nxb7, retaining all the advantages of his position.

3 Kf1!

White does not hurry, and centralizes his king. The immediate 3 b4 was also possible, but Rubinstein prevents . . . Nxd4 once and for all, while the b-pawn can always be advanced later.

3 . . .	Bd8
4 b4	f5

Black's K-side activity is easily neutralized by White, and leads merely to new weaknesses. Once Black had chosen passive tactics, he should have stuck to them as long as possible. A tenacious, planned defence would have been much more appropriate than unprepared counter-play. He should have played 4 . . . Kf8, but not 4 . . . Bc7 5 Bxc7 Nxc7 6 Nc5.

5 Nb2!

White keeps a careful eye on his opponent's counter-play. The transfer of the knight to d3 forces Black to abandon his active play on the K-side.

5 . . .	g5
6 Nd3	Kf7
7 Rc2	Bb6

Stronger was 7 . . . Ke7 with the idea of . . . Bb6, . . . Kd8 and . . . Bc7, taking the king to the defence of the Q-side.

8 Bd6!

Again Rubinstein skilfully suppresses

the opponent's counter-play, while continuing to cramp Black's position. Tackacs is unable to persist with his king manoeuvre, since after 8 . . . Rh8   9 Rec1 Ke8   10 a4 Kd8 White has the decisive sacrifice 11 Rxc6! bxc6 12 Nxc6+ Ke8 13 Nxa7 Bxa7 14 Rc8+ Nd8 15 Ra8 Bb6 16 a5.

8 ...	Nd8

Removing one of the attacks on c5, which White promptly exploits.

9 Nc5!	Nxc5
10 Bxc5	Bxc5
11 bxc5	

The position has simplified. Black's basic weakness — his b7 pawn — is fixed, the rook at a7 is still out of play, but for the moment White does not appear to have anything concrete. He needs to create a second weakness on Black's other wing. This is assisted by the position of the pawns at f5 and g5. Were these pawns on the 6th rank, White's task would be more difficult.

11 ...	Ke7

In an attempt to help out his rook at a7, Black marches his king to the Q-side, but this merely helps White's breakthrough on the K-side.

12 Rb2	Kd7
13 Reb1	Kc8
14 Ke2	Re7
15 Kf3	Re4
16 g4!	

The start of the attack.

16 ...	g6
17 Rg1	Nf7

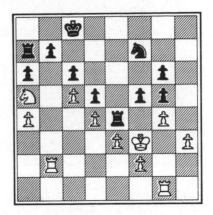

18 h4!!

Rubinstein sacrifices a pawn, to gain control of the g-file. It is this that will be the second weakness in Black's position.

18 ...	gxh4
19 gxf5	gxf5
20 Rg7	Nd8
21 Rg8	f4

This merely accelerates the end.

22 Rh8	fxe3
23 fxe3	Kd7
24 Rg2!	Re8
25 Rxh4	Re7
26 Rh8	Kc7
27 Rgg8	Rd7

Black resists to the last.

28 Nb3!

The transfer of this knight to e5 concludes the game.

28 ...	a5
29 Nc1	Ra8
30 Nd3	b5

A last try: White might just play 31 Ne5 Re7 32 Rxd8? Rxd8 33 Rxd8 Rxe5! Passive defence would not have saved Black, a possible continuation being 30 . . . a4 31 Ne5 Re7 32 a3!

Rc8 33 Kg4 Rb8 34 Kf5 Rc8 35
Re8 Rxe8 36 Rxe8 followed by Re7+
and the transfer of the king to b6.

31	cxb6+	Kxb6
32	Nc5	Rd6
33	a4!	Rc8
34	Kg4	Resigns.

Black has no defence against Kf5,
Rh7, Ke5 and Rxd8.

Saidy—Fischer

USA, 1964

Were it not for the pawns at d4 and
d5, White's chances would be in no way
worse. But the mutually isolated pawns
create an impenetrable barrier to the
white bishop, without restricting the
mobility of the black knight. White is
therefore faced with a difficult task in
trying to draw.

1	Kf1	Nf8
2	Ke2	Ne6
3	Kd3	

What plan should Black choose? First
he must activate his king. It would
appear that it should be brought to the
centre to d6. But the American grandmaster intends to play on the K-side
with the aim of creating a target for

attack there, and so he transfers the king
to f5 by the shortest route via h7.

3 . . .	h5!

In achieving the required set-up,
Fischer does not waste a single move. It
is advisable not to hurry only when the
projected plan has been carried out, or
when it has to be masked from the
opponent.

4 Be3

White sticks to waiting tactics. It
would possibly have been better to
activate his bishop by a3—a4, b2—b3
and Ba3 with his king at e3.

4	. . .	Kh7
5	f3	Kg6
6	a4	Kf5
7	Ke2	g5
8	Kf2	

Black has achieved his planned set-up,
and now sharply changes the tempo of
the play. In his *My 60 Memorable
Games*, commenting on a game from
Portoroz, 1958, Fischer writes: "Petrosian likes to play cat-and-mouse,
hoping that his opponents will go wrong
in the absence of a direct threat. The
amazing thing is — they usually do!" A
highly graphic exposition of the principle "do not hurry". The further course
of the game shows how well Fischer had
learned this particular lesson. Although
Saidy does not make any obvious mistakes, he also begins moving here and
there, not wishing to create any weaknesses in his position. But at the critical
moment, when immediate activity is required, White proves to be psychologically unprepared for it.

8	. . .	Nd8
9	Bd2	Kg6
10	Ke3	Ne6

11 Kd3	Kf5
12 Be3	f6
13 Ke2	Kg6
14 Kd3	f5

Note how slowly, almost unwillingly, the black f-pawn advances.

15 Ke2	f4
16 Bf2	Ng7
17 h3	Nf5
18 Kd3	g4!?

Unexpectedly Black makes a break, although he could have played his knight to e6 and his king to f5.

19 hxg4	hxg4
20 fxg4	Nh6
21 Be1?	

The critical point. What is now required of White is a concrete approach to the problems facing him. He should have immediately activated his bishop by 21 Bh4 Nxg4 22 Bd8, with the idea of a4—a5. True, after 22 ... Ne3 White loses a pawn, but 23 h3 Nc4 24 gxf4 Nxb2+ 25 Kc2 Nxa4 26 Kb3 b5 27 Kb4 a6 28 Ka5 Nc3 29 Be7 gives him every hope of a draw. Instead, through inertia, White continues his waiting tactics, and very soon finds himself in a hopeless position.

21 ...	Nxg4
22 Bd2	Kf5
23 Be1	Nf6
24 Bh4	Ne4
25 Be1	

It is now too late for Bd8, since after ... Kg4 the white king has to switch to the defence of the g2 pawn, and there can be no question of any activity on the Q-side.

25 ...	Kg4
26 Ke2	Ng3+

27 Kd3

The pawn ending is obviously hopeless, while after 27 Kf2 Black gains e4 for his king by 27 ... Kf5 28 Kf3 Ne4 followed by ... Ng5+. If 29 Bh4, then 29 ... Nd2+ 30 Ke2 Nc4 31 b3 Na5 32 b4 Nc6, and White loses a pawn.

27 ...	Nf5

It transpires that against the threat of ... Nh4 White has no satisfactory defence.

28 Bf2	Nh4
29 a5	

A belated attempt at activity.

29 ...	Nxg2
30 Kc3	Kf3
31 Bg1	Ke2
32 Bh2	f3
33 Bg3	Ne3

White resigns.

There is no defence against ... Nf5.

Lilienthal—Bondarevsky

Moscow, 1940

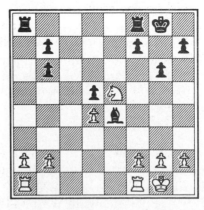

This game was played in the last round of the 12th USSR Championship, and had enormous significance regarding the final placings. Bondarevsky was leading, with Lilienthal a point behind. In such a situation, where a draw is equivalent to defeat, the majority of players begin complicating the position, burning all their boats behind them. But in this game White happily went for favourable simplification, and as a result gained a highly promising ending. The mutually isolated pawns in the centre give the advantage to the knight over the bishop. In addition, Black's doubled b-pawns are weak, so that it is dangerous for him to go into the minor piece ending.

1 Rfc1

Of course, not 1 Nd7?! Rfd8 2 Nxb6? Ra6.

1 ...	Rfc8
2 a3	Bf5
3 g4	Be6

The rook ending after 3 ... f6 4 gxf5 fxe5 5 dxe5 gxf5 6 f4 is also unfavourable for Black.

4 h3	f6
5 Nd3	g5
6 f3	Kf7
7 Kf2	Ke7?!

A routine move. Black follows the principle that the centralization of the king is always useful. This is correct, but first he should have suppressed White's attempts to give him weaknesses on the K-side. By 7 ... h5! Black could have gained counter-chances.

8 Ke3	Kd6?

And here ... h5 was simply essential. The natural king move is possibly the decisive mistake, allowing White to give his opponent a weakness on the K-side, in addition to those which he already has.

9 Rxc8!	Rxc8
10 h4!	

White opens and seizes control of the h-file, the invasion squares along which are a weakness in Black's position.

10 ...	h6

10 ... gxh4 is bad: 11 Rh1 f5 12 g5.

11 hxg5	hxg5

Perhaps 11 ... fxg5 was the lesser evil, but it was difficult for Black to decide on giving himself a backward pawn at h6 and weakening his control over e5.

12 Rh1	Re8
13 Kd2	Bd7
14 Rh6	Rf8

On 14 ... Ke6 White has the unpleasant 15 f4.

15 Ne1	Kc7
16 Nc2	Rf7
17 Ne3	Be6
18 Kc3	

White has completely tied down his opponent's forces on the K-side, and he now transfers his king to the Q-side to attack the weak b-pawns.

18 ...	Kd6
19 Kb4	Bd7
20 Nf5+	

In general the exchange of minor pieces eases Black's defence, but White has calculated that the rook ending is won after 20 ... Bxf5 21 gxf5 Kc6 22 a4 Rf8 23 Rh7 Rd8 24 Rf7 Rd6 25 b3 b5 26 a5 b6 27 a6.

20 ...	Kc7
21 a4	Be6

22 Ng3	Bd7
23 Nh5!	f5
24 Nf6!	

By this knight manoeuvre White wins a pawn, accurately judging that the counter-play obtained by Black is insufficient.

24 ...	fxg4
25 Nxd5+	Kb8
26 fxg4	

White avoids the tempting, but erroneous attempt to play for mate: 26 Rh8+? Ka7 27 Nc7 b5 28 a5 b6 29 a6 Bc6!, and Black defends against the mate at a8, simultaneously attacking the knight.

26 ...	Bxg4
27 Nxb6	Rf2
28 b3	Bd1
29 d5	Kc7

If 29 ... Rf3, then 30 d6 Rxb3+ 31 Ka5, and either Black is mated or the white pawn queens.

30 a5	Rd2
31 Rh7+	Kb8
32 d6!	

White concludes the game energetically. 32 ... Rxd6 fails to 33 Rh8+ Kc7 34 Rc8 mate.

32 ...	Rd4+
33 Kc5	Rh4
34 d7	Kc7
35 d8=Q++!	Kxd8
36 Rd7+	Resigns.

Fischer—Taimanov

Candidates ¼-Final Match
Vancouver, 1971

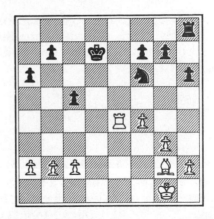

The position is an open one, and the bishop is clearly superior to the knight. It is true that realizing this advantage is very difficult, since the pawn formation is symmetric, and there is no possibility of setting up a passed pawn. First White restricts the knight's mobility and creates weaknesses in his opponent's position.

1 Re5	b6?!

1 ... Kd6 was preferable, and if 2 Bxb7?! Rb8.

2 Bf1!	a5
3 Bc4	Rf8

Just three moves have been made, and how the position has changed! The black rook is tied to the f7 pawn, Black's Q-side pawns have lost their mobility, and he has acquired a weak square at b5. Now White centralizes his king.

4 Kg2	Kd6
5 Kf3	Nd7
6 Re3	Nb8
7 Rd3+	Kc7
8 c3	Nc6
9 Re3	Kd6
10 a4	

White's play has proved successful — the black knight has no strong points, the white king is centralized, and Black's pawn weaknesses on the Q-side are fixed. But for a win this is insufficient. Black must also be given a second weakness on the K-side.

10 ...	Ne7
11 h3!	Nc6
12 h4	

Do not hurry! Remember the advice of Byelavyenets: "If there is a possibility of advancing a pawn two squares or one, advance it first one square, look carefully around, and only then advance it a further square."

| 12 ... | h5?! |

Black fails to withstand the tension. His desire to clarify the position as soon as possible is psychologically understandable. Unfortunately, he is now forced to place all his K-side pawns on white squares, and it is this that will constitute Black's second weakness. Up to a certain time it would have been better to stick to waiting tactics, leaving the K-side pawns in place. After 12 ... h5 White realizes his advantage in highly instructive fashion.

13 Rd3+	Kc7
14 Rd5	f5
15 Rd2	Rf6
16 Re2	Kd7
17 Re3!	

Black is practically in *zugzwang*.

| 17 ... | g6 |
| 18 Bb5 | |

Black's K-side pawns present an excellent target for the bishop, while on the Q-side the king can easily approach via c4—b5—a6, so that White's next problem is to exchange rooks.

| 18 ... | Rd6 |

| 19 Ke2 | Kd8 |

Black does nothing to hinder White's intention. He could of course have played 18 ... Rf6, but after 19 Kd2 he would have had to agree to the exchange, since to allow the white rook to reach e8 would be even less attractive.

20 Rd3	Kc7
21 Rxd6	Kxd6
22 Kd3	Ne7
23 Be8	

The knight is tied to the g6 pawn, and White's problem is to break through with his king to a6. If he can attain the following position, Black will be in complete *zugzwang*.

23 ...	Kd5
24 Bf7+	Kd6
25 Kc4	Kc6
26 Be8+	Kb7
27 Kb5	Nc8

Clever, but inadequate. White cannot of course take the pawn: 28 Bxg6?? Nd6 mate, but he is able to push back the black king by a subtle bishop manoeuvre.

28 Bc6+	Kc7
29 Bd5!	Ne7
30 Bf7	Kb7
31 Bb3!	

The bishop switches to the long diagonal.

31 ...	Ka7
32 Bd1	Kb7
33 Bf3+	Kc7

The a6 square has been won for the king. Black cannot play 33 ...Ka7, since he is in *zugzwang* after any waiting move by White.

34 Ka6	Ng8
35 Bd5	Ne7
36 Bc4	Nc6
37 Bf7	Ne7
38 Be8	

The required position has been attained. Black is in *zugzwang*.

38 ...	Kd8
39 Bxg6	

The tireless bishop now sacrifices itself.

39 ...	Nxg6
40 Kxb6	Kd7
41 Kxc5	Ne7
42 b4	axb4
43 cxb4	Nc8
44 a5	Nd6
45 b5	Ne4+
46 Kb6	Kc8
47 Kc6	Kb8

and **Black resigned.**

Keres—Portisch

Moscow, 1967

(See next diagram)

A complicated ending. White controls the only open file, but a careful study of the position shows that Black has the

more promising game, since White will not have any invasion squares on the d-file, while in the event of the exchange of rooks the Q-side pawns at a3, b2 and c3 may become an excellent target for the black bishop.

1 ...	Re8
2 Rd3	Raa8
3 Kf1	Rab8!

By this move Portisch reduces still further the value of a possible c3—c4, on which there follows ...b4!

4 Ne1	g6
5 Nc2	

The white knights rush around the board in search of strong points, and are quite unable to find any.

5 ...	h5
6 f3	

An important moment. The f3 square is now occupied by the pawn, which means that there is no longer any threat to the e5 pawn, and Black can exchange rooks. To some extent the pawn formation resembles that in the previous Fischer—Taimanov game, where on one wing all the weaker side's pawns are on squares of the colour of the bishop, and on the other wing — on squares of the opposite colour.

6 ...	Red8!
7 Rcd1	Rxd3
8 Rxd3	c5
9 Ne2	c4!

A subtle understanding of the position. Black paralyzes White's Q-side, after which he exchanges the second pair of rooks. There was no sense in maintaining the pawn tension on the Q-side, since the ... b4 break was not in the spirit of the position.

10 Rd1	Rb7
11 Nb4	Rd7
12 Ke1	Rxd1+
13 Kxd1	Bc5

First of all White must be deprived of counter-play involving an attack on the b5 pawn by Na6–c7. The c7 square will be guarded by the bishop, while the black king prepares to go to g5 via g7 and h6.

14 Nc6	Nd7
15 f4	

Keres does not wish to await the squeeze, and attempts to activate his game on the K-side, which leads to the creation of weaknesses for both players.

15 ...	f6
16 fxe5	

It is unlikely that 16 f5 gxf5 17 exf5 h4 was any better.

16 ...	fxe5

Now White has a weak pawn at e4, and Black — at e5.

17 Ng3	Kf7
18 Ke2	Ke6
19 Nf1	Bf8

The bishop is switched to h6 to attack

White's Q-side pawns, while the king takes on the defence of the b5 pawn.

20 Ne3	

Not 20 Na7? Kd6 21 Nxb5+ Kc6 22 Na7+ Kb6 23 Nc8+ Kb7, when the white knight is trapped.

20 ...	Kd6
21 Nb4	Nc5
22 Kf3	Bh6
23 h4!	Nd3

The end seems to be close. White cannot take the knight: 24 Nxd3? cxd3 25 g3 Kc5, and the black king breaks through to the Q-side pawns after the preliminary exchange on e3.

24 Nd1	Bc1
25 Ke2!	

A brilliant defence.

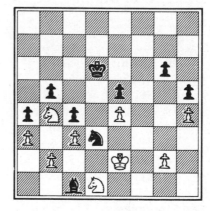

It transpires that 25 ... Nxb2 26 Nxb2 Bxb2 27 Kd2 Bxa3 28 Kc2 leads to a very pretty positional draw. White moves his king between c2 and b1. As soon as the black king goes to a5, he checks with his knight at c6, and if it goes to c5, he checks at a6. There is also no way of breaking through on the K-side: ... g5 is met by g2–g3. The pawn ending after the exchange on b4 is also drawn, in spite of Black's two extra pawns! Black is forced to retreat, and the battle flares up anew.

25 . . .	Nc5

Attacking the e4 pawn.

26 Kf3	g5!

Forcing White to open up the K-side, since 27 g3 is not possible due to . . . g4+.

27 hxg5	Bxg5
28 Na2	

Now after . . . Nd3 and . . . Bc1 White is no longer able to set up a fortress, and so Keres defends the c1 square.

28 . . .	Ke6
29 Nf2	Kf6
30 Nd1	Nd3
31 g3	Kg6
32 Kg2	

32 Ke2 fails to 32 . . . Nc1+.

32 . . .	Bd2
33 Kf3	Kg5
34 Ke2	Be1
35 Kf3	Bd2

Do not hurry!

36 Ke2	Be1
37 Kf3	Kf6!

Now Black pushes back the white king and breaks through to the e4 pawn. The game enters its decisive phase.

38 Kg2	Kg6!
39 Kf3	Kg5
40 Kg2	h4!

Obtaining control of f4.

41 gxh4+	Kf4!

Black has accurately calculated that he will be able to stop the h-pawn, while the loss of the e4 pawn will be fatal for White.

42 h5	Kxe4
43 h6	Nf4+
44 Kf1	Bh4
45 Nb4	Bf6
46 Ke1	Kf3!
47 h7	Bg7
48 Nc2	Nd5

It is time to pick up the h-pawn.

49 Kd2	Nf6
50 Ne1+	Ke4
51 Nf2+	Kf5
52 Ng2	Nxh7

Black has finally won a pawn. White's Q-side pawns are weak, and his second weakness is Black's passed e-pawn. Although the distance between these pawns is not great, Black's advantage is sufficient to win.

53 Ne3+	Ke6
54 Ne4	Bh6!

It is essential to simplify the position. The knight ending is won.

55 Ke2	Bxe3
56 Kxe3	Nf6
57 Ng5+	Kd5
58 Kf3	Nh5

Aiming for the b2 pawn.

59 Ne4	Nf4
60 Nf6+	Kc6
61 Ke4	Nd3
62 Ng4	Kd6
63 Nh6	Nxb2
64 Nf7+	Kc5
65 Nxe5	Nd1

66 Nd7+   Kd6
White resigns.

A highly interesting battle between two outstanding players, in which both attack and defence were of very high quality.

Andersson—Franco

Buenos Aires, 1979

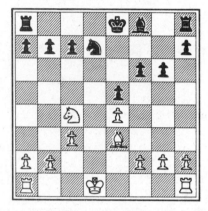

With the pawn formation symmetric, White has a slight advantage thanks to his better placed pieces, and in particular his bishop. But Black is threatening by . . . Bc5 to equalize completely, and so Andersson prevents the exchange of bishops.

1 b4!   Nb6
2 Na5   0—0—0+
3 Kc2   Be7
4 a3

White has a persistent positional advantage, which he intends to increase by the advance of his c-pawn. Painstaking work is required of Black to neutralize White's initiative. A set-up which deserves consideration is the following: . . . Kb8, . . . Nc8, . . . c6, and possibly . . . Rd7, . . . Bd8 and . . . Bc7. Instead Black decides to follow the principle of answering a flank attack by a counter-

blow in the centre.

4 . . .   f5?!

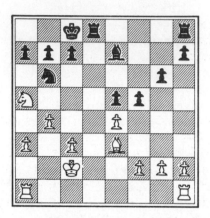

5 Bxb6!

The situation on the board has changed (the e5 pawn has been weakened), and Andersson immediately changes his plan, transforming a dynamic spatial advantage into a static one: a good knight against a bad bishop.

5 . . .   axb6
6 Nc4   Bf6

After this move White's idea is completely vindicated. Correct was 7 . . . fxe4! 8 Rae1 Rhf8 9 Rhf1 Bh4! 10 g3 Bg5 11 Rxe4 (*11 a4 Rd3 12 Rxe4 R8f3*) 11 . . . b5!, and White has only a minimal advantage in the rook ending after 12 Ne3 Bxe3 13 Rxe3 Rd5, since 12 Rxe5 bxc4 13 Rxg5 does not achieve anything due to 13 . . . Rfe8. Andersson would obviously have had to play 10 Rxe4 Rxf2+ 11 Rxf2 Bxf2 12 Rxe5, maintaining a minimal advantage.

7 a4!

The f-file is blocked, and White can delay defending his e-pawn. It is much more important to secure the 'eternal' post for his knight at c4.

7 ...	Bg7
8 Rhe1	Rhe8
9 b5	f4

Now White's hands are freed in the centre, but it is very difficult to suggest anything better for Black.

10 a5!

With the possibility of play on the Q-side and the prospect of an attack on the black king, together with the weakness of the e5 pawn and the advantage of knight over bishop, White's position can be considered won. It is interesting to follow the ease with which the Swedish grandmaster realizes his advantage, in which one senses his complete mastery of endgame technique.

10 ...	bxa5
11 Rxa5	b6
12 Ra7	Bf6

12 Nxb6+ was threatened.

13 Rea1	Re6
14 R1a6	

Now threatening 15 Na5 and 16 Nc6.

14 ...	Rde8
15 Kb3!	

Do not hurry! The opponent must be allowed a little play, since the slightest activity on Black's part will merely worsen his position.

15 ...	Bd8

Now the eighth rank is blocked.

16 Ra8+	Kd7
17 Ra2!	Bf6
18 Rd2+	Ke7
19 Ra7	Rc8

The co-ordination of Black's pieces has been completely destroyed, and he is literally hanging on by his last legs. It only needs one final effort by White to break Black's defences, and Andersson easily finds a winning piece set-up.

20 Rd5!	Ke8
21 h3!	

White intends to transfer his knight to d3, but does not hurry over carrying this out, so as not to allow counter-play with ... c6.

21 ...	Ke7
22 Nb2	Ke8
23 Nd3	Bg7

The last chance was 23 ... c6, although after 24 Rdd7 cxb5 25 Nb4 the outcome of the game is not in doubt.

24 c4	Bf6
25 c5!	bxc5
26 Nxc5	Re7
27 Ra6	Bh8
28 Kc4!	

Even here Andersson does not hurry, but strengthens his position to the maximum.

28 ...	Bg7
29 f3!	Rb8

Black tires of moving his bishop, and the game concludes even more quickly.

30 Ne6	Bf6
31 Rc6	Resigns.

On 31 ... Rc8 there follows 32 b6.

Miles—Byrne

Reykjavik, 1980

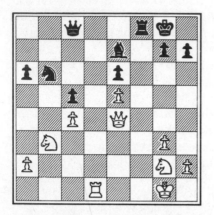

The advantage is with White, who has a spatial superiority and better placed pieces. Black must simplify the position, and he has two possibilities: 1 . . . Qa8 and 1 . . . Rd8. The American grandmaster chose

| 1 . . . | Qa8? |

which was evidently the decisive mistake. In the endgame the white rook becomes much stronger than its black colleague, with good prospects of invading along the open b- and d-files, and later along the f-file. The black knight has no strong points, and in the absence of the queens the white king can advance into the centre without fear, whereas the prospects for the black king are considerably more modest. All these factors indicate that White has a big advantage in the ending, whereas after the correct 1 . . . Rd8! he would have merely had an insignificant advantage.

| 2 Qxa8 | Rxa8 |
| 3 Na5 | Bf8 |

Black cannot contest the d-file, since 3 . . . Rd8 is met by 4 Rb1 and 5 Nc6.

| 4 Nf4 | Re8 |

5 Kf2!

Once White has brought his king to e4 and defended the e5 pawn, it will be possible for him to invade with his rook via b1. Byrne makes a desperate attempt to escape from the vice, but in doing so creates new weaknesses in his position.

| 5 . . . | g5 |
| 6 Nh5 | |

Pressure on the e6 pawn is exchanged for an attack on the weak squares on the f-file, which are in the immediate vicinity of the black king.

6 . . .	Be7
7 Ke3	Kf7
8 Rf1+	Kg6
9 g4!	

Now Black has not only to play the endgame without his king, but he must also constantly watch that he doesn't get mated.

9 . . .	h6
10 Rb1	Bd8
11 Ke4	Bc7
12 Rf1	Bd8
13 Rf3!	

Black is in *zugzwang*.

| 13 . . . | Be7 |

13 . . . Rh8 can be met by 14 Nc6, and if 14 . . . Nxc4 15 Rd3 Ba5 16 Rd7.

14 Rb3	Bd8
15 Nc6	Bc7
16 Rf3	Nd7

The white rook, by switching from the f-file to the b-file and back, has caused total confusion in the enemy ranks. With difficulty Black has parried the immediate threat of an invasion, but his pieces occupy pitiful positions. Now Miles embarks on a decisive strengthening of his position — the advance of his pawn to a5, after which it will be impossible to avert the invasion of the white rook down the b-file.

| 17 | a4! | Rf8 |

This loses material, but there is nothing better.

18	Ne7+	Kh7
19	Rxf8	Nxf8
20	Nf6+	Kg7
21	Ne8+	Kf7
22	Nxc7	Kxe7
23	Nxa6	

In the knight ending White is an outside passed pawn to the good and has a spatial advantage. All that he is required to demonstrate now is elementary technique.

| 23 | ... | Nd7 |
| 24 | Nc7 | |

It was still possible even to lose the game after 24 a5?? Kd8.

24	...	Nb6
25	a5	Nxc4
26	a6	Kd7
27	a7	Nb6
28	a8=Q	Nxa8
29	Nxa8	Kc6
30	Kd3	Kd5
31	Nb6+	Kxe5
32	Ke3	Kd6
33	Ke5	Kc6
34	Nc4	Kb5
35	Nd2	Kb4
36	Ke5	c4
37	Nxc4	Kxc4
38	Kxe6	Resigns.

Miles—Ljubojevic

Puerto Madryn, 1980

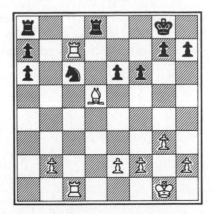

White's position is better. Black's extra doubled pawn is of no significance, the active placing of all the white pieces being more than sufficient compensation. Black has a difficult exchanging problem to solve, and has to choose between 1 ... exd5, 1 ... Rxd5 and 1 ... Nd4. The Yugoslav grandmaster chooses the most aggressive and least successful continuation.

| 1 | ... | Nd4? |

He should have gone into the rook ending. Best was 1 ... exd5, answering 2 R1xc6 with 2 ... Rf8, as suggested by Miles in *Informator* No. 30. In this case Black would have been able to cover his main weakness — the seventh rank — by ... Rf7, and White could hardly have hoped for more than a rook ending with four pawns against three on the K-side.

One can understand the unwillingness of the Yugoslav grandmaster to play for a draw without the slightest chance of anything more. A player normally finds it difficult to take this kind of decision. To do this, apart from an exact appraisal of all the details of the position, he needs great confidence in his own powers, and, if you like, a certain degree of courage. After all, if in such a cheerless, passive struggle he fails to gain a draw, he will be annoyed that he did not go in for more complicated play, where there would have been fair practical chances. But after Black fails to exchange the white bishop, a rook ending with an extra pawn for White on one wing becomes a mere dream.

2 Bc4!	Rd6
3 Kg2!	

Do not hurry!

3 ...	Kf8
4 Rd1	Rb8
5 b3!	

It is important for White to retain his b-pawn.

5 ...	Rbd8
6 Rxa7	Nb5
7 Rxd6	Rxd6
8 Rb7	

The position has stabilized. White has regained his pawn and obtained a big positional advantage. Black's a-pawn is weak, his king is cut off on the back rank due to his weakened seventh rank, and his rook and knight occupy passive positions. White's first problem is to create weaknesses in his opponent's position on the K-side.

8 ...	Nc3
9 Kf3	h6
10 g4!	Nd5
11 h4	Nc3
12 h5	Nd5
13 Bd3!	

White has fulfilled another task — he has fixed the g7 pawn and given Black a whole complex of weak white squares on the K-side. He already threatens Bg6.

13 ...	Ne7
14 Kg3!	

Black is completely deprived of counter-play, and in such situations, as is well known, it is very useful not to hurry but to strengthen the position to the maximum.

14 ...	Nd5
15 f3!	

White guards against a check on the third rank in the event of the exchange of the pawns at b3 and g7.

15 ...	a5

After 15 ... Ne7 Black, who was already in time trouble, would have had to reckon seriously with 16 Ra7.

16 Bg6	Rb6
17 Rf7+	Kg8
18 Ra7	Kf8
19 e4!	

To be considered was 19 Rxa5 Rxb3 20 Ra8+ Ke7 21 Rg8, but after 21 ... Kd6 22 Rxg7 Ke5 the threat of 23 ... Nf4 would have given Black some counter-play. The move chosen by the English grandmaster is significantly stronger and more energetic.

19 ...	Nb4

As shown by Miles, after 19 ... Ne3 20 Rf7+ Kg8 21 Rc7 Kf8 22 Kf2 Nd1+ 23 Ke2 Nb2 24 Rf7+ Kg8 25 Re7! Rb8 26 Re8+ Rxe8 27 Bxe8 followed by Kd2—c2 the knight is trapped.

(See next diagram)

20 e5!!

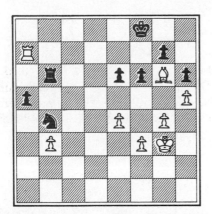

Excellent play. White had many tempting continuations, but analysis by Miles shows that all the rest were much weaker:

(a) 20 Rxa5 Nc6 21 Ra8+ Rb8.

(b) 20 Ra8+ Ke7 21 Rg8 Nc6 followed by . . . Ne5.

(c) 20 Rf7+ Kg8 21 Re7 Rb8 22 Rxe6 Nc2! (intending . . . *Nd4*) 23 Re8+ Rxe8 , 24 Bxe8 Nd4! 25 Ba4 Kf7, with drawing chances.

20 ..	Nd5

On 20 . . . fxe5 Miles had prepared 21 Ra8+ Ke7 22 Rg8 Kf6? 23 Rf8+ Kg5 24 Be4!!, when Black has no defence against Rf7, Rxg7, Rg6+ and Rxh6, since 24 . . . Nd5 is met by 25 Bxd5 and mate at f5 with the rook.

21 Ra8+	Ke7
22 Rg8	fxe5
23 g5!	

The decisive blow.

23 ..	hxg5
24 Rxg7+	Kf8
25 h6	Ne7
26 Rf7+	Ke8
27 Bh5	Kd7
28 h7	Rb8
29 Kg4	Kd6
30 Kxg5	Nf5
31 Bg6	Nd4

32 Be4	Nxb3
33 Rb7	Resigns.

Bogoljubov—Lasker

New York, 1924

Black's extra pawn is a considerable advantage. But the activity of the white pieces, the small amount of material left on the board, and the advantage of the bishop over the knight when there is play on both wings make Black's task of realizing his advantage very difficult. By his next move, preventing . . . f5, Bogoljubov makes it easier for his opponent to draw up a plan.

1 g4?!

Black can hardly hope that the a-pawn itself will queen. To win he must create a second weakness in White's position. After 1 g4 the pawn at h3 is significantly weakened. Black's problem is now to provoke a further advance of the white pawns, then fix and eliminate them. As we will see, it is fairly easy to describe Black's plan, but its implementation requires Lasker's supreme technique.

1 ...	Nd2
2 Rc8?!	Kh7
3 Ra8?!	

In the endgame it is normally advantageous to place a rook behind an enemy passed pawn. But for the time being Black has no intention of advancing his a-pawn. His aim is to attack White's K-side. Had Bogoljubov guessed at Lasker's plan, he would have hardly taken his rook away from the defence of the K-side.

3 . .ᐧ.	Ra2
4 Kg2	Nb3+
5 Kg3	Nd4!

Of course, Black does not play 5 ... a5. The scope of White's rook would immediately be widened, and he would gain counter-play, e.g. 5 ... a5? 6 Ra7 Kg6 7 h4! f6 8 h5+ Kh6 9 Bb6, with the threat of 10 Be3+ and 11 h6 (indicated by Alekhine). By the move in the game Black creates the strong positional threat of 6 ... Ne6 followed by 7 ... g5!, in the event of the bishop moving from d8. The h3 pawn would then be doomed, so that White's reply is practically forced.

6 h4

A serious achievement by Black. It remains for him to provoke the advance of the g-pawn, and the game will be practically decided. To this aim Lasker plans a new regrouping of his pieces. But, in order to mask his intentions and to achieve the maximum effect, for a certain time he follows the principle "do not hurry", dulling his opponent's vigilance.

6 ...	Ra3+
7 Kf2	Nc6
8 Bc7	Ne7
9 Bd6	Ra2+
10 Kf3	

10 Kg3 is more exact.

10 ...	Nc6
11 Bc7	Nd4+
12 Kg3	

Compared with the position after White's sixth move, the only change is that his bishop stands at c7 rather than d8.

12 ...	Ra3+
13 Kf2	Ra4!

Now Black starts to take positive action.

14 Kg3	Ne6
15 Bb6?!	

In the event of 15 Bd6 White was evidently afraid of 15 ... a5. But it would have been much better to permit the advance of the a-pawn that to allow his king to be cut off from the g- and h-pawns. Bogoljubov had obviously been lulled by Lasker's preceding series of manoeuvres, and he considered his defensive set-up to be perfectly correct.

15 ...	Ra3+
16 Kg2?	

Again a careless move, this time leading to a forced loss. Right to the last moment Bogoljubov fails to guess at Lasker's idea. 16 Kf2! was correct, so as to use the bishop to hinder the black knight from attacking the g4 pawn, e.g. 16 ... Nf4 17 Bc7 Nd5 18 Bd8.

16 ...	Nf4+

The outcome of the game is decided.

17 Kf2

White loses after 17 Kg1 Rg3+, or 17 Kh1 Rh3+. On 17 Kf1 Black does not play 17 ... Rf3+ 18 Ke1 Ng2+ 19 Ke2 Nxh4 20 Bf2 Rh3 21 Rxa6, but simply 17 ... Ra2!, with a decisive positional advantage.

17 ...	Nd3+!
18 Kg2	

Forced. On 18 Kg3 Black wins by 18 ... Ne5+ 19 Kf4 Ng6+ 20 Kg5 Rf3! 21 Bc7 f6+ 22 Kh5 Nf4+ 23 Bxf4 g6 mate.

18 ...	Ne5!
19 g5	

Black has carried out his plan. Now comes an energetic elimination of White's K-side pawns.

19 ...	Ng6!
20 Bf2	Nf4+
21 Kh2	Kg6
22 Ra7	a5

Only now does Lasker decide to advance his a-pawn, to divert White's forces from the K-side.

23 Bg3	Ra2+
24 Kh1	Nh5!

Lasker's knight manoeuvres in this ending are above all praise.

25 Be5

25 Be1 loses to 25 ... Ra1 26 Ra6+ (26 Re7 Kf5!) 26 ... Kf5! (stronger than 26 ... Kb7 27 g6+!) 27 Rxa5+ Rxa5 28 Bxa5 g6! 29 Kg2 Kg4 30 Be1 Ng7 (Euwe).

25 ...	Ra4!
26 Kg2	Rxh4
27 Ra6+	Kxg5
28 Rxa5	Kg6

The game could have concluded here. The finish was:

29 Kf3	f6
30 Bd6	Rd4
31 Bc7	Rc4
32 Bd6	Rc6
33 Bb8	Kh6

White resigns.

We will now analyze a more modern variation on the same theme.

Spassky—Petrosian

World Championship Match
Moscow, 1969

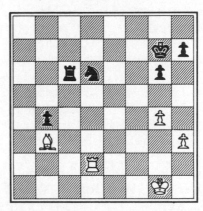

The first game of the match was adjourned in this position, with Black having to seal his move. In comparison with the Bogoljubov—Lasker game, Black's task looks more difficult. Firstly, White's rook is much more active than in the previous example, and secondly, the pawn structure on the K-side is symmetric, which also favours the defender. The publishing house *Fizkultura i Sport* brought out an interesting book on the match, written by the two players' seconds, grandmasters Boleslavsky and Bondarevsky. In spite of the fact that the grandmasters worked separately on the book, the majority of the variations coincide almost exactly. The book contains an exhaustive analysis of the given ending, and we will make use of it here.

1 ...   Ne4!

The commentators unanimously consider this stronger than the alternatives:

(a) 1 ... Kf6 2 Rd4, when Black achieves nothing by 2 ... Ke5 3 Rxb4 Ne4 4 Rc4 and 5 Bc2, while after 2 ... Rb6 his forces are too passively placed.

(b) 1 ... Rc3 2 Rxd6 Rxb3 3 Kg2 leads to a rook ending which Bondarevsky judges to be drawn. Accurate play is demanded of White, it is true. A possible variation is 3 ... Rc3 4 Rb6 b3 5 g5 Rc2+ 6 Kf3 b2 7 Rb7+ Kf8 8 Ke4 Ke8 9 Ke5 Rf2 10 Kd6, and White does not allow the black king to break through to the b2 pawn.

2 Rd7+

On 2 Rd4? Black had prepared 2 ... Rc1+ 3 Kg2 Nc5 4 Rxb4? Rb1.

2 ...   Kf6!

On 2 ... Kh6 White would have continued 3 Rd4! Rc1+ 4 Kg2 Nc5 5 g5+ Kg7 (*5 ... Kxg5 6 Rxb4*, or *5 ... Kh5 6 Bd5*) 6 Bd5 b3 7 Rf4 (Bondarevsky).

3 Rxh7   Rc1+
4 Kg2   Nc5

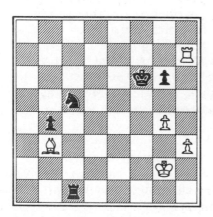

"What should White play? After 5 Bd5 b3 6 Bxb3 Nxb3 7 h4 Nd4! 8 g5+ Kf5 9 h5 gxh5 10 Rxh5 Kg4 11 Rh8 Rc2+ 12 Kf1 Nf3 he loses. We considered the most tenacious to be 5 Rf7+ Ke5 6 Rf3, but the rook ending after 6 ... Nxb3 7 Rxb3 Rc4 gives Black good winning chances", writes Boleslavsky. But Spassky had managed to find a brilliant saving manoeuvre.

5 Bf7!!   b3
6 g5+!

"The point of White's plan. He gains time to exchange the K-side pawns, and for the b-pawn he intends to give up his bishop" (Bondarevsky).

6 ...   Kxg5
7 h4+   Kf6
8 h5   Rc2+

"On 8 ... gxh5 there follows 9 Bxb3 Kg6 10 Bg8, while if 8 ... g5 9 Bg6 b2 10 Rf7+ Ke6 11 Rg7, and there is no win for Black" (Boleslavsky).

9 Kf3   b2
10 Ba2   gxh5

"If 10 ... Rc1, then 11 hxg6 Kxg6 12 Rh2 Na4 13 Rh4 Nc3 (*13 ... Ra1 14 Rxa4 Rxa2 15 Rb4* with a draw) 14 Rb4 Rc2 15 Bc4 Rd2 16 Ke3 etc." (Bondarevsky). On 10 ... g5 there would have followed 11 Rf7+ Ke5 12 h6.

11 Rxh5   Rc1
12 Rh6+?

"A blunder. Spassky knew that 12 Ke3 led to a draw, but the quite understandable desire to win the dangerous pawn as soon as possible suggested to him a 'second' solution. But 12 Rh2 would not have drawn: 12 ... Na4

13 Rh4 Nc3 14 Rh2 (if *14 Rb4 Rc2*)
14 ... Rf1+ 15 Kg3 (*15 Ke3 Ra1*)
15 ... Na4 16 Rh4 Ra1 17 Rxa4
Rxa2 18 Rb4 Ke5" (Bondarevsky).

"The position resembles a study, and
the draw could have been achieved by
12 Ke3 Na4 13 Rh4! Nc3 14 Rb4
Ra1 15 Kd3" (Boleslavsky).

These beautiful and instructive variations show just how complicated a
seemingly simple ending can be.

12 ...	Ke5

The king approaches one square
nearer to the b2 pawn, and this factor
acquires decisive significance.

13 Rb6	Na4
14 Re6+	

It transpires that after 14 Rb4 Ra1
15 Rxa4 Rxa2 16 Rb4 Kd5 17 Ke3
Kc5 and 18 ... Kc4 Black wins.

14 ...	Kd4!
15 Re4+	Kc5
16 Rxa4	Ra1

White resigns.

Smyslov—Karlsson

Las Palmas Interzonal, 1982

(See next diagram)

White's advantage is obvious. Black's
K-side pawn majority has no significant
role to play, whereas White's extra pawn
on the Q-side is a very serious factor.
The white knight is excellently deployed
in the centre, and Black's only 'trump'
is his possession of the d-file. Therefore
Smyslov first wrests the open file from
his opponent.

1 Rd3	Rxd3
2 Nxd3	Nh5

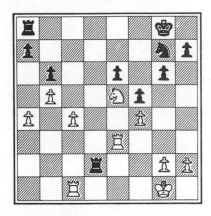

3 Kf2!

3 c5 looks good, but after 3 ...
bxc5 4 Rxc5 Rd8 Black obtains
counter-play.

3 ...	Nf6
4 Ne5	

Preparing Ke3 and preventing
... Ng4+.

4 ...	Rd8
5 Ke3	

After the exchange of one pair of
rooks the d-file is not of any great importance.

5 ...	Ne4
6 a5!	Nc5

On 6 ... Rd2 White has the unpleasant 7 c5!

7 a6	Kg7
8 Rc2!	

White takes control of the second
rank and threatens 9 Rd2.

8 ...	Ne4
9 g4!	

Smyslov does not miss the chance to
strengthen his position on the K-side too.

9 ...	Kf6
10 g5+	Kg7
11 Nc6	Rd7
12 Rg2	

White is not tempted by the possibility of 12 c5, winning a piece. After 12 ... Nxc5 13 Rxc5 bxc5 14 b6 axb6 15 a7 Rxa7 16 Nxa7 h6! 17 h4 hxg5 18 hxg5 e5! 19 fxe5 Kf7 Black has fair counter-play, whereas after the move in the game he has none at all.

12 ...	Kf8
13 h4	Ke8
14 Rh2	Kf8
15 h5	gxh5
16 Rxh5	Kg8
17 Rh1	Kg7
18 Ne5	Rd8
19 Rh6!	Rd6

Black's moves are very much forced, as he is almost in *zugzwang*. On 19 ... Nc5 White wins by 20 Rf6 with the threat of 21 Rf7+.

20 Ke2!

A move which is highly characteristic of the Soviet grandmaster. Smyslov does not trouble himself with calculating the consequences of 20 Nc6 Nd2, where Black threatens to capture on c4 with check.

20 ... Nc3+

After 20 ... Rd2+ 21 Ke1 Rd6 the move 22 Nc6 wins without any unnecessary complications.

21 Ke1	Rd1+
22 Kf2	Rd4
23 Kf3	Rd6
24 Rf6	

Further resistance is pointless. The game concluded:

24 ...	Kg8
25 Rf7	Rd3+
26 Nxd3	Resigns.

On 26 ... Kxf7 the manoeuvre of the knight to c6 via e5 is decisive.

Such games appear simple and clear, and they are easy to annotate. The only difficulty is in finding and making White's moves. It is possible that White could have won the game differently: his advantage in the initial position was obvious. However, it seems to us that the path chosen by Smyslov, by which the opponent was not allowed the slightest counter-play, is the most technically correct, and corresponds best of all to the aims of this book.

Petrosian—Ivkov

Bugojno, 1982

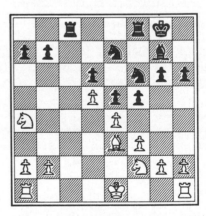

The players have exchanged only the queens, the white-squared bishops, and one pair of pawns, but the game has already gone into an ending.

The pawn chains will immediately tell an experienced player that the opening was a King's Indian Defence, in which the pawn formation often determines the plans of the two sides. White's pawn wedge in the centre creates the preconditions for play on the Q-side. By ... f4 Black can set up an analogous wedge on the K-side, but it is fairly obvious that he will be unable to obtain any serious counter-play on this part of the board. Summing up all that has been said, it is not difficult to decide that White has a positional advantage, but to convert it into a win is no easy matter. Let us see how Petrosian solves this problem.

1 Nc3!

Threatening to capture on a7, which was not possible immediately due to 1 ... Ra8.

| 1 ... | a6 |
| 2 Ke2 | Kh7 |

Ivkov plans to exchange off his bad bishop by ... h5 and ... Bh6.

| 3 Rac1 | Nd7?! |

Black is inconsistent. He should have continued 3 ... h5, with chances of a successful defence. In vindication of the Yugoslav grandmaster, it should be stated that to foresee Petrosian's subsequent manoeuvre was very difficult. Outwardly the position appears fairly blocked, and it is hard to imagine that on the next move it would already be too late to play ... h5.

4 Nb1!!

It is all wonderfully simple. Once this move has been made, everything becomes clear. But the plan of transferring the knight from c3 to c4, at the same time exchanging both pairs of rooks, could be found only by a player with a complete mastery of endgame technique, of which Petrosian is undoubtedly one.

4 ...	Rxc1
5 Rxc1	Rc8
6 Na3!	Rxc1
7 Bxc1	

With the disappearance of the rooks White's advantage has increased considerably, to a great extent due to the difference in the positions of the kings. Petrosian's problem now is to weaken the opponent's Q-side and create the preconditions for the approach of his king, exploiting the remoteness of the enemy king from the Q-side.

| 7 ... | h5 |

This attempt to exchange the black-squared bishop is obviously too late.

| 8 Nc4 | Nc8 |
| 9 Bd2! | Bf6 |

9 ... Bh6 would of course have been met by 10 Bb4.

10 Na5	b6
11 Nc6!	Kg7
12 Be3	Kf7
13 Nd3	Ke8
14 a4!	Bd8
15 Ndb4	a5
16 Na2!	

The way for the white king is prepared. Petrosian has carried out his plan with precision and consistency, and White now has a decisive advantage.

16 ...	f4
17 Bf2	g5
18 Kd3	Nf8
19 h3	Ng6
20 Nc3	Bf6
21 Kc4	Kd7
22 Kb5	Kc7
23 Ka6	

This concludes the king's march, and 23 Nb5+ is now threatened. Ivkov makes a desperate attempt at counter-play.

| 23 ... | g4!? |

24	hxg4	hxg4
25	fxg4	Bh4
26	Nd1!	

This puts an end to Black's counter-play. 26 Nb5+ would have been technically less correct.

26	...	Bxf2
27	Nxf2	Nce7

On 27 ... Nh4 White wins by 28 g5 followed by the transfer of his knight from f2 to f3 via h3.

28	Nxe7	Nxe7
29	g5	Ng6
30	Ng4	Nh4
31	Ka7	Ng6
32	Nh2	Nh4
33	Nf3	Ng6
34	b3	Nf8

and without waiting for 35 Nh4, **Black resigned**.

Svyeshnikov—Browne

Wijk aan Zee, 1981

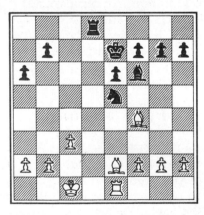

White has the advantage of the two bishops with a typical Q-side pawn majority. But it is not possible to exploit this advantage, since the black knight is very strong, and in the event of the white c-pawn advancing Black acquires an excellent strong point at d4. Black's rook, king and bishop also occupy excellent positions. This makes White's plan all the more interesting, a plan which he carries out in full without encountering any resistance on the part of the opponent, on account of its very originality.

1	Kc2	Rd5
2	Be3	g5
3	h3!	

White restrains his opponent's activity on the K-side.

3	...	Rd8
4	Bh5	Rd5!
5	Be2	Rd8
6	Kb3	Rc8
7	Bh5	

White's manoeuvres appear rather absurd, but, thanks to their very illogicality, they provoke Black into trying to seize the initiative.

7	...	Nd3?

Browne fails to guess at his opponent's plan. 7 ... Nc4 followed by ... Nd6 was correct, maintaining roughly equal chances.

8	Rd1	Nc5+
9	Kb4!	Ne4
10	Ka5!	Nd6
11	Kb6!	Rc6+
12	Ka7	

(See next diagram)

We are accustomed to the king being an active fighting unit in the endgame. But when White's entire army is back in camp, and the king alone goes into the attack, it must be agreed that this is not often seen. Nevertheless, the Soviet grandmaster's unusual evaluation of the

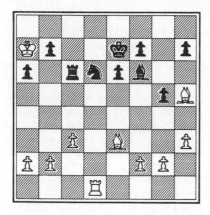

position proves to be correct. The white bishops now rush to the aid of their king, and the entire black army is imprisoned in its own camp.

12 ...	Rc7
13 Bb6!	

Parrying the threat of 13 ... Nc8+, which is decisively met by 14 Kb8!

13 ...	Rc6
14 Ba5	Be5
15 Bf3	Rc5
16 Bb4	Rc7
17 Kb6	Rd7
18 Re1	

Black is completely tied up, and loss of material is merely a question of time.

18 ...	f6
19 a4	Kd8
20 Bxd6!	Rxd6+
21 Kxb7	

The bold white king was first into the attack, and is the first to win spoils for its army. The ending with opposite coloured bishops and rooks is easily won for White, thanks to his two-pawn majority on the Q-side.

21 ...	Rd2
22 Rd1!	

The correct solution to the exchanging problem. The bishop ending is very easily won for White.

22 ...	Rxd1
23 Bxd1	a5

White only has to play b2—b4, and it will all be over. In the next few moves Svyeshnikov does not hurry, but seeks the most favourable moment for the advance.

24 Kb6	Bc7+
25 Kc6	Bf4
26 Kb7	Be5
27 Be2	Bd6
28 g3	f5
29 Kc6	Bb8
30 Bc4	e5
31 b4!	

The finish was:

31 ...	Ba7
32 Kb7	Bxf2
33 bxa5	Bxg3
34 a6	Bf2
35 Be6!	f4
36 Bd5	h5
37 Bf3	Resigns.

Larsen—Marjanovic

Bled/Portoroz, 1979

(See next diagram)

It is difficult to imagine that the game will end in a win for White. If he gives up his two knights for a rook and pawn, this leads to a drawn rook ending. But Larsen won the game, and, as we will see, this was no accident. The ending may seem tedious to the reader, but it is rather instructive, and after a study of the preceding chapters the turning points are not so difficult to understand.

197

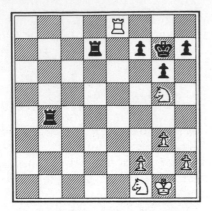

| 1 Ne3 | Rbb7?! |

As shown by Larsen, annotating this game in *Informator* No. 27, 1 . . Rb5! was correct. Marjanovic obviously reckoned that he would gain a draw as he pleased, and did not attempt to delve into the subtleties of the position. Indeed, there appears to be nothing threatening Black. If the Yugoslav grandmaster had tried to find a winning plan for his opponent, he would possibly have been able to forestall this plan.

| 2 Re4 | Re7? |

Black's first move was not the best, although quite reasonable, but his second is a direct mistake. In order to obtain winning chances, White has to weaken his opponent's position. There is no way of approaching the f7 and h7 pawns, which only leaves g6. The black pawn which is there is twice defended. In order to attack it, White must first provoke the advance of the black f- and h-pawns. By 2 . . . Rb5! Black could have forestalled this plan.

| 3 Rh4! | h6 |
| 4 Nf3 | |

Things are going well for White. For the success of his subsequent plan, Larsen carefully masks it and, following the principle "do not hurry", makes a series of harmless moves. We beg the reader, in making White's moves, not to fall asleep, since they were made with the aim of lulling only Marjanovic.

4 ...	Rb1+
5 Kg2	Rb2
6 Nc4	Rbe2
7 Ncd2	Rd7
8 Nb3	Rde7
9 Ra4	Rb2
10 Nbd2	Reb7
11 h3	

This pawn has to be advanced to h5. But there are no sharp advances, so as not to frighten the opponent.

11 ...	R2b4
12 Ra5	R7b5
13 Ra3	Rd5
14 Ra7	Rdb5
15 h4	Rb7
16 Ra6	R7b6
17 Ra3	R6b5
18 Rd3	Kh7

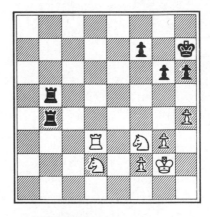

| 19 Ng1! |

The Danish grandmaster obviously decided that it was time to take positive action. Marjanovic does not sense this moment, and continues carelessly moving his rooks around the board, while the white knight begins stealing up on the h5 square.

19 ...	Kg7
20 Ne2	Ra5
21 Nf4	Rba4
22 Nb3	Ra7
23 Rd5	

Larsen evidently has a good understanding of his opponent's psychology, and he decides to advance h4—h5 in the most favourable circumstances. Now Black could himself have played 23 ... h5, and, in order to pierce Black's defence, White would have had to prepare the advance of his f-pawn. The immediate 23 h5 came into consideration, although then White would have had certain difficulties to overcome after 23 ... Ra3, with the threat of exchanging rooks by 24 ... Rb7. The best continuation for White would have been 24 hxg6 fxg6 (*24 ... Rb7 25 Nc5 Rxd3 26 Nfxd3*) 25 Ne6+ and 26 Nec5.

23 ...	R4a6?

The decisive mistake. As already mentioned, Black should have played 23 ... h5.

24 h5!	

Black's game is lost. Against the attack on his K-side he has no defence.

24 ...	Kh7
25 Nd4	Kg7
26 Nb5	Rb7

Black had to reckon with the threat of 27 Rd8 and Nd6—e8+.

27 Nd6	Rbb6?!

This allows the concluding attack, but even the better 27 ... Re7 would not have saved Black. Larsen gives the variation 28 Nc4 Rc7 29 Ne3 Rca7 30 Rd8 Ra8 (*Nc4—d6* was threatened)

31 Rd7 R6a7   32 Ne6+ Kg8 33 Nc7 Rc8   34   Ned5,   with a decisive advantage.

28 Ne8+	Kf8
29 Nc7!	Ra7
30 Rd8+	Ke7
31 Rg8!	Rc6
32 Ncd5+	Kd6
33 hxg6	fxg6
34 Nb4	Rb6
35 Nfd5	Rbb7
36 Rxg6+	Kc5
37 Rxh6	Rf7
38 Rc6+	Kb5
39 Rc2	Rad7
40 g4	Resigns.

The deftness with which Larsen directed his cavalry in this ending would have been the envy of any horseman.

Andersson—Stean

Sao Paulo, 1979

This game began with a currently popular variation of the English Opening, and almost immediately went into an ending, by-passing the middlegame stage:

1 c4	Nf6
2 Nf3	c5
3 g3	d5
4 cxd5	Nxd5
5 Bg2	Nc6
6 d4	cxd4
7 Nxd4	Ndb4
8 Nxc6	Qxd1+
9 Kxd1	Nxc6

(See next diagram)

10 Bxc6+!?	

In this age of rapid growth of opening information, it is difficult to guarantee

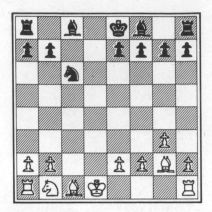

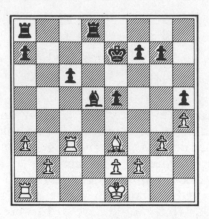

anything, but it would appear that the exchange of the bishop in this position was first employed in the game Miles—Tukmakov, Las Palmas, 1978, although the idea itself is by no means new. White breaks up his opponent's Q-side pawns, giving him in return the advantage of the two bishops, taking account of the fact that the side with the two bishops does not have a knight, and that White's position is therefore to be preferred. Subsequently White must aim to fix the opponent's pawn weaknesses and to provoke the exchange of one of the black bishops. Black's task is less specific — to organize piece pressure on White's position.

10 ...	bxc6
11 Nc3	e5

11 ... g6 came into consideration.

12 Be3	h5
13 h4	Bb4
14 Kd2!	

White allows his king's rook across to c1, and completes his development with his forces well co-ordinated.

14 ...	Ke7
15 Rhc1	Rd8+
16 Ke1	Be6
17 a3	Bxc3+
18 Rxc3	Bd5

The exchange of one of the bishops has taken place, but is White's advantage sufficient for a win? After all, there are opposite coloured bishops on the board, which foreshadow a draw. It is interesting to follow how Andersson realizes his advantage. First he must fix the opponent's weaknesses on the Q-side, i.e. not allow ... a5, and this must be done energetically.

19 b4!	Rdb8

19 ... a5 fails to 20 bxa5 and 21 Bb6.

20 Bd2!	Ke6

20 ... a5 again did not work, due to 21 bxa5 and 22 Re3.

21 Rc5!

It is useful to provoke ... Rb5, which will allow White to gain a tempo by a3—a4.

21 ...	Rb5
22 Rcc1	f6
23 a4	Rb7
24 Rc5	

By energetic play White has achieved a bind over his opponent's Q-side. Now he might try pressurizing the a7 pawn, say, by transferring his rooks to a5 and a6, his king to c3, and his bishop to c5. But White's advantage is not so great that he can achieve success by such straightforward play. Black would probably gain counter-play on the K-side. The next stage of White's plan should be to neutralize any possible initiative by the opponent on the K-side, and to create weaknesses there if the opportunity should arise. Note how 'gentle' and 'ingratiating' Andersson's moves become.

| | 24 ... | Rg8 |
| | 25 f3! | f5?! |

The first signs! Soon Black's other K-side pawns will also be forced to move onto white squares. It would have been better to defend against the threat of 26 e4 by 26 ... Kd6.

| | 26 Kf2 | Rd8 |
| | 27 Bc3 | e4 |

There is no other defence against 27 c4.

| | 28 Rd1 | Rdd7 |
| | 29 Ke3 | g6 |

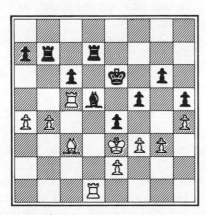

30 f4!

The final stage of White's plan commences. Since, in the event of a concentrated attack by White, it is unlikely that Black can save his a-pawn, there is

absolutely no need for White to have the option of play on two wings. Therefore Andersson decides not to try and give his opponent a second weakness, and blocks the K-side.

| | 30 ... | Rd6 |
| | 31 Rb1 | Rdd7 |

Black sticks to waiting tactics, since he has no basis at all for active counter-play.

| | 32 Bd4 | Kf7 |
| | 33 Rb2! | |

The Swedish grandmaster does not hurry with the decisive regrouping of his pieces, by which he deploys them in the most favourable positions. This reduces to a minimum the probability of any 'surprise' on the part of the opponent at the time of the regrouping itself.

	33 ...	Ke6
	34 Kd2	Kf7
	35 Kc3	Ke6
	36 Ra5	Kf7
	37 Ra6	

One white rook has reached its appointed place. With the arrival of the second rook at a5 the a7 pawn will fall.

	37 ...	Re7
	38 Bc5	Red7
	39 Rd2	Rbc7
	40 Be3	Rb7
	41 Bc5	Rbc7
	42 Rc2!	

Right to the end Andersson masks his intentions. The transit point for the rook is now occupied by the bishop, and the white king is on the c-file.

	42 ...	Rb7
	43 Kb2	Rdc7
	44 Ka3	Rd7

45 e3!

White suppresses even the most insignificant attempt by his opponent to gain counter-play. The bishop obtains a post at d4 and blocks the d-file. In addition, Black is obliged to forget about ... e3.

45 ...	Rdc7
46 Bd4	Rd7
47 Rc5	Rbc7

After this White is able to pick up the a7 pawn 'at his leisure'. 47 ... Rdc7 was slightly better, forcing White to win the pawn with his king at a3. But 48 Rca5 Bc4 49 Rxa7 Rxa7 50 Bxa7 would not have allowed Black any hope of saving the game.

48 Kb2	Rb7
49 Kc3	Rb6
50 Rca5	Rxa6
51 Rxa6	Ba2
52 Rxc6	Resigns.

Yusupov—Razuvayev

Kislovodsk, 1982

The previous move saw the conclusion of a mass exchange of pieces, and the game went into an ending which is slightly better for White. He can hope to win the weak black d-pawn, and if in doing so he can retain at least one pair of rooks, the opposite coloured bishops will not guarantee Black a draw.

1 ...	Rc7
2 b3!	

Yusupov sets a positional trap, into which Razuvayev falls.

2 ...	Rfc8?

This natural move is a positional mistake. 2 ... b5! was essential.

3 a4

The white bishop is now assured of an excellent post at c4.

3 ...	Kf8
4 Bd5	Ke7
5 Bc4	Rc5
6 Rd3	d5!?

Razuvayev does not wish to be tied to the defence of his d-pawn, and he decides to sacrifice it for the sake of exchanging one pair of rooks and activating his remaining rook.

7 Bxd5	Rc1+
8 Rxc1	Rxc1+
9 Kg2	Rc2
10 Bc4	Be5

The position has clarified. White is a pawn up, but it is difficult to realize his insignificant material advantage, in view of the active placing of his opponent's pieces and the absence of any defects in the opponent's pawn formation. Yusupov embarks on a lengthy phase of manoeuvring, with the aim of improving the placing of his own pieces and of creating weaknesses in the opponent's position.

11 Bb5	Bd6!

On 11 ... Rc7 there could have followed 12 Bc4!, when the black rook is cut off from the second rank.

12 Rd4	a5

All the same Black cannot get by without this move, but now his b6 pawn is weakened, and in the future he will have to reckon with an exchange sacrifice at b6 or c5 when the white king is at b5.

13 Re4+	Kf6
14 Bc4	Rd2
15 Re8	Bc5
16 Kf3	

On the Q-side the pawn structure has stabilized. Now changes can be expected on the K-side. White is preparing to attack the f7 pawn with his rook along the seventh rank, so Black has to take counter-measures.

16 ...	g5!?

Black vacates g6 for his king and moves his K-side pawns onto squares of the colour of his bishop. Passive defence, involving the transfer of his rook onto his second rank, was unpromising. In this case White could have prepared the advance of his king to b5 under the cover of his bishop at d5, supported by the pawn at e4.

17 g4	h6
18 Rc8	Kg6
19 h3	

White overlooks his opponent's counter-play. As indicated by Yusupov, he should have first checked at g8.

19 ...	f5!

White has markedly improved his position, and it is natural that Razuvayev is unhappy for the game to continue in the same vein. He therefore seizes the opportunity to set his opponent a difficult exchanging problem. It should also be taken into account that Yusupov had to solve it on the last move before the time control. (The initial position was reached after White's 21st move.)

20 Be6!

In endings with opposite-coloured bishops plus rooks, exchanging problems become of primary importance. In this example — and it is a fairly typical one — White had the possibility of winning a second pawn, exchanging rooks, but the opposite coloured bishops would have led to a draw. On the other hand, it often happens that transposing into a bishop ending with one extra pawn is a sure way to win.

In endings with opposite-coloured bishops without rooks, schematic thinking comes to the forefront. In the possible variation 20 Rc6+ Rd6 21 Rxd6+ Bxd6 22 Bd3 Kf6 White has two captures on f5: with the bishop or the pawn. In the event of the capture with the bishop Black's problem is simplified, and consists of not allowing the opponent to create two connected passed pawns advancing on black squares. Let us analyze the capture with the pawn,

23 gxf5. Now it is dangerous to allow the white king to reach h5, in view of the risk of ending up in *zugzwang*. Imagine this position.

Black's king is tied to the defence of his h-pawn, while his bishop has to restrain the advance of the white pawns in the centre. If it is Black to move he has to relinquish one of these tasks. Note that is bad to take on h4 due to Kg4! Therefore the best reply to 23 gxf5 is 23 ...h5.

Suppose now that White succeeds in provoking the advance of the black pawn to h4. The following is now a probable position:

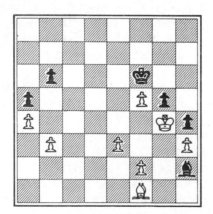

White can try playing for a win as follows: 1 f4 gxf4 2 e4! Bg3 3 Be2, to which Black does best to reply with the counter-sacrifice 3 ...f3! 4 Bxf3 Be1. After this White's only winning

attempt is 5 e5+! Kxe5 6 Kg5. Black again has to find a particular defensive set-up, shown in the next diagram.

As soon as the white pawn advances to f7, the black king stands at e7, while if the white king approaches the h4 pawn, the black bishop defends it from e1. Draw.

Let us now return to the game continuation.

20 ...	f4
21 Bf5+	Kg7
22 Rc7+	Kg8
23 Rc6	fxe3
24 fxe3	Rd6
25 Rc8+	Kg7

The pawn structure on the wings has become stable, while in the centre White has acquired a passed e-pawn. If he should succeed in advancing it to e5, without allowing the opponent any serious counter-play, his advantage will become sufficient for a win.

26 Rc7+	Kf6
27 Rh7	Ke5
28 Rh8	Rc6
29 Bd3	

The white bishop has two excellent posts at f5 and c4. Yusupov begins operating according to the principle "do not hurry". In doing so he keeps the position in a constant state of tension, threatening to advance e3—e4—e5 both with the bishop at f5, and at c4.

29 ...	Rf6+!
30 Ke2	Bf8
31 Rh7	Bc5
32 Bc4	Kd6

Black has successfully parried White's first onslaught.

33 Rh8	Ke7
34 Rh7+	Kd6
35 Rg7	Kc6
36 Ra7	Kd6
37 Rh7	Kc6
38 Bb5+	Kd5
39 Bd3	

White again prepares to switch his bishop to f5.

39 ...	Ke5
40 Bf5	Rd6
41 Rh8	Rc6

Black must all the time be on the alert: 41 ... Rf6 42 Re8+ Kd6 44 e4 is bad for him.

42 Bd3!

The indefatigable bishop again switches to c4.

42 ...	Bb4
43 Re8+	Re6
44 Rb8	Rd6

44 ... Bc5 came into consideration.

45 Bc4

Threatening the advance of the e-pawn.

45 ...	Kf6

Now 46 e4 is answered by 46 ... Ke5, with good counter-play.

46 Rf8+	Kg7
47 Rg8+	Kf6
48 Re8!	Bc3
49 e4!	

At last. For twenty-five moves Yusupov has been preparing this advance, improving the placing of his pieces and wearing down his opponent by constantly threatening it. White has chosen a very apt moment to commence positive action. The black pieces have lost their co-ordination, whereas all the white pieces, including the e-pawn, co-operate splendidly with one another.

49 ...	Bd4
50 Bd5	Kg7
51 Kd3	Bc5
52 Rg8+	Kf6
53 Re8	Kg7
54 Rc8	

Threatening a possible exchange sacrifice on c5. After 54 ... Kf6 there follows 55 Kc4, when the capture on c5 is a real threat to Black.

54 ...	Rf6
55 Rc7+	Kf8
56 e5	

The actions of the black pieces have finally lost all harmony. The outcome of the game is decided.

56 ...	Rf4
57 Be4	Rf7
58 Rc8+	Ke7
59 Bf5	

The white bishop, like a pendulum, oscillates between c4 and f5, the latter post being especially good.

59 ...	h5

This loses, but Black's position is already on the way downhill.

60	Rc7+!	Kf8
61	Rxf7+!	

The correct approach to the exchanging problem. In the given situation the transition into the bishop ending is the quickest way to win.

61	...	Kxf7
62	gxh5	Bf8
63	Ke4	Bg7
64	Kd5	Ke7
65	Bg6	Kd7
66	e6+	Ke7
67	Bf7	

Black is in an unusual form of *zugzwang*. He is forced to allow the advance of the h-pawn.

67	...	Bf6
68	h6	Bc3
69	Kc6	Bd4
70	h7	Resigns.

After 70 ... Kd8 71 Kb7 Ke7 72 Kc7 it is again *zugzwang*.

Andersson—Miles

Tilburg, 1981

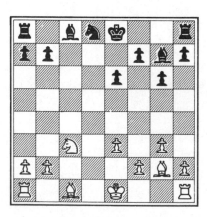

Material is level and the pawn formation symmetric. The position is roughly equal, but not drawn! We have already seen in numerous examples that maintaining the balance in a complex ending against a strong opponent is an extremely difficult matter. The Swedish grandmaster is renowned for his great skill in the playing of this type of ending. He has frequently succeeded in demonstrating that the concepts of equality and a draw are by no means synonymous.

1	Bd2	0—0

The choice of move in such apparently simple positions has to be approached with a great degree of responsibility. As shown by Kovacevic, annotating this game in *Informator* No. 32, 1 ... Bd7 was weaker due to 2 Ne4! Bc6 3 Nd6+ Kd7 4 Bxc6+ Kxd6 (*4...Kxc6 5 Nc4*) 5 Bf3 Bxb2 6 Rb1 Bg7 7 Ke2, with advantage to White. In this variation the black king may well come under a strong attack. Miles correctly removes his king from the centre, since 1 ... Ke7 2 Rc1 Bd7 3 0—0 Bc6 4 b4 favours White (Kovacevic).

2	Rc1	Bd7
3	0—0	Bc6
4	Rc2!	

A strong move. Andersson prepares for play on the Q-side, involving the exchange on c6 and the transfer of his knight to c5. In this case, in order to increase the pressure on the opponent's Q-side, White needs the c-file.

The routine 4 Rfd1 would have eased Black's problems.

4	...	Bxg2

The knight must be moved from d8, to co-ordinate the rooks.

5	Kxg2	Nc6

6 Ne4	Rfd8		11 ...	f5
			12 Nc5	Rd6

To be considered was Makarichev's suggestion of 6 ... a5 with the idea of 7 ... Nb4. Then 7 a3 could be met by 7 ... a4, and if 8 Nd6 Ra6 9 Nxb7 Rb6.

7 Bc3	Rac8
8 Bxg7	Kxg7
9 Rfc1	Rb8
10 a3	

By threatening to cramp Black on the Q-side with b2—b4, Andersson provokes a weakening of the opponent's pawn formation on this part of the board.

10 ...	a5

Not 10 ... Ne5 11 Rc7 Nd3 12 R1c3 Nxb2 due to 13 Ng5.

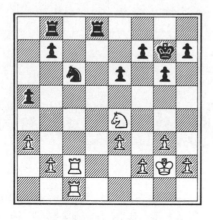

11 Rc3!

There would not seem to be anything difficult about this move. But this simplicity is merely apparent, and we would invite the reader to try finding such a move. The position has hardly changed, but it is not at all easy for Black to decide what to play. The white rook has gained access to b3, and an attack on the b7 pawn may become a reality.

12 ... Kf6 was to be considered.

13 Rb3	b5
14 Rd3	Rxd3
15 Nxd3	Rb6
16 f4	

White's initiative has transformed into a stable positional advantage, which he has consolidated with his last move. But Black has few real weaknesses, and there is very little material left on the board, so that the game is still closer to a draw than to a win for White.

16 ...	Kf6
17 Kf3	e5!

Not 17 ... b4 18 a4 followed by Rc5, or 17 ... g5 18 e4. Miles goes into a rook ending. It is interesting that on the previous move Andersson could have prevented this by 17 Rc5, but he considered the rook ending to be favourable. Objectively speaking, 17 Rc5 would seem to be stronger than 17 Kf3, but the final result of a game is often influenced by subjective factors no less than by objective ones. This is confirmed once again by the present game.

18 fxe5+	Nxe5+
19 Nxe5	Kxe5
20 Rc5+	Kd6?!

It can be assumed that Miles was short of time. 20 ... Kf6 looks much more natural, depriving the white king of the possibility of approaching the K-side via f4 and g5.

21 b4	Rb7
22 h4	a4
23 Kf4	Ke6
24 h5	Kf6

25 Rc6+   Kf7

Kovacevic shows that 25 ... Kg7 was objectively stronger, not allowing h5—h6. As confirmation he gives the following variation: 26 hxg6 hxg6 27 Kg5 Re7   28 Rxg6+ Kh7   29 Kxf5 Rxe3   30 g4 Rxa3   31 Rb6 Rf3+   32 Kg5 Rf7!   33 Rxb5 Ra7 with a draw. The variation is correct, but it should be added that in time trouble it is unlikely that anyone would play 25 ... Kg7. One could say that, when pressed for time, an experienced player's hand would itself make the king move to f7.

26 Rc5!!

Kovacevic shows that White does not win by 26 h6. Here are the variations given by the Yugoslav grandmaster: 26 h6 (*26 hxg6+ hxg6 27 Kg5 Re 7*) 26 ... Rd7!   27 Rb6 Rd3   28 Rxb5 (*28 Rb7+ Kf6   29 Rxh7 g5+   30 Kf3 Kg6*)   28 ... Rxa3   29 Ra5 Kf6   30 Ra6+ Kf7   31 b5 Rb3   32 Rxa4 Rxb5   33 Kg5 f4+   34 Kxf4 Rh5, with a draw. All these variations demand serious consideration, and it is possible to find them in a calm situation, but not in time trouble. In our opinion, what happened was that, after playing 25 ... Kf7, Miles saw the possibility of 26 h6, and began feverishly seeking a way out. He obviously overestimated some possibilities on the part of his opponent, and

he did not like his position. It would seem that Andersson also investigated the consequences of 26 h6, but he considered them insufficiently clear and decided to repeat the position, taking account of the fact that the opponent did not have anything better. The two exclamation marks are attached for White's excellent understanding of psychological subtleties.

26 ...   Rd7?

The decisive mistake. Remember Byelavyenets: "The repetition of moves in the endgame plays an important role. Disregarding the fact that it gains time for thinking, it can be mentioned that, by repeating moves, the active side acquires certain psychological gains. The defender, whose position is inferior, often cannot stand it, and creates a further weakening which eases his opponent's task. In addition, repeating moves enables the position to be clarified to the maximum extent."

27 Rxb5!   Rd3
28 Rb7+   Kf6

28 ... Kg8 is hopeless: 29 h6! Rxa3 30 Rg7+ Kh8   31 Re7 Kg8   32 Kg5, with the threat of Kf6.

29 Rxh7   g5+
30 Kf3   Rxa3
31 Ra7   Ra2
32 Ra6+   Ke5
33 g4

The rest is not so difficult.

33 ...   fxg4+
34 Kxg4   Rg2+
35 Kh3   Rb2
36 Rxa4   Ke4
37 Kg3   Rb1

On 37 ... Kxe3 White wins by

208

38 h6 Rb1	39 Ra3+ Ke4	40 Kg4

Rg1+ 41 Rg3 (Kovacevic).

38	h6	Rg1+
39	Kf2	Rh1
40	Ra6	Kd5
41	Kg3	Rh4
42	Rg6	Ke4
43	b5	Kf5
44	Rc6	Re4
45	Kf2	Re7
46	b6	Rb7
47	Kg3	Resigns.

Vaganian—Rashkovsky

Moscow, 1981

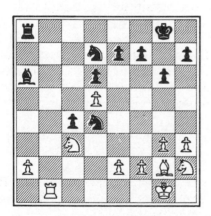

In this complicated ending White has the advantage. The black c4 pawn is cut off from the main chain, and White can quickly bring his king to the centre.

1 . . .	Rb8

The unpleasant 2 e3 was threatened, driving the black knight into the corner.

2	Rxb8+	Nxb8
3	a4!	

Black must not be allowed to dislodge the white knight from its excellent blockading position by . . . Nb5.

3 . . .	Kf8
4 Nf3	Nxf3+

4 . . . Nb3 was preferable, with a complicated game.

5	Bxf3	Nd7
6	Be4	Ke8?

This natural move proves to be a mistake. Black aims to transfer his king to c5. If he should succeed in this, he will have a perfectly reasonable, and perhaps even more promising, position. But the plan proves to be impracticable. 6. . . e5 was better, with chances for both sides.

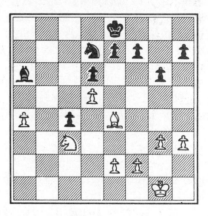

7 f4!

Vaganian begins carrying out a far from obvious, but highly effective counter-plan, involving the advance of his K-side pawns. In doing so White had to work out the consequences of sacrificing his passed pawn on the Q-side.

7 . . .	Kd8
8 h4!	Kc7
9 a5!	

The pawn is sacrificed, so as to gain several tempi and to squeeze the opponent's position on the opposite wing.

9 . . .	Nc5
10 Kf2	Nb3

11 g4	Kd8

The black king returns to the defence. White's threat of advancing his pawn to h6 and then breaching Black's defences by f4–f5 is highly dangerous.

12 h5	Ke8

On 12 ... gxh5 there would have followed 13 g5.

13 h6!	Nxa5
14 f5	

It is not often in the endgame that one sees such a furious pawn attack. The double capture on g6 is threatened, and so Black's king, which is the sole defender of his K-side, is forced to take one further step back.

14 ...	Kf8
15 g5	Nb3
16 Ke3	Nc5
17 Bc2	Bc8

Black wishes to clarify the position on the K-side. In the event of 17 ... Nd7, with the aim of preventing f5–f6, White would first have strengthened his position by 18 Kd4, and then all the same played 19 f6, meeting 19 ... gxf6 with 20 Ba4.

18 f6	Bh3
19 Ba4!	

Vaganian forestalls Black's threat to play 19 ... Nd7 20 Ne4 Bg2!

19 ...	exf6
20 gxf6	Nxa4

Black could hardly have avoided this exchange. White was threatening 21 Bc6 followed by 22 Nb5.

21 Nxa4	

Black is a pawn up, with a bishop against a knight, two passed pawns on the c- and g-files, and. . . nevertheless a lost position.

21 ...	g5

Passive tactics would not have changed anything. White would have placed his king at d4 and knight at c3, and by Ne4 or Nb5 would have won the d6 pawn.

22 Nc3	g4
23 Kf2	Ke8
24 Nb5	Kd7
25 e4	

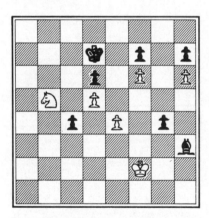

A pretty *zugzwang* position. On his next move Black is forced to give up something.

25 ...	Kd8

Rashkovsky pins his last hopes on his passed pawns.

26 Nxd6	c3
27 Nxf7+	Kc7
28 Ne5	

The black pawns are easily stopped, whereas White's three passed pawns in the centre are impossible to stop.

28 ...	g3+

| 29 Kxg3 | c2 |

29 . . . Bf1 30 f7 would have won quickly for White.

30	Nd3	Bf1
31	Nc1	Kd7
32	e5	Bc4
33	d6	Be6
34	Kf4	Kc6

and **Black** resigned without waiting for his opponent's move. White brings up his king and eliminates the c2 pawn, after which further resistance is pointless.

Miles—Yusupov

Vrbas, 1980

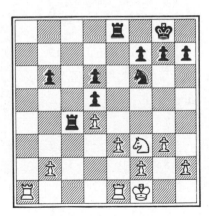

The only serious defect in Black's position is his compromised central pawn formation. Were the d6 pawn at e6, the game would be absolutely level. The drawback to Black's position, which amounts to his having one extra pawn island, is highly insignificant, but the presence on the board of knights gives White the preconditions for exploiting his advantage. First he has to exchange one pair of rooks and suppress Black's temporary activity.

| 1 Re2 | |

Miles plans the set-up: Re2, Ne1, f2—f3 and Kf2, with the aim of co-ordinating his K-side pieces. By his control over c2 White intends to reduce to the minimum the effect of the black rooks on the c-file, while by his active rook on the a-file he intends to worry the opponent and force him to exchange.

1 . . .	Rec8
2 Ne1	Rb4
3 f3	g5

Yusupov makes an active attempt on the K-side. The threat is 4 . . . g4.

4 g4!	Rb3
5 Kf2	Kg7
6 h3	

Before switching to active play on the Q-side, the English grandmaster makes all the useful moves on the K-side.

| 6 . . . | h5 |

Yusupov creates a slight weakness in his opponent's position — the pawn at h3.

| 7 Ra3! | Rxa3 |

Black cannot avoid the exchange of rooks. On 7 . . . Rb5 there could have followed 8 Nd3 with the threat of 9 b4.

8 bxa3	Rc3
9 Ra2	h4
10 Ke2	

Although White is still engaged in defence, it is already apparent that Black's activity has reached an impasse. Very soon his pieces will be completely thrown back. Yusupov tries to latch onto White's weakness at h3.

| 10 . . . | Rc1 |

11 Nd3!   Rh1
12 Rb2!

Miles demonstrates a concrete approach to the position. He does not try to defend his h-pawn, since variations indicate that its capture favours White: 12 ... Rxh3 13 Nf2! Rg3 14 Rxb6 h3 15 Rb1 h2 16 a4 Rg1 17 Rf1 Ne8 18 a5.

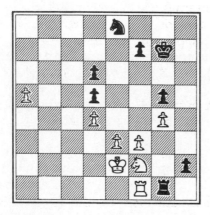

If now Black tries to stop the a-pawn with his knight, White gains a decisive advantage on the K-side: 18 ... Nc7 19 Nh1 Rg2+ 20 Rf2 Rg1 21 Rxh2 Ra1 22 Rh5 and 23 Ng3.

Therefore 18 ... f6, but then 19 a6 Nc7 20 a7 Kf7 (*20 ... Kg6 21 Nh1 Rg2+ 22 Rf2 Rg1 23 Rxh2 Ra1 24 Rb8 Rxa7 25 Ng3*, with a decisive advantage) 21 Nh1 Ke7 22 Kf2 Rxf1+ 23 Kxf1 Kd7 24 Kg2 Kc6 25 Ng3 Kb7 26 Nf5 Ne8 27 Ne7 Nc7 28 Kxh2 Kxa7 29 Nc8+, and White wins.

All these complicated variations are given by Ugrinovic, annotating the game in *Informator* No. 30.

12 ...   Ra1

A sad necessity.

13 Rxb6   Rxa3

13 ... Ra2+ 14 Nb2 does not

change anything.

14 Rxd6   Ra2+
15 Kf1   Ra1+

After 15 ... Ra3 White holds onto his pawn by tactical means: 16 Nb4!, and 16 ... Rxe3 fails to 17 Rxf6!

16 Ne1   Ra3
17 Nc2

It becomes clear that White has managed to retain his extra pawn. Black's game is lost.

17 ...   Ra2
18 Nb4   Ra5

18 ... Rh2 is no better.

19 Ke2   Rb5
20 Nd3   Ra5
21 Rb6   Ra2+
22 Rb2   Ra1
23 Ne5!

Aiming at f7.

23 ...   Ra7
24 Rb5   Ra2+
25 Kd3   Ra7
26 Kc3   Rc7+
27 Rc5   Rb7
28 Ra5   Kf8
29 Ra6   Ne8

29 ... Kg7 was more tenacious, but all the same Black would be unable to prevent e3—e4.

30 e4!   Nc7
31 Ra5   f6
32 Nc6   dxe4
33 fxe4   Ne6
34 Rf5   Kg7
35 e5!

The endgame play of grandmaster

Miles is characterized by unhurried manoeuvring and the painstaking accumulation of small advantages, according to all the demands of the principle "do not hurry". But when his advantage attains decisive dimensions, the English player is transformed, and he uses all his tactical skill to reach his goal by the shortest path, although quieter, more lengthy roads might be found. A player from the past who acted in this manner was the outstanding Russian Champion Alexander Alekhine.

35 ...	fxe5
36 Rxe5	Nf4

Not 36 ... Kf7 37 Rxe6.

37 Rxg5+	Kh8
38 d5	Nxh3
39 Rf5!	Kg7
40 Nd8	Ra7
41 Ne6+	Kg8
42 g5	

Black resigned, in view of the variation 42 ... Rf7 43 Rxf7 Kxf7 44 g6+ Kxg6 45 d6.

Kasparov—Ivanov

Moscow, 1981

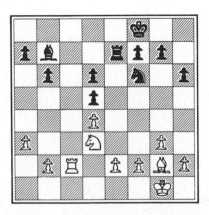

In contrast to the Miles—Yusupov game, White, apart from his superior pawn formation, also controls the c-file. Black is faced with a difficult defence.

1 h4	Ke8
2 Nf4	Kd8
3 Bf3?!	

An inaccuracy. As shown by Kasparov, annotating this game in *Informator* No. 32, he should have played 3 h5, securing the post for his knight at f4.

3 ...	Rc7?

A mistake in reply, possibly caused by time trouble. 3 ... g5 was correct.

4 Rxc7	Kxc7
5 g4!	

It is easier for White to exploit his advantage in the minor piece ending than with the rooks on.

5 ...	g5

5 ... Ne4 does not solve Black's problems: 6 Bxe4! dxe4 7 Nh5 g6 8 Nf6.

6 hxg5	hxg5
7 Nh3!	Nh7
8 e3	f6
9 Be2	Bc8?

The decisive mistake. As shown by Kasparov, Black should have tried to hold the position by 9 ... Nf8 10 f4 Ne6.

10 f4!

Now the black knight is tied to the defence of the g5 pawn, and Black has no way of preventing the transfer of the white king to g3 followed by Bd3.

10 ...	Kd8
11 Kf2	Ke7
12 Kg3	Be6
13 Bd3	gxf4+
14 exf4	Bg8

On 14 ... Nf8 White was intending 15 f5 Bg8 16 Ba6 Nd7 17 Nf4 Nb8

18 Bb7, winning the d5 pawn.

15 Bxh7!	Bxh7
16 f5!	Resigns.

In view of the possible variation: 16 ... Bg8 17 Nf4 Kf8 18 Kh4 Kg7 19 g5 (Kasparov).

INDEX OF PLAYERS

INDEX OF MATERIAL

Several examples appear under more than one classification, reflecting transitions from one type of ending to another. Important endings reached in analysis are indicated by parentheses.

Rook Endings

Bishop Endings

Knight Endings

Pawn Endings —